DIALOGUES
AND A DIARY

Also by Mr. Stravinsky and Mr. Craft

CONVERSATIONS WITH IGOR STRAVINSKY

MEMORIES AND COMMENTARIES

EXPOSITIONS AND DEVELOPMENTS

Dialogues
and A Diary

IGOR STRAVINSKY

and

ROBERT CRAFT

Garden City, New York

DOUBLEDAY & COMPANY, INC.

1963

Portions of this book have appeared in the following periodicals: Encounter, The Observer, Musical America, Mademoiselle, Show, HiFi-Stereo Review, Perspectives of New Music.

Lines from Exile & Other Poems, Seamarks, *and* Winds, *by St.-John Perse, reprinted by permission of Bollingen Foundation.*
Lines from Four Quartets, *by T. S. Eliot, reprinted by permission of Harcourt, Brace & World, Inc., and Faber and Faber Ltd.*

Library of Congress Catalog Card Number 63–20511
Copyright © 1961, 1962, 1963 by Igor Stravinsky
All Rights Reserved
Printed in the United States of America
First Edition

To

WYSTAN AUDEN

CONTENTS

LIST OF ILLUSTRATIONS

PART 1

Dialogues

A GREEK TRILOGY

OEDIPUS REX

R.C.: What do you recall of the circumstances that led to the composition of *Oedipus Rex*? To what extent did you collaborate with Cocteau on the scenario and the text? What was your purpose in translating the libretto into Latin, and why Latin rather than Greek—or, if Latin, then why not directly from Greek? What were your original ideas for staging the work and why have they never been realized? What did you mean by opera-oratorio? How would you identify the religious character of the work, if you agree with those people who profess to hear religious elements in it? Would you discuss what you call the musical manners of the piece? And, what more can you contribute to performance knowledge, and to the history of the work in performance?

I.S.: I date the beginnings of my *Oedipus Rex* from September 1925, but at least five years earlier than that I had been aware of the need to compose a large-scale dramatic work. Returning from Venice to Nice that September, I stopped in Genoa to renew memories of the city in which I had spent my fifth wedding anniversary, in 1911. There, in a bookstall I saw a life of Francis of Assisi which I bought and, that night, read. To this reading I owe the formulation of an idea that had occurred to me often, though vaguely, since I had become *déraciné.* The idea was that a text for music might be endowed with a certain monumental character by translation backwards, so to speak, from a secular to a sacred language. "Sacred" might mean no more than "older," as one could say that the language of the King James Bible is more sacred than the language of the New English Bible, if only because of its greater age. But I thought that an older, even an imperfectly remembered, language must contain an incantatory element that could be exploited in music. The confirming example from Francis of Assisi was that of the Saint's hieratic use of Provençal, the poetic language of the renaissance of the Rhône, in contrast to his quotidian Italian, or Brass Age Latin. Prior to that moment of illumination in Genoa, I was unable to resolve the language problem in my future vocal works. Russian, the exiled language of my heart, had become musically impracticable, and French, German, and Italian were temperamentally alien. When I work with words in music, my musical saliva is set in motion by the sounds and rhythms of the syllables, and "In the beginning was the word" is, for me, a literal, localized truth. But the problem was resolved, and the search for *"un pur langage sans office"* (St.-John Perse) ended with my rediscovery of Ciceronian Latin.

The decision to compose a work on the play by Sophocles followed quickly upon my return to Nice, but the choice was preordained. I wanted a universal plot or, at least, one so well known that I would not have to elaborate its exposition. I wished to leave the play, as play, behind, thinking by this to distill the dramatic essence and to free myself for a greater degree of focus on a purely musical dramatization. Various Greek myths came to mind as I considered subjects, and then, almost in automatic succession, I thought of the play that I had loved most in my youth. In a final moment of doubt I reconsidered the possibility of using a modern language version of one of the myths, but only *Phèdre* fulfilled my conception of the statuesque, and what musician could breathe in that meter?

I invited Cocteau's collaboration because I greatly admired

his *Antigone*. I told him my ideas and cautioned him that I did not want an action drama, but a "still life." I also said that I wanted a conventional libretto with arias and recitatives, though the conventional, I knew, was not his strongest suit. He appeared to be enthusiastic about the project except for the notion that his phrases were to be recast in Latin, but the first draft of his libretto was precisely what I did not want: a music drama in meretricious prose.

"Music drama" and "opera" have long since blurred together, of course, but they were firm categories in my mind at that time, and I even used to argue such extenuating notions as that the orchestra has a larger and more exterior interpretive role in "music drama." I would now replace these terms by "verse opera" and "prose opera," identifying the new categories with such pure examples as *The Rake's Progress* for the type of the former and *Erwartung* for the type of the latter. Divisions of this sort, no matter how factitious, are necessary to my forming processes.

Cocteau was more than patient with me and my criticisms. The whole book was rewritten twice, and even after that he submitted it to a final shearing. (I am a topiarist at heart, and my love for clipping things sometimes amounts to a mania.) What is purely Cocteau's in the libretto? I am no longer able to say, but I should think less the shape of it than the gesticulation of the phrasing. (I do not refer to the practice of repeating words, which is habitual with me and which dates only from the time when I begin to compose.) The speaker device is Cocteau's and the notion that the speaker should wear a *frac* and comport himself like a *conférencier* (which has too often meant, in practice, like a master of ceremonies). But music goes beyond words, and the music was inspired by the tragedy of Sophocles.

I had begun to visualize the staging as soon as I started to compose the music. I saw the chorus first, seated in a single row across the stage and reaching from end to end of the proscenium rainbow. I thought that the singers should seem to read from scrolls, and that only these scrolls and the outlines of their bearers' cowled heads should be seen. My first and strongest conviction was that the chorus should not have a face.

My second idea was that the actors should stand on pedestals and wear cothurni, each person at a different height, behind the chorus. But actors is the wrong word. No one "acts," and the only individual who moves at all is the narrator, and he merely to show his detachment from the other stage figures. *Oedipus Rex* may or may not be an opera by virtue of its musical content, but it is not at all operatic in the sense of movement. The people in the play relate to each other not by gestures, but by words. They do not turn to listen to each other's speeches, but address themselves directly to the audience. I thought that they should stand rigidly, and in my original version I did not even allow them exits and entrances. My first conception was that the people of the play should be revealed from behind small individual curtains, but I realized later that the same effect might be accomplished more easily by lighting. Like the Commendatore, the singers should be illuminated during their arias and become vocally, though not physically, galvanized statues. Oedipus himself should stand in full view throughout, of course, except after the "*Lux facta est*," when he must change masks. (He could be recountenanced behind his individual curtain or in the dark.) His self-violence is described, but not enacted: he should not move. Those directors who whisk him offstage and then bring him back realistically staggering in an unreal, stylized, costume have understood nothing of my music.

I am often asked why I should have tried to compose a waxworks opera. My answer has been that I abhor *verismo*, but a complete reply would be more positive and more complex. For one thing, I consider this static representation a more vital way to focus the tragedy not on Oedipus himself and the other individuals, but on the "fatal development" that, for me, is the meaning of the play. Oedipus, the man, is a subject for a type of symbolic treatment which depends upon the interpretation of experience and is principally psychological. This did not attract me as musical material, and if it had, I would have constructed the drama differently—for example, by adding a scene from the childhood of the prince. My audience is not indifferent to the fate of the person, but I think it far more concerned with the person of the fate and the delineation of it which can be achieved uniquely in music. But so far as visualization may give support, the stage figures are more dramatically isolated and helpless precisely because they are plastically mute, and the portrait of the individual as the victim of circumstances is made far more starkly effective by this static presentation. Crossroads are not personal but geometrical, and the geometry of tragedy, the inevitable intersecting of lines, is what concerned me.

I have also been asked why I failed to take one more step and use puppets, as my late friend Robert Edmond Jones once did for a performance of my *Oedipus* in New York. This notion did occur to me, in fact, and I had been impressed by Gordon Craig's puppets when he showed them to me in Rome in 1917. But I am also fond of masks, and while composing Oedipus' first aria, I already imagined him wearing a roseate, ogival one, like that of a Chinese sun-god—just as, when I composed the Devil's music in *The Flood*, I imagined a singer made to seem transparent, like a scorpion.

My staging ideas[1] were not realized simply because Diaghilev lacked time to mount the work at its premiere; and because the first performance was unstaged, many people assumed that I preferred the work to be given that way. *Oedipus Rex* was composed as a twentieth-anniversary present for the Diaghilev Ballet—"*Un cadeau très macabre,*" Diaghilev called it. Its existence was kept secret from him until the last moment, and I was late in finishing the score, so late that the singers hardly had learned the notes before the piano preview performance, which took place at Edmond de Polignac's a few

[1] The *Avant-Propos* in the score only partly represents them.

days before the public one. At this Polignac soirée I accompanied the singers myself, and from the reactions of the guests I foresaw that *Oedipus* was not likely to succeed with the Parisian ballet audience. But my austere vocal concert, following a very colorful ballet, was an even greater failure than I had anticipated. The audience was hardly more than polite, and the Sganarelles of the press were a lot less than that: "*Celui qui a composé Petrouchka nous présente avec cette pastiche Handelienne . . . Un tas de gens mal habillés ont mal chanté . . . La musique de Créon est une marche meyerbeerienne,*" etc. Performances were rare in the next two decades, but since then they have been more and more frequent.

I should note that Diaghilev himself was cool to *Oedipus* at the premiere, but I think that this may have been because of Cocteau. A very handsome, very young man was deliberately chosen to be the speaker, at any rate, and this was certainly to spite Cocteau, who, when composing the play, must have thought of that part for himself.

I have participated as a conductor in only a few staged performances, and I have seen few other stagings. (Of recent ones I should mention the Vienna Opera's, where the "*e peste*" sounded as though the singers really did have the plague, and the Washington Opera's, where the white faces of the chorus glistened from rectangular towers like holes in Emmentaler cheese.) The performance that has pleased me most, visually, was Cocteau's in the Théâtre des Champs-Élysées, in May 1952. His huge masks were very striking, and so, though it contradicted my idea, was his use of symbolic mime. I wince when I recall the first staged performances, in the Kroll Opera, Berlin, though they were musically well prepared by Otto Klemperer. The speaker wore a black Pierrot costume. I complained to the director that this did not seem relevant to the *Oedipus* story, but his answer permitted no further argument: "Herr Professor Strawinsky, in our country only the *Kappelmeister* is allowed to wear a *frack*." Hindemith and

Schoenberg were in the audience at the Berlin performance, the former *hingerissen*, and the latter—who must have heard in it nothing but empty *ostinato* patterns and primitive harmonies—*abgekühlt*.

In what sense is the music religious? I do not know how to answer because the word does not correspond in my mind to states of feeling or sentiment, but to dogmatic beliefs. A Christianized *Oedipus* would require the truth-finding process to resemble an *auto-da-fé*, and I had no interest in attempting that. I can testify, though, that the music was composed during my strictest and most earnest period of Christian Orthodoxy. At the beginning of September 1925, with a suppurating abscess in my right forefinger, I left Nice to perform my piano Sonata in Venice. I had prayed in a little church near Nice, before an old and "miraculous" icon, but I expected that the concert would have to be canceled. My finger still was festering when I walked onto the stage at the Teatro La Fenice, and I addressed the audience, apologizing in advance for what would have to be a poor performance. I sat down, removed the little bandage, felt that the pain had suddenly stopped, and discovered that the finger was—miraculously, it seemed to me—healed. (Now I grant that minor "miracles" are more disconcerting than even the most farfetched "psychosomatic" rationale, and the reader who has come this far will probably decide that all I had was a *maladie imaginaire*. A miracle is what seemed to have happened to me, however, and if it was no such thing, and another word is used to describe it, then the fact that I took it for a miracle is at least as significant to the reader. I do, of course, believe in a system beyond Nature.)

A few days after this Venetian concert, I discovered the book about St. Francis and decided after reading it to use the language that is also the language of the Western Church, and shortly after that I chose the archetypal drama of purification. I also composed a Russian liturgical-style *Pater Noster* at the same time as *Oedipus Rex*, and I was certainly influ-

enced in composing the *"Gloria"* chorus by Russian Church
ritual: the Holy Trinity is symbolized by the triple repetitions,
just as it is in the *Kyrie* of the Mass. But, to begin with, the
character of the *"Gloria"* music itself is ecclesiastical.

Although I have been concerned with questions of musical
manners all my life, I am unable to say precisely what these
manners are. That, I think, is because they are not precompositional, but of the essence of the musical act: the
manner of saying and the thing said are, for me, the same. But
am I not unusually conscious of the manner question, nevertheless? All I can say is that my manners are my personal
relations with my material. *Je me rends compte* in them.
Through them I discover my laws. The direction of the next
melodic interval is involved with the musical manners of the
whole work. Thus, the clarinet trill at *"lux facta est"* is a mani-
festation of my *Oedipus* manners: the trill is not just a trill but
an indispensable mannerism. I have been told that such things
merely indicate the culture-consciousness found in all *emi-
grés*,[2] but I know that the explanation is deeper than that,
as I worked and thought in exactly the same way in Russia.
My manners are the birthmark of my art.

I began to compose according to a plan of gradation for
the musicodramatic development, a recitative-aria scheme in
which each aria was to mark a crucial development in the
story. My first idea was that each dramatic progression was
to be accompanied by a downward pull of the key-center,
somewhat in the tradition of the Baroque composers, though
in saying this I must quickly add that I did not refer to any
models. I do not now recall any predatory attractions to other
composers at the time, though, if another composer is sug-

[2] And I am a double emigré, born to a minor musical tradition and twice
transplanted to other minor ones. I myself, and not political circumstance or
the revolution, helped to exhaust and scuttle the limited tradition of my birth-
right, but the dead end of "Russian music" was the reason for my removal to "French music," which, at the time, was almost as eclectic as
"Russian music" and even less "traditional." My second removal was to
America.

gested in my score, he is Verdi. Much of the music is a
Merzbild, put together from whatever came to hand. I mean,
for example, such little games as the offbeats at No. 50 and
the Alberti-bass horn solo accompanying the Messenger. I
also mean the fusion of such widely divergent types of music
as the *Folies Bergères* tune at No. 40 ("The girls enter, kicking") and the Wagnerian 7th-chords at Nos. 58 and 74. I
have made these bits and snatches my own, I think, and
of them a unity. "Soule is form," Spenser says, "and doth the
bodie make." (And I would apply that quotation to *Le Baiser
de la fée* as well. Listening to a concert of the saccharine
source material for that work the other day, I almost suc-
cumbed to diabetes.)

What were my first musical ideas for *Oedipus*? Well, what
are musical ideas? An idea is already a formulation, is it not,
and does not something happen before that? I, at any rate,
am aware of a precognitive sense of my material long before
I have any "ideas" of how to use it. I know also that this
material cannot be imposed upon by "ideas," but that something very like the contrary takes place. All of my "ideas" for
Oedipus Rex were in one sense derived from what I call the
versification—though by "ideas" I may mean nothing more
than what I have already described as manners. And what do
I mean by "versification"? I can answer only by saying that
at present I make my "versification" with series as an artist of
another kind may versify with angles or numbers.

The *Oedipus* music was composed from beginning to end
in the order in which it now stands. I was not conscious of
the manner question as I composed the first chorus, and when
I did begin to understand it, in Oedipus' aria, I may have
established it too exaggeratedly, which is to say, too conven-
tionally. This, I think, was because I realized that it would
have to be fixed then and there for the whole work. The King's
manner conceals the King's "heart," though not, perhaps, the
tail feathers of his pride.

I frame the word heart with diacritical marks because I
do not believe the Greeks would have used it in our sense or,

at least, with our emphasis, and even if they did temperamentalize it, they were careful to balance it in their cosmogony of affective organs by the *hepar*. (The Greeks must have divined that the liver is a regenerative organ, incidentally, though medical science has only recently determined the fact, for otherwise Prometheus' punishment would have had no retributive meaning—the birds would have had of him no more than an *hors-d'oeuvre*.) But whereas journalists may claim utility for "heart" and "heartless," "cold," the key word in most attacks on *Oedipus*, is propaganda, verbicide through the simple-minded wish to evaluate rather than to describe. What is "warm," please? *Schmaltz*? And is the first canon in the "Goldberg" Variations cold or warm?

Useful criticism should seek to discover the effect produced by the fact that the harmonic dominant is so often in the minor. It should also analyze the nature of the music's rhythmic manners, the hint for which came from Sophocles himself or, more precisely, from the meters of the chorus (especially the simple choriambics, the anapests and dactyls rather than the glyconics and dochmii). No one seems to have noticed that where Sophocles has used what may be called a 3/8 rhythm I have used the 6/8, and that just as his chorus sings of the gods in 4/4 dactyls, my Créon, who is on the side of the gods, sings in the same meter. And, in general, I exploit rhythmic staticity in the same way as Sophocles. Listen, for example, to the choral passage in his play just before the appearance of the Shepherd. The rhythms in *Oedipus* are more static and regular than in any other composition of mine to that date, and the tension created by them in the "*Mulier in vestibulo*" chorus, for instance, is greater than any tension that irregular, upset rhythms could produce. But precisely that chorus—I call it a mortuary *tarantella*—has been cited as a piece of inappropriate gaiety, a ballet coda, even as a cancan—by people who have no manners of their own. The rhythms are the principal source of dramatic tension and a major element of the dramatic method. If I have succeeded in freezing the drama in the music, that was accomplished largely by rhythmic means.

My musical performance notes are few. I repeat the "*Gloria*" chorus after the narrator's speech both because I like the chorus and because I prefer to go directly, without narration, from *tutti* G major to *solo* flute and harp G minor. And in stage performances I like to acknowledge the audience's realization that the Queen Mother must have a lot to say by giving them a pause before she says it. I should mention, too, that I prefer the 1948 version of the score. The revisions are not mere copyright changes, but improvements instituted in my manuscript immediately following the first performance. I refer to such things as the added horns and tuba in the "*Aspikite*" chorus, and the added trumpet in the "Beckmesser" aria, "*Nonne Monstrum*." I would also advise conductors that the part of Oedipus himself should not be sung by a large operatic voice, but by a lyrical one. The Oedipus singer must exploit dynamic contrasts, and his gradations in volume are extremely important. The first aria, for example, must be quiet, not bellowed, and the melismata must be given strict and full rhythmic value.

My criticisms of *Oedipus Rex*? Criticism is too easy after thirty-five years, and, what is worse, too late, but I detest the speaker device, that disturbing series of interruptions, and I do not much like the speeches themselves. "*Il tombe, il tombe de haut*"—from where else, indeed, given the gravity situation? (The English is not much better, though: "He falls headlong" sounds like the description of a swan dive.) The line "And now you will hear the famous monologue, 'the Divine Iokaste is dead,'" is intolerable snobbery. Famous to whom? And no monologue follows, but only a four-word singing telegram. Another line mentions a "witness to the murder, who steps from the shadows," and I have always wondered who that interesting character might be and what might have become of him. But the final "*on t'aimait*" is the most offensive phrase of all, for it is a journalist's caption and a blot of sentimentality wholly alien to the manner of the work.

But alas, the music was composed with the speeches, and is paced by them.

The music? I love it, all of it, even the Messenger's fanfares, which remind me of the now badly tarnished trumpets of early 20th Century-Fox. Neoclassicism? A husk of style? Cultured pearls? Well, which of us today is not a highly conditioned oyster? I know that the *Oedipus* music is valued at zero by present progressive-evolutionary standards, but I think it may last awhile in spite of that. I know, too, that I relate only from an angle to the German stem (Bach—Haydn — Mozart — Beethoven — Schubert — Brahms — Wagner — Mahler—Schoenberg), which evaluates solely in terms of where a thing comes from and where it is going. But an angle may be an advantage.

R.C.: Did you choose Jean Daniélou to make the Latin translation of *Oedipus*? Would you comment on his work?

I.S.: Daniélou was a friend of Cocteau. I did not know him, and in fact we have never met. He was attached to a monastic order in India then, or so I think, but I may be confusing him with his brother Alain, the orientalist and musicologist. Jean Daniélou eventually became a priest, in any case, and an author of books on patristic typology, especially the *Sacramentum futuri* (Paris, 1950), which contains an absorbing study of Philo and Alexandrian Judaism. His only work in English that I know is an essay on Gregory of Nysa.

I used Latin rather than Greek, to answer your earlier question, because I had no notion of how to treat Greek musically (or Latin, Latinists will say, but there I did at least have *my* idea). I sometimes read in program notes that the language of my *Oedipus* is "medieval Latin," a rumor no doubt derived from the fact that the translator was a Catholic cleric. But the Latin, judging by the sentence structure, the placement of modifiers, and the use of the historical infinitive, is Ciceronian. I have found only one "ecclesiastical" word in the whole libretto, and that—the *omniscius pastor*—can be called such only by association. (*Why* the shepherd should be omniscient I do not know.) Unusual grammatical situations can be found—for example, the ablative form "*Laudibus Regina*," which Daniélou may have borrowed from an old text—but they are rare. Idiomatically, the language is all pre-Boethian. But the Latinist is already horrified by the first letter of my score, the "K", which does not exist in the language he knows. The purpose of this barbarian orthography was to secure hard, or at least non-Italianized, sounds instead of the usual potpourri of classic and ecclesiastic. I have misspelled a word, too, because of an error in transliteration from Russian: "*Miki*," at rehearsal number 50, is a mistake for "*Mihi*."

"Stravinsky's scansion of the Latin syllables is sometimes rather unorthodox." I quote a much quoted criticism. In fact, however, my scansion is entirely unorthodox. It must break every rule, if only because Latin is a language of fixed accents and I accentuate freely according to my musical dictates. Even the shift from "*OEdipus*" to "*OeDIpus*"(which must be pronounced "*OYdipus*" by the singers and "*EEdipus*" by the speaker[3]) is unthinkable from the point of view of speech though that, of course, is *not* my point of view.

I have noted in my own score that "*Vale*" should be "*Ave*" in the salute to Créon, as to say "good-bye" at this point would be an incongruous intrusion of low comedy; that the grammar, and therefore the meaning,[4] is obscure in the passage from "*Non reperias*" to "*istum pellere*," and that later in this same speech the construction "*Polliceor divinabo*"—"I promise," or "I shall guess"—is freakish; that "*accusat*" and "*accusas*" in the Oedipus-Tiresias exchange are misspelled; that the string of plosive consonants in Tiresias' "*Dicam, dicam quod dixit deus*" is good sound but bad Latin, though for this I claim musical license; that the accent shift on the last syllable of each of the final "*Glorias*"—in the salute to the Queen—should

[3] The "pus" must rhyme with deuce, "Tiresias" must be pronounced "Tyreesias," and Jocasta in three syllables—"Iokaste."
[4] I no longer posses a copy of the French text, and I can only guess at the original meaning.

be avoided by exaggerating the tonic accent; that "Ment*ian*-tur*," in Iokaste's aria, is a printer's error, but a grave one: the Queen is supposed to say "They lie"—"Ment*iuntur*"—not "they may lie"; that *"Oedipoda"* is an unusual form and should perhaps be changed to *"Oedipodem"* or *"Oedipum."*

APOLLO

R.C.: What do you recall of the genesis of your *Apollo,* the circumstances of the commission, the choice of subject, the career of the work in performance? Was the idea to imitate Alexandrines melodically—you once referred to *Apollo* as an exercise in iambics—your first musical idea? Your own performances of *Apollo* differ rhythmically from the printed score in many ways. Would you comment on these corrections, if that is what they are?

I.S.: *Apollo* was commissioned by Elizabeth Sprague Coolidge for performance in the Library of Congress. Or, more precisely, Mrs. Coolidge asked for a work of thirty minutes' duration—a condition I satisfied with the exactitude of a film composer—employing an instrumentation appropriate to a small hall. The choice of the subject and the choice of the string ensemble were my own.

Diaghilev was very much annoyed when he learned that I had composed a ballet for someone else, and though he acquired it gratis after the Washington premiere, he never forgave my (as he thought) disloyalty:

> *"Cette Americaine est complètement sourde."*
> *"Elle est sourde, mais elle paye."*
> *"Tu pense toujours à l'argent."*

The *"argent,"* though, was only one thousand dollars. My monetary discussions with Diaghilev were always the same and always unresolvable. What he called stinginess I called economy. I was never, and am not now, wildly dispendious, to be sure, though neither was my only goal the promise of numismatic bliss, as Diaghilev pretended. (Diaghilev also used to pretend that the *or* in Igor meant gold.) But Diaghilev disliked the music so much that he cut the Terpsichore variation when the company was on tour, and would have done so in Paris, too, had I not conducted all twelve performances there myself.

In *Apollo* I tried to discover a melodism free of folklore. The choice of another Classical subject was natural after *Oedipus Rex*, but Apollo and the Muses suggested to me not so much a plot as a signature, or what I already have called a manner. The Muses do not instruct Apollo—as a god he is already a master beyond instruction—but show him their arts for his approval.

The real subject of *Apollo*, however, is versification, which implies something arbitrary and artificial to most people, though to me art is arbitrary and must be artificial. The basic rhythmic patterns are iambic, and the individual dances may be thought of as variations of the reversible dotted-rhythm iamb idea. The length of the spondee is a variable, too, and so, of course, is the actual speed of the foot. The *pas d'action* is the only dance in which patterns of iambic stress are not immediately apparent, but the subtlety of that piece, if I may say so, is in the way the iamb is saved for the subsidiary key and then developed in augmentation at the return of the original key. I cannot say whether the idea of the Alexandrines, that supremely arbitrary set of prosodic rules, was precompositional or not—who can say where composition begins?[5] —but the rhythm of the cello solo (at No. 41 in the Calliope variation) with the pizzicato accompaniment is a Russian Alexandrine suggested to me by a couplet from Pushkin, and it was one of my first musical ideas. The remainder of the Calliope variation is a musical exposition of the Boileau text

[5] One's forms are a stamp of oneself, of one's physical, bilateral apprehension of experience, and form and function are the same. Composition begins when some one thing preponderates over another, a statement I cannot elucidate because my outer mind is a better superintendent than observer of my inner mind and because I am overwary of concepts that I suspect of being word mirrors and no more.

that I took as my motto.[6] But even the violin cadenza is related to the versification idea. I thought of it as the initial
solo speech, the first essay in verse of Apollo the god.

The success of *Apollo* as a ballet must be attributed to the
dancing of Serge Lifar and to the beauty of Balanchine's
choreography, especially to constructions such as the "troika"
in the Coda and the "wheelbarrow" at the beginning, in which
two girls support a third carrying Apollo's lute. But was it a
success? The journalists, with characteristic perception, pointed
out that it wasn't "Greek," and the English and Americans
pretended to be disturbed by melodies which, they said,
sounded like college songs (at No. 89, at the fourth bar after
No. 31, and at No. 22—"shout to the rafters three"). The
French were appalled at the suggestion of Delibes (at No. 68,
for example) and Tchaikovsky (in Polyhymnia's variation, and
at No. 69). And some people said that the *pas de deux* beginning had been stolen from Debussy's *Clair de lune*, and
that the beginning of the whole work had been taken from
the *"miserere"* of *Il Trovatore*.[7] The score was generally dis-
missed as light and even empty. I was hurt by this—as I considered it—misunderstanding. *Apollo* is a tribute to the French
seventeenth century. I thought that Frenchmen might have
taken the hint for this, if not from my musical Alexandrines,
at least from the décors: the chariot, the three horses, and the
sun disc (the Coda) were the emblem of *le roi soleil*.[8] But if
a truly tragic note is sounded anywhere in my music, that
note is in *Apollo*. Apollo's birth is tragic, I think, and so is
his ascent to Parnassus, and the Apotheosis is every bit as
tragic as Phèdre's line when she learns of the love of Hip-
polyte and Aricie—*Tous les jours se levaient clairs et sereins*

---

[6] *Que toujours dans vos vers le sens coupant les mots*
    Suspende l'hemistiche et marque le repos.
[7] *Il Trovatore*, the "Anvil Chorus," is also supposed to be the source of the
trombone march tune two measures before No. 187 in *Perséphone*, though I
am certain I did not think of it at the time, as I did not know the "London
Bridge Is Falling Down" tune when I wrote the latter part of *Danses con-
certantes.*
[8] This chariot was attractively designed by Bauchant, and so was the curtain
with bouquet *à la* Odilon Redon, but the costumes had to be remade, by
Chanel.

pour eux—though, of course, Racine and myself were both absolutely heartless people, and cold, cold.

Apollo was my largest single step toward a long-line polyphonic style, and though it has a harmonic and melodic, above all an intervallic, character of its own, it nourished many later works as well. (For example, the last seven measures of Apollo's first variation might equally have come from *Orpheus*, and the section at No. 212 in Act II of *The Rake* is purely Apollonian, and I do not mean the "philosophy," but the notes. Bits of old pieces are always turning up in new ones, however, and two other examples have just occurred to me: the string theme in the *Scherzo fantastique* is recalled in the *Firebird* by the trumpets two measures before No. 14; and, though composed almost forty years apart, the cembalo octaves at No. 196 in Act III of *The Rake* have certainly come from the same wellsprings as the octaves in Death's music one measure after No. 123 in *The Nightingale*.) *Apollo* also was my first attempt to compose a large-scale work in which contrasts of volumes replace contrasts of instrumental colors. Volumes, incidentally, are all too rarely recognized as a primary musical element, and how few listeners have remarked the real joke in the *Pulcinella* duet, which is that the trombone has a very loud voice and the string bass almost no voice at all.

My *Aufführungspraxis* is concerned chiefly with rhythmic articulation, and if I had time to prepare a new edition now, I would mark every note to be played on or off the string, and give the bowing. The figure

from the beginning to No. 6, and from No. 15 to the end should be played as though double-dotted, and the thirty-second notes should be played as sixty-fourth notes. The same double-dotting should apply from No. 99 to the end, as well as in the cello solo at No. 59, the bass solo four measures before No. 63, and the violin solo at the upbeat to No. 2. The notation of *fermati* is misleading two measures before No. 67, where the hold should apply only to the first cellos and four measures

before No. 23, where it is intended only for the solo violins.
At No. 23 the violin cadenza should be played as a strict 3/8
measure grouped as follows: seven even notes on the first
eighth;

on the second eighth;

on the third eighth. I would also like to warn cellists that the
B-natural harmonic in the little homage-to-Saint-Saëns solo in
Calliope lies very far back on the string, and is therefore usually
played flat.

What do I love most in *Apollo*? The last six measures of
Calliope; the coda of the Coda; the augmentation in the *pas
d'action* and the cadence that leads from it to the violin solo;
the false-relation cadence in the *pas d'action* (measures 4–5 of
No. 29, and especially the viola E flat); the entire second variation of *Apollo* and the entire Apotheosis.

PERSÉPHONE

R.C.: What do you recall of the original staging of *Perséphone*
and what are your present ideas for staged presentations of
the work?

I.S.: The unstaged preview performance at the Polignacs' is
clearer in my recollection than the actual premiere, and I can
still see the Princess' salon, myself groaning at the piano,
Suvchinsky singing a loud and abrasive Eumolpus, Claudel
glaring at me from the other side of the keyboard, Gide
bridling more noticeably with each phrase.

The actual performance was visually unsatisfactory, which
must be why my memory is so discreet about it, but the fact
that I fail to remember the staging is surprising because the
music was composed and timed to a fixed plan of stage action.
The form is so specifically theatrical, in fact, that at least two

episodes make little sense in concert performances: Pluto's
mute march-aria for oboe and bass instruments, and the sarabande of the *raccourci* ending with the appearance of Mercury.

Perséphone is described in the score as a melodrama, a term
C. S. Lewis defines as "the tragic in exile." It is, in fact, a
masque or dance-pantomime co-ordinated with a sung and
spoken text. Ida Rubinstein declaimed the text at the premiere,
but she did not dance, which was as it should be, or so I
now think. The mime should not speak, the speaker should not
mime, and the part should be shared by two performers. I say
this not only because few mimes, or dancers, are trained speak-
ers as well (an argument refuted by Vera Zorina, who is
skilled both as a dancer and *diseuse*, and who is beautiful to
look at as well—what a superorbital ridge!), but also, and
principally, because the division of labor allows greater freedom for mimetic movement. This is important if only for the
reason that Perséphone's longest soliloquies are musically motionless, but also because I now think it stylistically wrong to
grant one stage figure unique powers of speech: the sound of
Perséphone's voice is always a shock, for a moment, after a
wordless section of mimed or danced movements.

The speaker Perséphone should stand at a fixed point antip-
odal to Eumolpus, and an illusion of motion should be established between them. The chorus should stand apart from and
remain outside of the action. The resulting separation of text
and movement would mean that the staging could be worked
out entirely in choreographic terms. (Balanchine would have
been the ideal choreographer, Tchelitchev the ideal decora-
tor.) At the premiere, Eumolpus stood deep downstage on a
tall pedestal, just out of sight of my beat and just out of
hearing. The chorus did not move, though this was not in
accord with any aesthetic plan, but only because their union
wouldn't let them. Pluto and Mercury did not appear in the
original production, but they should appear, I think, and
Tryptolemus and Demeter as well, if only because any embod-
iment will help to dramatize Gide's undramatic narrative.
Demeter must be related both by costume and stage position

to Eumolpus, who is her priest. But narcissuses and pome-
granates are better kept in the cupboard of comic props now
associated with the Gide-Wilde age.

My first recommendation for a *Perséphone* revival would
be to commission Auden to fit the music with new words, as
Werfel did *La forza del destino*. The rhymes are leaden-
eared:

> *Perséphone confuse*
> *Se refuse*

(I composed the music for this couplet on a train near
Marseille whose rhythm was anapestic.) And the text borders,
at times, on unconscious comedy; *"ivre de nuit . . . encore mal
reveillée,"* for example, sounds like the description of a hang-
over.

But whether *Perséphone* is the patchwork and the bonbon
that its critics claim is not for me to say, and time will tell no
more than a circumstantial truth. As for the critics, I must
remark that no one has cited as stylistically discordant the
section that I grafted whole from a sketch book of 1917 (the
G-minor flute and harp music in Eumolpus' second aria in
Part II). But then, neither has anyone noticed that the two
clarinets in the middle section of the Sarabande anticipate
boogie-woogie by a decade.

Perséphone begins tentatively, the B-flat music in 3/8 meter
near the end is long, and the melodramas beget large stretches
of *ostinato*. I no longer can evaluate such things, or ever again
be as I was when I wrote *Perséphone*. But I still love the music, especially the flutes in Perséphone's final speech (this needs
stage movement!), and the final chorus (when it is played and
sung in tempo, and quietly, without a general *crescendo*). I
love the chord before the C minor Russian Easter music, and I
love the lullaby, *"Sur ce lit elle repose."* I composed this
berceuse for Vera de Bosset in Paris during a heat wave, and
I wrote it originally to my own, Russian, words.

PERSONAL

THOUGHTS OF AN OCTOGENARIAN

"And in his old age the wisdom of his song shall exceed even the beauties of his youth; and it shall be much loved" (Psellus Akritas of Alexandria, *De Ceremonies*, XIV, 7). I am not so sure.

I was born out of time in the sense that by temperament and talent I would have been more suited for the life of a small Bach, living in anonymity and composing regularly for an established service and for God. I did weather the world I was born to, weathered it well, you will say, and I have survived—though not uncorrupted—the hucksterism of publishers, music festivals, recording companies, publicity, including my own ("Self-love is unquestionably the chief motive which leads anyone to speak, and more especially to write respecting himself."—Alfieri, *Memoirs*), conductors, critics (with whom my real argument is that the person who practices the vocation of music should not be judged by the person who has no vocation and does not understand musical practice, and to whom music must therefore be of infinitely less fundamental consequence), and all of the misunderstandings about performance the word concerts has come to mean. But the small Bach might have composed three times as much music.

At eighty I have found new joy in Beethoven, and the Great Fugue now seems to me—it was not always so—a perfect miracle. How right Beethoven's friends were when they convinced him to detach it from opus 130, for it must stand by itself, this absolutely contemporary piece of music that will be contemporary forever. (I wonder, do these statements surprise students of my own later work, the Great Fugue being all variation and development whereas my later music is all canonic and therefore static and objective—in fact, the antithesis of Beethoven's fugue? Do students of my music expect me to cite something like Josquin's *Hic me sidereo* as my "favorite" piece?) Hardly birthmarked by its age, the Great Fugue is as rhythm alone more subtle than any music composed in my own century—I mean, for example, the consequences implied by the notation

as Herr Webern knew. It is pure interval music, this fugue, and I love it beyond any other.

An example of a musical antithesis to me in my own time is *Wozzeck*, though it is a masterpiece of an entirely different sort than the Great Fugue. What disturbs me about *Wozzeck*, a work I love, is the level of its appeal to "ignorant" audiences, with whom one may attribute its success to: 1) the story; 2) Bible, child sentiment; 3) sex; 4) brevity; 5) dynamics, pppp to ffff"; 6) muted brass, ∧ , ▼ , *col legno*, etc.; 7) the idea that the vocal line ⌒⌒ =emotion; 8) the orchestral flagellation in the interludes; 9) the audience's feeling that it is being frightfully modern.

But "passionate emotion" can be conveyed by very different means than these, and within the most "limiting conventions." The Timurid miniaturists, for example, were forbidden to portray facial expression, and in one of my favorite scenes, from the life of an early Zoroastrian king, the artist shows a group of totally blank faces. The dramatic tension is in the way the ladies of the court are shown eavesdropping, and in the slightly discordant gesture of one of the principal figures. In another favorite miniature, two lovers confront each other with stony looks, but the man unconsciously touches his finger to his lips, and this packs the picture with, for me, as much passion as the *crescendo molto* in *Wozzeck*.

The dualism of the self and the body-container widens, as though I had become the demonstration instrument in a platonic form-argument, and the container is more foreign each day, and more of a penance. I wish to walk faster, but my unwilling partner will not execute the wish, and one imminent tomorrow it will refuse to move at all, at which time I shall insist upon an even sharper distinction between the alien form instrument and myself. At four-score, the alienation of the body image is a necessary psychological safety device, and those Lourdeses of glandular and cellular rejuvenation are indispensable articles of belief.

The brain cells are unique in that they cannot be renewed. May I adduce from this that we are born with our talents, that we may "think" or "will" ourselves into command of them, but the thinking and willing potentiality, or call it the cerebral biochemistry, is given? That I was born with the possibility of becoming a composer, and the circumstances of my formation have made me this composer?

I regard my talents as God-given, and I have always prayed to Him for strength to use them. When in early childhood I discovered that I had been made the custodian of musical aptitudes, I pledged myself to God to be worthy of their development, though, of course, I have broken the pledge and received uncovenanted mercies all my life, and though the custodian has too often kept faith on his own all-too-worldly terms.

Creation is its own image and thought is its own mirror. As I think about this metaphor language—it gives me claustrophobia—the word mirror frightens me. Seventy-five years ago as a child alone in my room, I once saw my father instead of myself in the looking glass, and my already strong case of father-fears became mirror-fears as well. I expect Purgatory to be full of many-dimensional mirrors.

What about the much publicized "infinity of possibilities" in connection with the new art material of electronically produced sound? With few exceptions "infinite possibilities" has meant collages of organ burbling, rubber suction (indecent, this), machine-gunning, and other—this is curious—representational and associative noises more appropriate to Mr. Disney's musical mimicries. Not the fact of possibilities, of course, but choice is the beginning of art. The sound lab is already a part of the musical supermarket, however. (Especially in the field of publicity. The structure of a new piece by Xenakis is advertised as having been "worked out on the IBM 7090 electronic computer" as though that were a guarantee of quality.) I know of a composer who wanted "something electronic, kind of middle range, bassoon-trombone like"—these were his only instructions to the sound engineer, who nevertheless flipped a toggle switch, made a few connections, and handed the composer an envelope containing a tape of the desired noise. The composition, I am told, sounds like "electronic Brahms."

Sounds by themselves may be aesthetic, or, at least, painful or pleasurable, but to me they are only a putative material of music. They have another use, too, and a fascinating one, in the new field of audio-analgesics. But a composer is not, by intention, a musical therapist.

An electronic machine cannot dehumanize (whatever that may be); indeed, it can only do what it has been directed to do. It may extend memory functions, for example, when a man has established its memory locations and devised the means to signal and connect them. But the most nearly perfect musical machine, a Stradivarius as well as an electronic synthesizer, is useless until joined to a man with musical skill and imagination. The stained-glass artists of Chartres had few colors, and the stained-glass artists of today have hundreds of colors but no Chartres. Organs, too, have more stops now than ever before, but no Bach. Not enlarged resources, then, but men and what they "believe."

What is the "human measure" in music? And is this a possible question? Isn't the wish to prescribe merely another instance of the fear of becoming other, of changing the past? And, in any case, won't the "human measure" *be* whatever we agree it ought to *be*? As for myself, I am no more concerned with a definition Man than I am with subjective grunts like "good" and "bad." My "human measure" is not only possible, but also exact. It is, first of all, absolutely physical, and it is immediate. I am made bodily ill, for example, by sounds electronically spayed for overtone removal. To me they are a castration threat.

Time, too, is a physical measure to me, and in music I must feel a physical here and there and not only a now, which is to say, movement from and toward. I do not always feel this sense of movement or location in, say, Boulez's *Structures* or those fascinating score-plans by Stockhausen (I have not yet heard his *Momente* for voices and thirteen instruments, but the title augurs well), and though every element in those pieces may be organized to engender motion, the result often seems to me like the essence of the static. A time series may very well postulate a new parable about time, but that is not the same thing as a time experience, which for me is the dynamic passage through time. Nor, of course, are these composers concerned about "dynamic passage through," which betrays an essentially dramatic concept, Greek in origin, like all of my ideas of musical form. The very phrase exposes the gulf between myself and the Teddy Boys of music, and between me and the Zen generation as a whole, and so does their favorite word, vector, which for me is a metaphor in no way analogous to a musical experience, vector being a spatial concept to me, music a purely temporal art.

Anyone who survives a sixty-year span of creative activity in our century must sometimes feel a satisfaction merely in being able to metabolize new experience, to "stay with it"; or, at any rate, this appears to be a greater feat now, where the "ins" are in for a shorter term than in the time of such octogenarians (so far as one can judge other times and generalize about octogenarians) as Sophocles, Voltaire, and Goethe, and where no one can be *primus inter pares*, or hold not only the historical center but even the redoubts for more than two or three years.

I was born to causality and determinism, and I have survived to probability theory and chance. I was born to a world that explained itself largely in dogmatic terms and I have lived, through several changes of management, to a world that rationalizes itself almost entirely in psychoanalytic terms. Educated by simple fact—the trigger one squeezed was what shot the gun—I have had to learn that, in fact, the universe of anterior contributing possibilities was responsible. But I was also born to a non-progressivist notion of the practice of my art, and on this point, though I have survived into a musical society that pursues the opposite idea, I have not been able to change. I do not understand the composer who says we must analyze and determine the evolutionary tendency of the whole musical situation and proceed from there. I have never consciously analyzed any musical situation, and I can follow only where my musical appetites lead me.

And how are we to know "the whole musical situation"? I am something of an aldermanic figure in music today and a composer still considered to be capable of development in some

departments of musical practice, yet recently, trying to read
an essay on current techniques by a foremost scholiast of su-
praserial music, I discovered that I understood hardly a word
—or, rather, hardly a diagram, for the essay looked like an
IBM punch card. Whether I am a forefront or rear-guard or
road-hog composer is beside the point, which is the disparity
between the doer and the explainer. I as a doer have not been
able to "keep up" even in my own specialized and ever-nar-
rowing preserves. And because anything one writes is already
out of date on publication (reread the first page of these
pensées and you will see that they have become quite moldy),
the professional literature of the future (which is now) can
consist only of summaries and supplements—developments in
the field during the previous week. Dr. Toynbee's last book
was called "Volume Twelve: Reconsiderations." And Volume
Thirteen? Further Reconsiderations? And so on.

"Mortify the past." The past as a wish that creates the probability pattern of the future? Did John of the Cross mean that,
and the fear of changing the past which is fear of the present?
I mortify *my* past every time I sit at the piano to compose, in
any case, though I have no wish to go back or to relive a day
of my life. But I have relived much in recent years, perhaps
because four cerebral thromboses have unshuttered the re-
motest reaches of memory or spilled a restorative chemical
over the palimpsest of my baby book. I have been able to roam
in the Phoenix Park of childhood as I could not a decade ago,
but I tug at my memory as a mountain-climber tugs at his
rope: to see how and where it is tied; I do not go back, in the
threat of time, because of a wish to return. And even though
my subconscious may be trying to close the circle, I want to
go on rectilinearly as always: the dualism again. The archaeologist's dream—Renan's—of the past recaptured, is another of
my visions of Purgatory, and the poet's dream—Coleridge's—
of restoring the collective experience of a mind's whole past
existence is, to me, an insanity threat.

My agenbite of inwit is that I do not know while composing, am not aware of, the value question. I love whatever I am now doing, and with each new work I feel that I have at last found the way, have just begun to compose. I love all of my children, of course, and like any father, I am inclined to favor the backward and imperfectly formed ones. But I am actually excited only by the newest (Don Juanism?) and the youngest (nymphetism?). I hope, too, that my best work is still to be written (I want to write a string quartet and a symphony), but "best" means nothing to me while I am composing, and comparisons of the sort that other people make about my music are to me invidious or simply absurd.

Were Eliot and myself merely trying to refit old ships while the other side—Joyce, Schoenberg—sought new forms of travel? I believe that this distinction, much traded on a generation ago, has disappeared. (An era is shaped only by hindsight, of course, and hindsight reduces to convenient unities, but all artists know that they are part of the same thing.) Of course we seemed, Eliot and myself, to have exploited an apparent discontinuity, to have made art out of the *disjecta membra*, the quotations from other poets and composers, the references to earlier styles ("hints of earlier and other creation"), the detritus that betokened a wreck. But we used it, and anything that came to hand, to rebuild, and we did not pretend to have invented new conveyors or new means of travel. But the true business of the artist *is* to refit old ships. He can say again, in his way, only what has already been said.

CONTEMPORARY MUSIC AND RECORDING

Con-tempo: "with the times." Con-tempo music is the most interesting music that ever has been written, and the present moment is the most exciting in music history. It always has been. Nearly all con-tempo music is bad, too, and so it was ever. The "lament of present days," as Byron called it, is as old as the first antiquarian.

Modern: *modernus, modo*: "just now." But, also, *modus,*

"manner," whence "up-to-date" and "fashionable." A more complex word, and evidently of urban origin, though I shall have to look this up in Latin and French poets. (Rimbaud: "*Il faut être absolument moderne.*")

And "new music"? But surely that misplaces the emphasis. What is most new in new music dies quickest, and that which makes it live is all that is oldest and most tried. To contrast the new and the old is a *reductio ad absurdum*, and sectarian "new music" is the blight of contemporaneity. Let us use contempo, then, not technically, in the sense that Schoenberg and Chaminade lived at the same time, but in my meaning: "with the times."

To the performer, a recording is valuable chiefly as a mirror. He is able to reflect himself in it, to walk away from his subjective experience and look at it. A recording session is a shuttling from subjective to objective, and the performer is like the muralist who has to back away from his work to see it in perspective. In my case the perspective of the object, the playback, dwindles to a point of identity when I conduct, and the located object, myself conducting the music, is replaced by, simply, the music—or, rather, as it is my music, myself in the music, for I am always aware of my being in my music. This mirroring is the main point, I think, and not whether a recording extends the range of peripheral hearing or canalizes hearing selectively (dangers as well as advantages): a record is a lever that can lift one outside of one's performance involvement, or "far out" enough, at least, to establish the illusion.

Mirrors are also mnemonic devices. One sees what one was rather than what one is; the immediate has too many shadings. One looks into one's mirrors and is aware only of the subtraction; one listens to oneself to compare. The recognition of a time seam and its point of view is evident to me in other people's recordings of other composers, too, of course, though there my reaction is more passive. But I imagine that any still-growing performer must be similarly disturbed.

By definition, contemporary music is unfamiliar, and, by deduction, it is more difficult than other types of music to record. (I do not say that it is more difficult to perform; it is and it isn't, in different ways.) The fifty recordings of the Beethoven symphony are fifty different angles of distortion, but these distortions actually protect the scope of the work: the larger the variorum, the greater the guarantee that Beethoven himself will remain intact. The recording of the contemporary, on the other hand, lacking comparison, fixes the music at a single angle, and the gravest danger of this fixed angle, which is that the truly contemporary exists on the precarious edge of the comprehensible, is not obvious. What is wrong with the Beethoven performance is evident and cannot damage the work, but what is wrong in the performance of the unfamiliar work is not at all evident, and the line between sense and nonsense in it may, and often does, depend upon its performance. The difference between a Kandinsky and a doodler, a Schoenberg and a lunatic, was apparent to only a few imaginative and highly trained perceivers in 1912. We know that even such a close disciple as Alban Berg could not at that time readily follow *Pierrot lunaire*. I state as axiomatic, then, that performance of the unfamiliar is a greater responsibility and must seek higher standards than performance of the familiar. Every first recording is a risk.

The question of value in repertory versus non-repertory: I see no artistic reason to proliferate recordings of music that is widely performed live. I mean the concertos in B-flat Minor, the tone poems in E-flat Major, the symphonies in E Minor. A recording is, or should be, a performance, and who can suffer exactly the same set of performance limitations more than once—at least with familiar music? I do suffer them when the music is unfamiliar, but with less pain because they do not distract unduly from the learning process, the becoming familiar. The recording of non-repertory, of what is not generally available live, should be the *raison d'être* of the industry.

How many people in the United States have heard live performances of Schoenberg's larger dramatic works? The answer —in full figures for per capita comparison—is 000,000,000, and the conclusion is obvious: recordings, rather than isolated and sporadic concerts, are the chief means of communication between the contemporary composer and his audience.

A footnote on non-repertory with another meaning of that term: non-existent. An advertisement for a new disc from the current catalogue says something about "Stokowski's Bach." But no such Bach ever existed. "Bach's Stokowski" would make far more sense historically. And I have just received an album with a blurb about "The great conductor" von K.'s "Mozart." But what does von K.'s conducting really do to Mozart? It opens his bier, unclasps his hands from his bosom, and folds them behind his head.

I have just received some programs of a concert series in Leningrad dedicated to my later music. Every musician—composer, conductor, music educator—to whom I have shown them has pronounced the same comment: "I wonder what the performances sounded like, as no one there has heard the music." In other words, the printed page is no longer self-sufficient, but should be supplemented by a recorded guide.

What are my attitudes to my own recorded performances? I have already said that I only listen to them critically and that I could not do any of them the same way again. But even the poorest are valid readings to guide other performers, and the best, like the new *Zvezdoliki* and *Symphony in C*, are very good indeed. What are the poorest? Those pieces which were too new to me, and for which I had no settled ideas and technical habits of performance. The recordings of *The Rake's Progress*, *Lulu*, and *Moses und Aron* have very effectively helped to kill those operas in America, where—the latter two, anyway—they are known only by records.

What, to a composer, is most important about a recorded performance? The spirit, of course, the same as in any performance. The spirit of the London recordings of my music has fallen arches, for instance, the spirit of the Mercury recordings has been propped up in Adler elevator shoes, and the spirit of the L'Oiseau-Lyre *Dumbarton Oaks* is that of a very slow choochoo. Next to the spirit come the two chief questions of the flesh: tempo and balance. I am annoyed by the violin solo in my *Agon* recording. It seems to emanate from the bedroom, while the trombone accompaniment sounds as though it is in my lap. But imbalances of this sort were common in early stereo recordings, and whereas a monaural was a closet, an early stereo was three closets. We also heard things we had never heard before, but we didn't always want to. Now we have learned to let backgrounds be backgrounds, like bygones, and we know that acoustics pretends to be, but is not yet, a science. But I am even more irritated by an impossible tempo. If the speeds of everything in the world and in ourselves have changed, our tempo feelings cannot remain unaffected. The metronome marks one wrote forty years ago were contemporary forty years ago. Time is not alone in affecting tempo—circumstances do too, and every performance is a different equation of them. I would be surprised if any of my own recordings follow the metronome markings.

"Live music is at least a performance"—which is meant to imply that recordings are not. In fact, though, performers can be inspired even in recording studios and concentration there is at least as great as it is in concerts. But with technically complex contemporary music, true performance on records, though it should always be the goal, is difficult to attain. The published version usually, in fact, is a pastiche of excerpts from the best of several forays. I can make this clear only by a description of such a session.

It lasts three hours. The music has not been rehearsed, of course, and the first two hours are therefore used in spot-rehearsing it. During this time, microphones are adjusted, balance tests are made, positions of instruments are changed, and sometimes the whole orchestra is reseated. The conductor's faculties are entirely concentrated on the problem of when to stop and explain or correct—on deciding what a player or an orchestra is likely to resolve the next time around on its own and what it will never understand without prompting and explanation. This is a matter of the conductor's and the orchestra's experience, but not entirely of that, and some part of the decision will always be a gamble. When this perfunctory contact with the music is over and the actual recording has begun, the attention of the conductor is turned to the clock. From then on he becomes a machine for making decisions. Can this section be improved if it is played once more, and how much time remains, and how much music has still to be recorded? The recording director will advise him to go on, of course, telling him that the section may be repeated "if time is left at the end" (quotation from the standard A-&-R recording director's manual), but every recording session is a photo finish, and even if one could return to something recorded earlier, the sound levels would not match.

(Editing and preparing the master record from such a session is an equally interesting non-musical exercise, largely because such a charming vocabulary has developed: scrub the tuba, dip the room noise, dig for the cellos, echo the splice. But if I were to expose the realities of editing, I would bury the bluff about performance and kill the sale of records.)

If the conductor is the surgeon in this three-hour operation, his anesthetist is the A-&-R supervisor. This accomplice must be a virtuoso listener and score-reader, a child psychologist, and a liar ("Marvelous take, everybody"). He also must know his artist to such an extent that he can keep him directed toward a performance that the artist himself may have lost sight of. And he must hide his boredom, too, for he spends most of his time recording the Liberaces of classical music, and the contemporary music he does do (in this case not contemporary, but modern) is likely to be the gimmick pieces for vibraphones, *Sprechstimme*, and *ponticello*—in other words, sound effects rather than music. Qualified recording supervisors are rare, and the opportunity to collaborate with them is rarer still. I have such a collaboration at present—Mr. John McClure of Columbia—and I hope to make many more records.

SOME PEOPLE

WRITERS

R.C.: What are your personal recollections of Evelyn Waugh, Gerald Heard, Christopher Isherwood, Aldous Huxley?

I.S.: When I met Mr. Waugh, in New York in February 1949, his popping blue eyes looked upon me as an oddity, and I soon found that the cutting edge in the books was even sharper in the person. I was an admirer of Mr. Waugh's talent for dialogue and the naming of characters (Dr. Kakaphilos, Father Rothschild, S.J., etc.). In person I admired, even while suffering from, the agility with which he caused my remarks to boomerang. But whether Mr. Waugh was disagreeable, or only preposterously arch, I cannot say. Horace Walpole remarks somewhere that the next worst thing to disagreeableness is too-agreeableness. I would reverse the order of preference myself while conceding that on short acquaintance disagreeableness is the greater strain. I addressed Mr. Waugh in French, and he replied that he did not speak the language. (His wife contradicted him charmingly, and was rebuked.) I asked whether he would care for a whisky and was told that "I do not drink whisky before meals," stated as a fact I should have known. I made an admiring remark about the Constitution of the United States and was reminded that Mr. Waugh is a Tory. I used the word music and was immediately informed that music is physical torment to Mr. Waugh. We talked at length only about United States burial customs, and here Mr. Waugh's impressive technical knowledge led me to believe he was gathering material for a doctorate on mausoleums. (I visited Forest Lawn and the Hollywood Pet Cemetery after reading *The Loved One,* and I esteem the book even more highly after viewing the sources of its inspiration.) At dinner I recommended chicken, but this was a new *gaffe.* "It's Friday," Mr. Waugh said. But by the time the meatless meal was over and he had peeled, sucked, and blown a cigar, the clipped conversation was succeeded by whole sentences of almost amiability. I still much admire Mr. Waugh.

Gerald, Christopher, and Aldous are dear and intimate friends—loved ones, in fact, though not in Mr. Waugh's sense. I should not talk about my friends, I know, but my excuse for doing so is that I want to record my pride and pleasure in having these three.

Gerald is a virtuoso talker, the most brilliant I have ever Heard, and he *likes* to talk, just as Artur Rubinstein *likes* to play the piano. (Isaiah Berlin is even faster and funnier—an ironical gaiety underlies everything he says—but Isaiah tends to speak in spurts, like a ticker tape. Wystan Auden, by comparison, fishes, though profoundly, between words, and Aldous is too serenely high in tessitura, and in volume too suavely soft.)

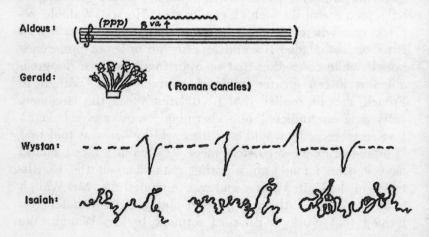

I first saw Gerald lecture in 1950, and regularly, thereafter, attended his Sunday sermons in Hollywood's Ivar Street Temple. He was, all of him, a stunning performer: blue eyes, red beard, long, thin fingers. Especially the fingers. He would grip the sides of the pulpit until the knuckle skin whitened, then flex and spread a skeletal hand. He would direct his index finger aloft in a terrifying gesture of admonishment, then line up four darning-needle digitals from the other hand, and as points one to four were enumerated, strike them down like bowling pins. Before each sermon, Gerald would clear the spiritual decks with a minute of meditation. He managed to electrify that minute, too.

I was frightened when we first met, of course, and when we dined together after his talks, I said hardly a word. At that time I would unkindly think that, though the Guru regarded his listeners intently in the short intervals allowed for reply ("yes" or "no"), he was in fact already preparing new paragraphs that were not entirely contingent on their answers. Later, when Gerald discovered that I had no idea what his talk was *about*—he used to lead off with questions like "Have you seen Semov's latest work on the engram complex?" and then go on about the thalamus, which, for all I knew, could have been a vegetable—we relaxed and became the closest friends.

I first heard the name Christopher Isherwood from André Maurois, and I read the *Berlin Stories* on his recommendation. Later, when I knew Isherwood, I was astonished by how exactly like the "Chris" of the stories he was. The question of 1) "my art" and 2) "my life" did not exist for him. His books were himself, and he stepped in and out of them without so much as zipping a zipper.

Everything about Isherwood is boyish: his looks, his laugh, his candor, even the Americanisms—"gee," "gosh"—in his speech. His eyes are his most striking feature; they look through you and beyond—all the way up to Karma, in fact. But one also remembers the sharply notched nose, the side-of-the-mouth smile that quickly gives way to full-faced grins, and the high, resonant voice, more resonant after alcohol and accompanied then by a marked decline in diction, a peculiar wagging of the knees, and a protrusion of the tongue suggesting that the owner is being garroted. We have often been drunk together—as often as once a week, in the early 1950s, I should think—and in such different climes as Sequoia Park and Santa Monica beach.

On Christopher's first visit to my home, he fell asleep when someone started to play a recording of my music. My affection for him began with that incident. I soon discovered that conversation with him may appear to be relaxed, but is actually full of undertow. "Serious" conversation, that is; Christopher has a weakness for movieland Hollywood, and about that he can talk without undercurrent trouble. But Christopher is not now, nor ever could have been, a camera. His reflective processes are too agonizingly acute, and however natural his gifts, writing can only be a torture to an intellectual self-awareness of his kind, though, of course, a commensurate satisfaction, too. Christopher's intelligence can clear a path of lucidity through even the fuzziest of subjects, and his merciless eye can pierce every disguise of hypocrisy and cant. This much I know from his journals, that Domesday Book in which, I fear, my own sins, especially those of vanity and intellectual ambiguity, lie bared. But Christopher is a passionately loyal friend, and I feel very close to him.

Aldous Huxley is the most aristocratic man I have ever known, and I do not mean in the sense of birth, though few people since J. S. Mill can have been so intellectually well-bred; or in appearance, though he has a truly noble head. Aldous is an aristocrat of behavior. He is gentle, humble, courageous, intellectually charitable.

Of the learned people I know, he is the most delectable conversationalist, and of that breed he is one of the few who are always droll. True conversation requires a matching of participants, of course, and though I myself am far from a match for Aldous, I have attended him with equals—his brother Julian, for instance—and come away uplifted from

Olympian hours of learning and wit. (Julian is a good friend, too, though I have not seen him since 1957 when we listened to a performance of Bach's *"Aus der Tiefe"* together with Arthur Waley, but Julian's is the Other Culture, and though I love to hear him on the joys of eutelegenesis—artificial insemination by an admired donor—his discourse is too recondite for me, and he himself is too much the cynosure of science.)

I met Aldous in London at the time of the publication of *Point Counter Point*, through our mutual friend Victoria Ocampo. We saw a film together on that occasion, Tolstoy's *Resurrection*, but concerning Aldous I remember only his strongly lenticular *lunettes* and, through them, his eyes like the magnified eyes of fish in an aquarium. When I saw him next, in Hollywood a dozen years later, the spectacles had disappeared, but he was able to see only by force of mind and by such tricks as memorizing the numbers of steps to his friends' front doors. (I have seen Aldous identify desert flowers from a speeding car, nevertheless, and I know that he discovered an unknown and unsigned Catherwood in a flea market from a distance of twenty feet.) The fact of his weak eyesight undoubtedly accounts for certain of his feats of memory and for his ability to add large sums and solve complex numerical problems "in his head," operations he performs with as much velocity and considerably less noise than a Univac robot.

I encountered Aldous only rarely in my first years in California—at that time, the period of *The Perennial Philosophy*, he lived in the desert—but we did exchange letters. Then, in the summer of 1949, we began to meet and lunch together at the Farmer's Market as often as three times a week. We also attended concerts, plays, and film previews, and we explored Southern California's museums, zoological gardens, architectural oddities. I remember Aldous in an art gallery diagnosing through his magnifying glass the pituitary disease of a stoatish, school-of-Brueghel peasant. I remember him in the San Diego Zoo referring to each caged creature by its Latin name, while revealing fascinating facts about its sexual habits and I.Q. I remember him peering at a huge Los Angeles bank in construction next to a tiny church and murmuring something about "God and Mammon in the usual proportion."

Aldous' "point-of-view" is more nearly "synoptic" than that of anyone else I know, and he is my only friend who is equally at home in either Culture. In his home I have met hypnotists, economists, parasitologists, speleologists, industrialists, physicists, occultists (the Lebanese magician, Tara Bey), holy men from India, actors, anthropologists, educators (Robert Hutchins), astronomers (the late Edwin Hubble), and even an occasional literary gent.

What is Aldous "like"? Well, he is "like" Beerbohm's willowy drawing, especially the long, ever folding and unfolding legs. He is passionate about music. He is morbidly shy. He cannot resist new gadgets, whether spiritual ones like LSD or physical ones such as the vibrating chair in his study which relaxes me about as much as would a raft ride in the English Channel. Other Aldine characteristics are the tendency to lip-smack over the short, black future of the human race, and the little expressions of shock at each day's discovery of each new example of human genius and/or bestiality ("One doesn't know what to think . . . The mind boggles . . . Absolutely extraordinary . . ."). Aldous addresses everyone with the same gentleness, and he always assumes that other people possess as much knowledge and intelligence as himself; whether considering the history of the Baptist Church in Burma or Stendhal's recipe for *zabaglione*, Aldous assumes that you know all this, even though, momentarily, you may have forgotten—which is the Socratic method, after all. But in spite of twenty-five years in Southern California, he remains an English gentleman for whom the ultimate and most wanton demonstration of affection for an old friend is a pat on the shoulder. The scientist's habit of examining everything from every side and of turning everything upside down and inside out is also characteristic of Aldous. I remember him leafing through a copy of *transition*, reading a poem in it, looking again at the title of the magazine, reflecting for a moment, then saying, "backwards it spells NO IT ISN(T) ART."

A decade ago Aldous' friendship was a great comfort to me.
And more; Aldous is a healer, a skillful masseur who cured me
of insomnia. Since then Aldous has suffered the tragic loss of
his wife, Maria. He has also suffered from a Hollywood fire
that destroyed his home and all its contents, including his
journal about D. H. Lawrence, that more emotionally com-
bustible man than Aldous who, I think, was the one human
being Aldous completely admired. But Aldous is an aristocrat,
as I have said, and therefore a stoic, and stoicism takes an
inward toll. The day after the conflagration, Aldous' only comment was: "Well, you know, it *is* inconvenient."

Aldous once introduced a catalogue of my wife's paintings.
I quote it both out of family pride and because it contains
Aldous' finest qualities:

Fantasy in painting is of many kinds and runs the whole gamut,
from dramatic and symbolic imagination at one end of the scale
to purely formal imagination at the other. The imagination which
animates Vera de Bosset's work lies somewhere between the two
extremes and partakes, in some measure, of both. At the formal
end of the scale, she possesses a wonderful gift for inventing
colored patterns; but this gift is combined with another, the gift
of transforming her formal inventions into an amused and amusing commentary on the realities around her—an oilfield, for example, a fishbowl, a boulevard at night with all its headlamps
and neons. She sees the heavenly oddity in things, she is touched
by their absurd and pathetic loveliness; and she proceeds to ren-
der these aspects of reality, not directly, not in terms of impressions caught on the wing and recorded in calligraphic shorthand,
but at one remove, through what may be called their visionary
equivalent. This visionary equivalent of the world's preposterous
beauties is a specially created universe of flat houses, depth-
less landscapes, two-dimensional aquariums—a private universe,
where the colors glow with preternatural brilliance, where the
darks are like lacquer and the lights like so many small apoca-
lypses from another world of angelic gaiety and paradisal en-
joyments. Here is a happy art, and as Jeffrey once ventured to
tell Carlyle, "You have no mission on earth (whatever you may

fancy) half so important as to be innocently happy." In these paintings Vera de Bosset has certainly done her duty and fufilled her mission.

R.C.: What are your recollections of Cocteau and St.-John Perse?

I.S.: I believe that I first was introduced to Cocteau at a rehearsal of the *Firebird*, but it might have been some time after the *Firebird*, in the street; I remember someone calling my name in the street—"*C'est vous IgOR?*"—and turning around to see Cocteau introducing himself. In any case, Cocteau was one of my first French friends, and in my first years in Paris we were often together. His conversation was always a highly diverting performance, though at times it was rather like that of a feuilletonist out to make a "career." I soon learned to appreciate Cocteau's many sterling qualities, however, and we have remained dear and lifelong friends—indeed, he is the only close friend I have of the *Firebird* period. Just before my first London visit, in the spring of 1912, I moved to the Crillon. (I remember that an electric sign in the Crillon lobby flashed reports of Channel weather conditions, and that Diaghilev used to watch for these reports in a perpetual state of alarm.) As Cocteau lived nearby, we began to dine together. I remember that we used to frequent a certain café at which stamps were sold as well as drinks and food, and that once when the waiter said "*Cognacs, messieurs?*" Cocteau replied, "*Non, merci, je préfère les timbres.*" In 1914 Cocteau came to Leysin to try to enlist my collaboration in a ballet he proposed to call *David*. A young Swiss artist, Paulet Thévenaz, accompanied him on this trip and painted a portrait of my wife and me. Cocteau's letters to me afterward are covered with attractive sketches for the never-to-be-realized ballet. But Cocteau is a master designer whose quick eye and economical line can fix the character of any quarry in a few loops. His best caricatures are as good as any but Picasso's, I think, and much modified by erasure, Cocteau scrawled his with photographic speed. When Cocteau first discussed his costumes and masks for the 1952 *Oedipus* with me, he ended each description by scribbling the design on a piece of paper. Though this took him only a few seconds the drawings—I have them still—are each a talented print of his personality.

And his personality is generous and disarmingly simple. Artistically, he is a first-rate critic and a theatrical and cinematographic innovator of a high order. The invention of his that I like best is the angel Heurtebise in *Orphée*. Heurtebise was the name of a well-known elevator company in Paris, and the word thus gave the necessary suggestion of levitation. But Cocteau also made Heurtebise a glazier who carries wing-shaped slats of glass.

Giraudoux, Morand, and St.-John Perse, when I first knew them, were all three employed by the Foreign Ministry (Quai d'Orsay). I was personally closer to Morand than to the others, until the 1939 war, but I was greatly attracted to the theater of Giraudoux. Giraudoux was the last person I saw in Paris before leaving France in September 1939. I sometimes met him with St.-John Perse, as I met Morand with Édouard Herriot. Perse worked directly with Briand, and thanks to his connection I was able to obtain permission to travel out of France for concerts when I came to live there, in 1920, which as a depatriated Russian I could not otherwise have done.

I came to know St.-John Perse more closely in his later Washington years, and not only himself, but also his work, and I admire him for the way he has continued to live, with all of his laurels, in that loneliest of cities.

I first read him—the hot Caribbean colors of *Pour fêter une enfance*—in 1911 or 1912. I followed his work thereafter, but at long intervals, which were not my fault, but his. His poems are a doxology of botany, of winds and seas, of stones and earth, of third-person man, and though one should not excerpt from an epic, his epics are temptingly full of memorable lines:

La mer elle-même comme une ovation soudaine!

for example, and,

> *un couple d'aigles, depuis hier, tient la Ville sous le charme de ses grandes manières,*

which might have been by Rimbaud, and

> *des jeunes veuves de guerriers, comme de grandes urnes rescellées,*

and

> *nous avons si peu de temps pour naître à cet instant*

which reminds me that I must get back to work.

COMPOSERS

R.C.: Were you aware in your St. Petersburg years of the work of such Russian experimental composers as Rebikov, with his whole-tone structures, unresolved dissonances, fourths *à la* Schoenberg's *Kammersymphonie*; Gnessin, with his *Sprechgesang*; and Roslavetz, with his "non-dodecaphonic serial sets"?

I.S.: I was indeed acquainted with the work of these stepping-stone composers and though I did not meet Roslavetz, I was much interested in certain compositions of his that I heard in St. Petersburg. The now so-called serial-set music, such as *Three Compositions for Piano*, was all written after I left Russia, and I have only recently seen it. Roslavetz came from Tchernigov, incidentally, which is where my father was born; "Tcherni" means "black," and "gov" means "soil." I did not know Rebikov personally, either, but his innovations were familiar to me in my Rimsky-Korsakov years and I much admired at least one of his works, the ballet *Yelka*.

Roslavetz and Rebikov were "Moscow composers," but Gnessin was a Petersburg pupil of Rimsky-Korsakov. I knew him well. I do not think his composer's gifts were strong or original—at least, everything of his that I heard sounded perfectly anonymous—but he was the liveliest and most open-minded spirit of the Rimsky group (though when I consider that the others were Steinberg, Glazunov, Gretchaninov, and Tcherepnin, the compliment sounds less generous than I intend it to be). Gnessin's *Sprechgesang* was only of passing interest, however, because, unlike Schoenberg's, it did not grow out of a musical necessity. But Gnessin himself was a striking character. He dressed as an Orthodox Hebrew, but at the same time was identified with radically antisectarian political and social views. I once sent him a note, after we had dined together, saying that I was delighted by our "sympathetic understanding." He answered me in a surprised and slightly shocked tone saying that he was sorry but I had been mistaken; he had felt no such sympathy. That was typical of Gnessin and, I suppose, it explains why I remember him.

R.C.: What recent composition by an American-born composer has most attracted you?

I.S.: Elliott Carter's Double Concerto, I think, but you would have to know what other music I have heard to evaluate the preference (and Heaven forbid that I should list it; American music will soon need a Ford Foundation for the Suppression of Unpromising Composers)—and how frequently I have heard it. Foss's *Time Cycle*, for example, does not, on one hearing, require such strong criticism as that of the English newspaper that described it as "appealing to teen-age taste" and called it "an undergraduate parody of modern music from B to X (Boulez to Xenakis)." One naturally thinks of large-scale pieces, too, Sessions' *Theocritus* and Wolpe's *Symphony*, which I haven't heard; and the symphonies of X and Y and Z, which, alas, I have—they always take the same half-hour to perform and, one supposes, rather less than that to write. I therefore neglect the many excellent smaller examples of—what seems to me anyway—a distinctly American and very lovely pastoral lyricism: Ruggles' *Angels* and *Lilacs*, Babbitt's *The Widow's Lament in Springtime*, Copland's Dickinson songs.

I like the mood of Carter's Concerto, first of all. It is full of new-found good spirits, as his quartets were not. But the success of the piece is owing to the listener's eventual involvement and satisfaction in its form. That the Double Concerto should suggest Berg's towering example in general ways is not surprising, but I hear direct references to the Berg in it, too. (Carter is certainly not a naïve composer, but I think these Berg bits are unknowing.) The passage from 432 (the piano entrance here is one of the finest things in the piece) to 460, and especially the flute at 436 and the bassoon at 441, remind me of the Berg, and the architectural plot of the solo instruments—their roles as alternate soloists, duo soloists, parts of ensemble groups—also is reminiscent of the Berg. The Concerto presents many interesting performance problems, not so much in instrumental technique—not in the wind and string parts anyway, though the percussion is a different matter—as in rhythm. The score introduces no metrical difficulties, and as the proportionalisms of tempos are easy to hear if the orchestras are reversed from the composer's seating plan so that the conductor stands next to the harpsichord, it is easy to conduct. Incidentally, the most effective example of an interlocking of tempos by a held-over beat pattern is precisely where it is most apparent (loudest): the percussion at measures 143–144. I do not think the chief rhythmic difficulty is in the notation—though I can imagine orchestra players complaining about that, and perhaps fidelity to the writing of the rhythmic series does make the instrumental parts momentarily more difficult to read: I mean, for example, four dotted sixteenths to the dotted quarter rather than "four for three" without the dots, as I would now do it. The rhythmic problem of the Concerto is the old one common to most contemporary music. The player manages the notes, but cannot count the rests or feel irregular pulsations—or regular ones, but without simple patterns—when he is not playing.

I like not only the shape but also the sense of proportion in the Concerto, and I like the harpsichord and piano writing very much, too. And the intended high point, the coda, is the real climax of the piece. (This section is unclear, though, in the recording, where the rhythm is a blur and the dynamic plan is without profile. The question of dynamics in recording practice must be criticized more strongly than anyone has criticized it so far. The harpsichord is weak in volume by nature, or so the engineer assumes; but this weakness is overcompensated by about ninety percent in the recording.) I cannot comment upon or add to the composer's own analysis, but analysis as little explains a masterpiece or calls it into being as an ontological proof explains or causes the existence of God. There, the word is out. A masterpiece, by an American composer.

R.C.: What are your memories of George Gershwin?

I.S.: I met Gershwin in New York in 1925 and spent an evening with him at Paul Kochanski's. He knew a few words of Russian, but no French, and therefore we had to talk through Kochanski. I remember him as a tall man—taller than I am, anyway—and very nervously energetic. At that time I hardly knew who he was and I was totally unacquainted with his music. He played the *Rhapsody in Blue* for me at the piano that night and some other pieces whose titles I forget, but none of the music interested me. I saw him again in Hollywood shortly before his death, at a dinner given for me by Edward G. Robinson, with Chaplin, Paulette Goddard, Marlene Dietrich. Gershwin was very *à la page* then, but he had not been spoiled by that.

But the popular story about myself and Gershwin regrettably is untrue. Gershwin is supposed to have come to me in Paris and to have asked me how much I would charge to give him lessons. I am then supposed to have asked how much he earned, and after he had supposedly said $100,000 a year, my supposed reply was, "Then I should take lessons from you." A nice story, but I heard it about myself from Ravel a year before I met Gershwin. One rather bad moment of pure Gershwin in my own music, incidentally, though it anticipated the Brooklyn composer by a decade, is the Emperor's *"Bonjour à tous"* in *Le Rossignol.*

R.C.: You have so far said little about Hindemith and Křenek. What do you recall of your associations with these composers?

I.S.: I met Hindemith for the first time in Amsterdam, I believe in 1924, at a concert by the Amar Quartet, of which he was the violist. I remember him as short, stocky, and even at that time almost bald. He was already widely discussed as a composer, but I had not heard any of his music, and I am no longer certain which piece of his I did hear first, though I think it must have been the attractive unaccompanied Viola Sonata, opus 11, played by himself. (*"Hindemith kratzt auf seiner Bratsche,"* the Schoenbergians said.) I encountered Hindemith often in the late 1920s but I knew him well only after 1930, when we were both published by Schott, which was then under the guidance of Willy Strecker, who was to become my close friend. Strecker was extremely effective in promoting Hindemith's music after World War I and in advancing the idea of a Stravinsky-Hindemith team. He once persuaded me to publish a favorable opinion about Hindemith's *Das Unaufhörliche*, a work I really only thought very appropriately named, just as, years later, he induced me to sign a squib recommending Henze's *Boulevard Solitude.*

In Berlin, one day in 1931, I was invited to the Hindemiths' for lunch, but when I arrived the housekeeper said the esteemed composer and his wife had not yet returned from their daily exercises. Just then they came running up the stairs, both in white linen shorts and both out of breath. They had been trotting in the Grünewald with their athletic instructor and, judging from the panting, they must have run home from there. I think of this incident every time I hear one of those setting-up-exercise concertos by Hindemith, though the whole scene seems as remote to me now as a period piece by Isherwood.

Hindemith and I traveled the same concert circuit in the

1930s, and our paths often crossed. We were neighbors for a time, too, in Positano in 1937, when I was composing my Concerto in E Flat, and he the ballet St. Francis, which I heard later that year in Paris. I recall with pleasure an excursion to Paestum which we took together then. Our friendship continued to develop in the United States during World War II, but we have seen each other only rarely since then—at a concert in New York in 1953 in which he conducted his Trakl song-cycle, in Munich at the time of his opera *Harmonie der Welt*, and at Santa Fe in 1961.

I am not entitled to an opinion of Hindemith's music, as I know next to nothing of it. I have seen none of his operas and have heard but few examples of his concert music. I liked his ballets *The Four Temperaments* and *Hérodiade*, I liked the *Schwanendreher* when I heard him play it in Paris in 1935 or 1936, I liked the Wind Quintet, and I found the *Ludus Tonalis* interesting to look at. But I have also heard pieces of his that were as arid and indigestible as cardboard and as little nourishing. I am ashamed of my ignorance of Hindemith, though, for he is a loyal friend, a man of elegant conduct and a truly delightful fund of humor. His only crime, in fact, is that he has refused to speak a new lingo, and those who do speak it—many of them just in time—have turned their backs on him. Now, though I would enjoy shielding Hindemith from the unaesthetic view of some of those backs, I know my shield is not needed. In another decade, when the new lingo has become the old lingo, when *Diarrhoea Polacco, Kontakte, Mobiles for Shakespeare*, etc., are gathering dust next to Hindemith's *Der Ploner Musiktag*, we shall see whether the authors of those masterpieces behave with the dignity of Paul Hindemith.

Křenek was a chubby, cherub-faced young man when he came to call on me in Nice one day in the late 1920s. I knew of him then only as the *Wunderkind* composer of *Jonny spielt auf*. He brought me a gift, a rare orchestra score of a Strauss waltz, and thus began an acquaintance that in our mutual California years was to develop into an affectionate sympathy. I do not remember the exact occasion of our next meeting, but I think it was at one of Klemperer's Bach concerts in Los Angeles or at a small concert honoring Schoenberg's seventy-fifth birthday. We saw each other regularly thereafter, and exchanged visits to each other's homes. Křenek lives in a Kokoschka mountain-landscape in the Tujunga Hills, north of Los Angeles. His dining room there is decorated with his own somewhat Kokoschka-like painting, incidentally, and his attractive watercolors of desert views hang throughout the house. I knew little of Křenek's music a decade ago, but I knew and liked the Symphonic Elegy for Strings and the *Lamentations of Jeremiah*. Perhaps my own *Threni* shows contact with the *Lamentations*. Křenek's short treatise on twelve-tone counterpoint was the first work I read on that subject, too, and his *Spiritus Intelligentiae Sanctus* was the first electronic "score" I had an opportunity to study.

Křenek is an intellectual and a composer, a difficult combination to manage, and he is profoundly religious, which goes nicely with the composer side, less nicely with the other thing. He is also a gentleman and a scholar—an authority on Offenbach as well as Ockeghem—and that is an even rarer combination, or so I would think, judging from the scholarly journals I read.

Křenek's sixtieth birthday was celebrated recently by the whole musical world—a unit that does not include his adopted city, where he can sometimes be seen conducting for no remuneration at certain interesting small concerts, but never at the "Philharmonic." (He should not be unhappy about this though, for to be ignored by the "Philharmonic" puts him in good company: Schoenberg was totally disregarded by the local orchestra for the whole of his seventeen years in Los Angeles.) But Křenek will be honored one day even at home, and I look forward to reading Charles Eliot Norton lectures by him on—may I suggest a subject?—"The Psychological

Principles of Auditory Form"; something of that sort is needed, by a musician, in the line of Ehrenzweig's *Psychoanalysis of Artistic Vision and Hearing*.

R.C.: Have you any further personal recollections of Arnold Schoenberg?

I.S.: I had heard Schoenberg's name as early as 1907, but *Pierrot lunaire* was my first contact with his music. I had not seen any score by him either, and to my recollection nothing by him was played in St. Petersburg while I lived there. I do not know how the Berlin meeting with him came about, but the initiative for it must have been Diaghilev's; Diaghilev wanted to commission Schoenberg. I remember sitting with Schoenberg, his wife Mathilde, and Diaghilev at a performance of *Petroushka*, and I have a clear memory of Schoenberg in his green room after he had conducted the fourth performance of *Pierrot lunaire* in the Choralion-saal, 4 Bellevuestrasse, Sunday, December 8, 1912, at twelve o'clock noon; I still have my canceled ticket. Albertine Zehme, the *Sprechstimme* artist, wore a Pierrot costume and accompanied her epiglottal sounds with a small amount of pantomime. I remember that and the fact that the musicians were seated behind a curtain, but I was too occupied with the copy of the score Schoenberg had given me to notice anything else. I also remember that the audience was quiet and attentive and that I wanted Frau Zehme to be quiet too, so that I could hear the *music*. Diaghilev and I were equally impressed with *Pierrot*, though he dubbed it a product of the *Jugendstil* movement, aesthetically.

I encountered Schoenberg several times during my short stay in Berlin, and I was in his home more than once. I arrived at the Adlon Hotel from Switzerland on November 20, 1912; I remember that I had been working on the orchestra score of *Le Sacre* on the train. Eduard Steuermann, the pianist of the first *Pierrot*, recalls a dinner with me in Schoenberg's house at which Webern and Berg were present but, alas, I have no recollection of this, my First and Last Supper with the hypostatic trinity of twentieth-century music.

When I met Berg in Venice in September 1934, at the concert in which I conducted my *Capriccio* and Scherchen *Der Wein*—two pieces as different as Eros and Agape—we did not mention an earlier meeting. Someone told me that after hearing the *Capriccio*, Berg said he wished he could write "such light-hearted music," but when he introduced himself to me in the artists' room after the concert his manner seemed slightly condescending—though short men often feel they have been condescended to by tall men.

Schoenberg was small in stature. I am five feet three inches and weigh 120 pounds. These measurements were exactly the same fifty years ago, but Schoenberg was shorter than I am. He was bald, too, with a wreath of black hair around the rim of his white cranium, like a Japanese actor's mask. He had large ears and a soft, deep voice—not so *basso* as mine—with a mellow, Viennese accent. His eyes were protuberant and explosive, and the whole force of the man was in them. I did not know then what I know now, which is that in the three years prior to *Pierrot*, Schoenberg had written the *Five Pieces for Orchestra*, *Erwartung*, and *Die glückliche Hand*, a body of works we now recognize as the epicenter of the development of our musical language. (By "we" I mean a small group still, for most composers are still bumping into each other in the dark.) The real wealth of *Pierrot*—sound and substance, for *Pierrot* is the solar plexus as well as the mind of early twentieth-century music—were beyond me as they were beyond all of us at that time, and when Boulez wrote that I had understood it *d'un façon impressioniste*, he was not kind but correct. I *was* aware, nevertheless, that this was the most prescient confrontation in my life, though "the future" is never an idea in one's mind, is never part of one's speculations at such moments. Time does not pass but only *we* pass and I do not know *more* now than I did then, for the quality of my knowledge is different, but I did know and recognize the power of the man and his music at that meeting half a century ago.

Shortly after the performance of *Pierrot*, Schoenberg left for St. Petersburg to conduct his *Pelleas und Melisande*. We were on good terms at parting, but we never met again. In Morges, in 1919, I received a very cordial letter from him asking for pieces of my chamber music to include in his Vienna concerts "The Society for Private Performances." I wrote and he wrote again. Then, in 1920 or 1921, I heard *Pierrot* in Paris, conducted by Darius Milhaud, and performed by Marya Freund. After that, incredibly, I did not hear another note by Schoenberg until the *Prelude to Genesis*, in Hollywood in November 1945, at which time we might well have met, for we were in the recording studios on the same day and we sat on opposite sides of the Wilshire Ebell Theater at the premiere of the *Genesis Suite*. Schoenberg conducted his Serenade in Venice in September 1925, and I played my Piano Sonata there the next day, but neither of us heard the other's music. Years later, when I knew the Serenade, I realized that, as reported to me at the time, Schoenberg probably did like my *Histoire du soldat*. When I came to Los Angeles in 1935, Klemperer and other mutual friends tried to bring us together, but only after 1948 did a meeting seem possible. I saw Schoenberg for the last time in 1949 when he appeared onstage at a concert and read a delicately ironic speech acknowledging the honor of the freedom of the city of Vienna just conferred on him, a half-century too late, by the Austrian consul. I remember that he repeatedly addressed the consul as "Excellency" and that he read from large sheets of paper which were extracted one by one from his pocket, his eyesight being very poor then, and each page containing but a few words. Even on such an occasion, instead of an all-Schoenberg program only the early *Kammersymphonie*[9] was played.

[9] I admire the *Kammersymphonie*, but am not attracted by the sound of the solo strings—they remind me of the economy-sized movie-theater orchestras of the 1920s—though I agree that the multiple-string version tames and blunts the piece unduly. At times the *Kammersymphonie* sounds to me like a joint creation of Wagner, Mahler, Brahms, and Strauss, as though one of these com-

Two days after Schoenberg's death, I happened to visit Mrs. Mahler-Werfel's home and to see there Schoenberg's not-yet-dry death mask. Less than a year later, his *Erwartung* and my *Oedipus Rex*—an unthinkable juxtaposition a few years before—were performed together in Paris by the late Hans Rosbaud, as a double bill. I hope Schoenberg would have been pleased. I know I was.

R.C.: Would you comment on the popular notion of Schoenberg and Stravinsky as thesis and antithesis?

I.S.: Like every arbitrary argument, that one is easy to develop, but in terms of large and not very waterpoof generalities. For example:

SCHOENBERG:	STRAVINSKY:
1. The way to the future.	1. The uses of the past.
2. A palace revolution.	2. Restoration.
3. Evolution.	3. Adoption.
4. "Today I have discovered something which will assure the supremacy of German music for the next hundred years." Schoenberg, July 1921, telling a friend of the discovery of the tone-row.	4. Reaction against "German music" or German "romanticism." No "*Sehnsucht,*" *no "ausdrucksvoll."*
5. Hedgehog. (Moses)	5. Fox (eclectic and abundant variety). (Aaron)
6. "Music expresses all that dwells in us . . ."	6. "Music is powerless to express anything at all."
7. "Ballet is not a musical form."	7. Chief production is of ballets.
8. Essentially polyphonic.	8. Essentially homophonic.

posers had written the upper line, one the bass, etc. But the triplets were written not by Brahms, whose triplets are lyrical but by Mahler, whose triplets are rhetorical. Nevertheless the *Kammersymphonie* is more polyphonic than the music of any of these composers.

SCHOENBERG:

9. Virtually no repetition.

10. A teacher. Large amount of writing on musical theory. Hardly anyone has escaped his school. (But the philosophy of teaching is: "Genius learns only from itself; talent chiefly from others. Genius learns from nature, from its own nature; talent learns from art.")

11. Never composed at the piano.

12. Composed fitfully, at lightning speed, and in the heat of "inspiration." Therefore, many unfinished works.

13. Contemporary subjects (protest music): *Survivor from Warsaw*.

14. Much use of *rubato*.

15. An inclusive view of the past.

16. Chromaticism.

17. *Espressivo*. Scores full of expression marks.

18. *Legati*.

STRAVINSKY:

9. Much use of repetition (*ostinato*) in all of the music before the *Movements*.

10. Never a teacher. No writing about musical theory.

11. Composes only at the piano.

12. Composes every day, regularly, like a man with banking hours. Hardly a scrap unfinished or unused.

13. Remote-in-time subjects: *The Rake's Progress*.

14. Metronomic strictness, no *rubato*. Ideal is of mechanical regularity (*Octuor, Piano Concerto, etc.*).

15. An exclusive (highly selective) view of the past.

16. Diatonicism.

17. *Secco*. Scores contain minimum of expression marks.

18. *Staccati*.

SCHOENBERG:	STRAVINSKY:
19. Preferred dense eight-part counterpoint (the choruses, op. 35; the *Genesis Prelude* canon).	19. Prefers spare, two-part counterpoint.
20. "A Chinese philosopher speaks Chinese, but what does he say?" ("What is *style*?")	20. "What the Chinese philosopher says cannot be separated from the fact that he says it in Chinese." (Preoccupation with manner and style.)

A nice parlor game, no more, but the parallelisms are more interesting. For example:

1. The common belief in Divine Authority, the Hebrew God and Biblical mythology, Catholic culture.
2. The success obstacle of the first pieces, *Verklärte Nacht* and *The Firebird*, which remained the most popular of all our works, all our lives and after.
3. The close parallel development over the span of sixty years.
4. The common exile to the same alien culture, in which we wrote some of our best works (his Fourth Quartet, my *Abraham and Isaac*) and in which we are still played far less than in the Europe that exiled us.
5. Both family men and fathers of several children, both hypochondriac, both deeply superstitious.
6. For both of us, numbers are things.
7. Both of us were devoted to The Word, and each wrote some of his own librettos (*Moses und Aron*, *Die glückliche Hand*, *Jacobsleiter*, *Les Noces*, *Renard*).
8. Each of us composed for concrete sounds, unlike the later Webern, in which choice of sound is a final stage.
9. For both of us, the row is thematic and we are ultimately less interested in the construction of the row, *per se*, than is Webern.

R.C.: Would you amplify your remarks in *Memories and Commentaries* concerning Edgar Varèse and his music?

"Sounds may be, and most of those that we hear are, public objects."

P. F. STRAWSON: *Individuals; an Essay in Descriptive Metaphysics*

I.S.: Varèse himself is so vivid—his electrified hair makes me think of Struwelpeter or the Wizard of Oz—and his words are so concrete that I would rather quote than attempt to describe. One striking phrase of his—"I like a certain awkwardness in a work of art"—reveals more about him than I could in an essay. That is the remark of a humanist (if I can use the word without its contemporary overtones of conservativism), and it is the humanist aspect of Varèse which I propose to consider. Varèse has made a new adjustment of the limits between "human" and "mechanical," and not merely theoretically, but by the force of his own humanizing creations. In fact, he has little theory, and in his lifelong crusade to emphasize sound over scheme he has avoided codification and description wherever possible. "Flowers and vegetables existed before botany," he says, "and now that we have entered the realm of pure sound itself we must stop thinking in the frame of twelve tones." Those of us who have not stopped thinking in that frame he calls *"les pompiers de douze sons."* Few composers have dedicated themselves with such singularity to the "purity of sound" ideal, and few have been as sensitive to the totality of sound characteristics.

We are naturally curious about the antecedents of such a man. They are either not apparent or else too apparent, by which I mean that the most obvious of them are likely to appear as solecisms. This is the case with his frequent references to Debussy—in measures 73-74, horns and trumpet, in *Deserts*; in the choral melody at No. 12 in *Equatorial*, a melody that reappears in *Density 21.5*; and in *Arcana*, at Nos. 13-14, at two measures before No. 20, and at five measures before No. 28, in the trumpets. But Varèse's melodic characteristics, whether lyrical as in the *Offrandes*, or popular as in the marching tunes in *Arcana*, are always Gallic. Perhaps some of *me* peeks through in *Arcana,* too:[10] *Petroushka* at No. 9; *The Firebird* at three measures before No. 5—this, a variant of the first motive of the piece, is what Varèse calls the *idée fixe,* but the real *idée fixe* is the figure of five repeated notes which occurs in nearly all of his music; and *Le Sacre du printemps,* at two measures before No. 17, and one measure before No. 24, and in the section beginning at No. 19. And Varèse's motorized metrical scheme may also owe something to my example. The many changes of tempo in *Arcana* involve, because of metrical proportionalism, few changes of beat. Echoes of the jazz age survive in *Arcana* and *Amériques,* too, though Varèse has eliminated some of them in the revised (1960) version of *Arcana.* (See the original score at Nos. 33–34. The revision cuts repetitions, replaces *tutti* with silence, and avoids the final C-Major triumph, the musical low point of the original score, but succeeded there by a skillful use of the mediant.)

One learns, at first with surprise, that Varèse is solidly grounded in seventeenth-century music and in "early" music in general, and that Ingegneri and Goudimel are among his favorite composers. Perhaps this may be attributed to his background as a choral conductor rather than to his formal musical education. By the contretemps of French *fin-de-siècle* birth, Varèse's teachers were d'Indy, Roussel, and Widor. He recalls some of these *barbes* as vividly as I warned he would: "*Ils n'étaient pas simplements des cons, ils étaient des generaux des cons. . . . Ils ont pensé que Marc-Antoine Charpentier avait composé 'Louise.'*" Varèse says that he fled France to escape academic stupidity on the one hand ("*Les professeurs étaient reglés comme du papier à musique*") and the "vice of intellectualism" on the other.

Varèse has been recognized, but is a lonely figure still. This is partly because he preferred composing to the career of being a composer; and instead of lecturing to ladies' clubs, writing articles on the state of music, participating in symposia,

[10] And perhaps some of him peeks through in my *The Building of the Ark,* and in the use of the gongs in my *Prayer.*

traveling on fellowships, he has remained at home and gone his own way, alone.

I knew of Varèse as a pioneer in the 1920s, and again, with *Deserts* in the 1950s, as a prophet of "spatial music." I sometimes think I understand what he means by sound depth, at least in *Deserts*, in which some of the electronically realized sounds do seem to come from a distance and as though from the ends of spirals, and where presence and distance are apparent structural factors in the composition. But Varèse has achieved other, more obviously tangible things as well: in *Deserts*, a form based on patterns of recurrence and incidence, and a purely intervallic harmonic structure. As an electronically organized and electronically produced sound composition, *Deserts* was possibly the first piece to explore the liaison characteristics between live instrumental music and electronically recorded sound. I refer to the transitions between the four instrumental portions and the three taped segments of electronically organized sound which connect and interpolate them; these transitions, exploiting the border country between the live and the electronically attenuated suggestion of the live, are, I believe, the most valuable development in Varèse's later music.

Varèse was among the first composers to employ dynamics as an integral formal element (the dotted-line sections in the first part of the *Deserts* score), and to plot the intensities of a composition, the highs and lows in pitch, speed, density, rhythmic movement. As Webern is associated with small volumes, so Varèse is identified with large ones. "Turn it up," he will say. "I like it louder." One thinks, not without sympathy, of the listener who wrote on his program of the London performance of Haydn's "Military" Symphony in 1795: "Grand but very noisy" (H. Robbins Landon: *Supplement to the Symphonies of Joseph Haydn*). Now that I have mentioned Webern, I should note that Varèse was aware of Schoenberg and Webern thirty-five years ago, which is to say that he had experienced long ago the now familiar stagefright attend-

ing the discovery of how vastly more difficult composition is
after those masters.

In the use of percussion and wind instruments, Varèse is
an innovator of the first rank. *Deserts* discovers a world of
possibilities for the tuba, and Varèse and Schoenberg, between them—Schoenberg in the *Seraphita* song—have created
new roles for the trombone. With percussion instruments
Varèse's knowledge and skill are unique. He knows them and
he knows exactly how to play them. Speaking for myself, I
weary of wood blocks and snare drums, but I love the guiro,
the gongs, the anvils of *Ionization*; the thundering metal
sheets, the lathes, the *claves* of *Deserts*; the parabolas of siren
music that make *Amériques* sound like an old-fashioned air
raid. I also love the scurrilous string drum in *Nocturnal*; the
doubling of flute, piccolo, and piano in *Deserts*; and the most
extraordinary noise of all, the harp attack ("heart attack," I
almost said, and that is what it almost gives one) at measure
17 in *La Croix du sud* and at various places in *Amériques*.
Varèse's most original large-orchestra sonorities are, I think,
in the extreme upper instrumental ranges throughout *Arcana*.

Varèse's music will endure. We know this now because it
has dated in the right way. The name is synonymous with a
new intensity and a new concretion, and the best things in
his music—the first seven measures from No. 16 in *Arcana*, the
whole of *Deserts*—are among the better things in contemporary music. More power to this musical Brancusi.

SOME OLDER COMPOSERS

R.C.: Will you list some of your favorite events in the symphonies and quartets of Beethoven?[11]
I.S.: The Eighth Symphony is a miracle of growth and development and I am therefore reluctant to cite my particular admirations out of context. Nevertheless, the entrance of the
trumpets and drum in F major in the last movement, after the

[11] Stravinsky's "answer" is a composite of remarks made at my rehearsals of
four Beethoven symphonies. The identifying measure numbers were added
later.

F-sharp-minor episode, is the most wonderful moment. I actually had the temerity to imitate this in the March that is No. six of my Eight Instrumental Miniatures. For me, the Ninth Symphony contains no event of comparable force. But then, for me, nothing in the Ninth is as perennially surprising and delightful as the development section of the last movement of the Fourth Symphony, or the repeated B-flat-A in the Trio of the Fourth, or the *tutti*, measures 50–54, in the *Adagio* of the Fourth.

What are my criticisms of the Ninth? Consider the *Adagio* without prejudice—or try to. The echo-dialogue of winds and strings lacks variation, and the *Andante moderato*, with the pedal A and the repeated octaves, sixths, thirds, is harmonically heavy. (The metronome markings must be at fault here, incidentally, for the *Adagio molto* is 60 and the *Andante moderato* only 63.) I find the movement rhythmically monotonous, too—for Beethoven—except in its finest episode, the E-flat *Adagio,* but the effect even of that beautiful episode is deadened by the rhythmic inanity of the subsequent 12/8. Another weakness, or miscalculation, is the repetition, after only six measures, of the heroics at measure 121. What has happened to Beethoven's need for variation and development? The movement is the antithesis of true symphonic form.

The failure of the last movement must be attributed, in large measure, to its thumping theme. As the composer cannot develop it—who could?—he spreads it out like a military parade. I am ever surprised in this movement by the poverty of the *Allegro ma non tanto*, as well as by the riches of the *Allegro energico* (especially measures 76–90, which, oddly enough, anticipate the world of Verdi). I am undoubtedly wrong to talk this way about "The Ninth," of course, or to question "what everyone knows." "The Ninth" is sacred, and it was already sacred when I first heard it in 1897. I have often wondered why. Can it actually have something to do with a "message" or with a so-called proletarian appeal?

The quartets, in any case, are addressed not to the great

unwashed, but to a select few, and the later sonatas speak to an intimate two or three, or perhaps only to the composer himself (the A-flat sonata, for example, which might also have been a string quartet and could become one by an adjustment of the ranges). The music of the opus 59 quartets is always so marvelously sustained and the substance to be sustained is so good that I cannot cite out of context, yet what a stroke is the A flat in measure 266 of opus 59, number 1, or, in the second movement, what marvels are measures 65–68, 394–404, and 290–294 (on the strength of this last passage alone Beethoven must be considered first among rhythmic innovators). But the last movement of this quartet, the *Kazatchok*, is often badly played because the dotted notes are held too long. For me the most astonishing passages in opus 59, number 2, are measures 210–226 in the first movement, and measures 64, 79, 84 (the A natural!) in the second movement; one could write a book *Beethoven and the Octave* on this second movement. The *Adagio* is another instance of a piece often destroyed by poor performance: the 16ths that follow dots and rests should be shortened in more places than the three measures in which Beethoven specifies 32ds. The long B-flat bass in the last movement is a wonderful surprise, and so is the passage in measures 344–350. In opus 59, number 3, the *Andante* movement anticipates Schumann and Mendelssohn, neither of whom was capable of anything as original as the *pizzicato* idea itself or as mighty as the upbeat to measure 66 and the great arc from measure 127 to measure 135.

The "Harp" quartet is slighter than the "Rasumovskys," I think, and its final movement, in spite of the sixth variation with the amazing D flat in the cello, breaks the empyrean flight that began with opus 59, number 1. I seldom listen to the "Harp" quartet because of the habitual bad performance of it. The *Adagio ma non troppo* is usually played "*troppo*"; and the figure in the *Presto* sounds in most performances like a sloppy 6/8 or like

because instrumentalists commonly do not cut the dots of the dotted notes. My favorite places in the quartet are measures 110 to the "harp" episode in the first movement, and the modulation at measures 192–193.

As for the *"Quartetto Serioso,"* the most wonderful event occurs in measures 47–65 of the *Allegretto.*

And the last quartets? Like the greatest beauties, they are a little flawed, and except for opus 127 and the Great Fugue, each has its *ennuis.* The three final movements of opus 130 are as pedestrian as anything bearing the stamp of the master, and so are the second 6/8 movement of opus 131, the first 3/4 movement of opus 132, the *Lento* movement of opus 135 (how like Tchaikovsky is the beginning of that movement!). The delights of opus 132 are, for me, the Schubertian *Allegro appassionato* and the quarter-note canon, which I sometimes think Schoenberg may have remembered when he composed the second episode of the String Trio. My particular pleasures in opus 127 are the modulation in the second movement (measures 75–78); measure 91; measures 97–101; and the whole *presto* of the *Scherzando,* but above all measures 244–270. What I find least attractive in the last quartets is the Ninth Symphony-style recitative in the finale of opus 135, in the violin cadenza in opus 132, and in the *ritenuto* passages in the finale of the music drama, opus 131.

R.C.: You have often declared your taste for Weber and Mendelssohn, and you have even avowed a kinship with these composers. When were you first aware of this attraction? And what are your sympathies for Schubert, Schumann, Chopin?

I.S.: Mendelssohn's elegance attracted me early in my career, as my *Scherzo fantastique* indicates, but my appreciation of Weber did not come until the 1920s, with a performance of

Der Freischütz in Prague conducted by Alexander von Zemlinsky. I acquainted myself with all of Weber's music after that *Freischütz*, with the result that his piano sonatas may have exercised a spell over me at the time I composed my *Capriccio*; a specific rhythmic device in the *Capriccio* may be traced to Weber, at any rate. The Weber of the *Invitation to the Dance*, the overtures, the *Konzertstück*, and the Mendelssohn of the "Italian" Symphony, the Octet, the *Rondo capriccioso*, and other piano pieces, the *Midsummer Night's Dream*[12] Overture; these are the Beau Brummells of music.

I will say nothing about Chopin now except that my opinion is very like Schoenberg's, but Schubert is, I think, infinitely the richest of the composers you mention. As a student in St. Petersburg I knew his songs, piano music, quintets, quartets, trios, the last two symphonies, but little else. I was especially fond of the song cycles, though I considered that Schubert abused—was too ready to go to—the minor key, and that the strictly harmonic function of the piano and the resulting eternally arpeggiated piano accompaniments were monotonous.

Other young St. Petersburg musicians knew even less Schubert, which did not keep them from dismissing him as a "peasant musician" and, in one case, from asserting that Tchaikovsky had improved the theme of the "Unfinished" Symphony in the theme song of *Swan Lake*. Few of my fellow students listened more deeply than that, though to compare the Schubert B-minor symphony with *Swan Lake* is to learn, among many

---

[12] The *Midsummer Night's Dream* incidental music ought to be used only for Schlegel's version of the play, the production of which should then be clothed in the provincial German court style of the period. No one can build a story ballet on a play whose substance is poetry and whose plot is a peg, though Balanchine has made a gallant attempt. The most successful episode in Balanchine's ballet is the Divertimento danced to the String Symphony No. 9, but this is smuggled into the second act and has nothing to do with the story. Mendelssohn is banal only when he reaches for dramatic pathos, and when he does that he tends, unsuccessfully, to anticipate Brahms—the passage in the *Melusine* that almost becomes a passage in Brahms's second symphony. I was disturbed, at Balanchine's ballet, by intemperate lengths in the *Dream* music. Even the flute *Scherzo* would be twice as magical if it were half as long. That is the impression of an elderly and economical composer, of course, and Mendelssohn was a freely-spending young one.

other things, that the Austrian peasant at least re-assigns orchestral roles when he repeats and that he is never as square of phrase as my compatriot.

Schubert's most astonishing symphonic achievement, the Fourth Symphony, mocks the nonsense that the composer was unable to sustain large-scale developments but could only string together song forms. One cannot catalogue the *momenti lirici* of this masterpiece, but can only look at the musical whole. In the symphony, Schubert's feeling for the largest-extending tonality relationships, his harmonic skill, his powers of development, are to be compared only to those of Beethoven. And the symphony points to never-to-be-developed contrapuntal gifts, while at the same time it far surpasses the other composers you mention in the ripeness of its chromatic idiom (see measures 90–105, and the corresponding place, in the *Andante* movement; and compare the introduction with the introduction of Mozart's quartet in the same key; and look at measures 431–451, and the corresponding place, in the last movement; and the whole of the scherzo; and the change of key in the last movement, which, as timing, can be matched only by Beethoven. The chromatic idea is sustained through all four movements, too, and with a maturity that Mozart might have envied, at that precocious age of eighteen).

Schumann is a composer for whom I have a personal weakness,[13] but the symphony is not his domain. If I compare a symphony of his, say the D-minor, which I have just heard, with the Schubert Fourth (admittedly an invidious comparison like all such), the Schumann seems not to be a symphony at all, in the Beethoven sense. It is naïve in construction and it was not conceived instrumentally, and these are a craftsman's remarks, as Gilbert Ryle would say, not public highway remarks. But, however far from Beethoven, the theme at measure 305 must have derived from the *Larghetto* in Beethoven's Second Symphony. The trio of the *Scherzo* is my favorite ep-

13 I saw Clara Schumann, plain, in the summer of 1895 when my father took me as a translator—he did not speak German—to call upon her in a villa near Hamburg-vor-der-Höhe. I remember a very old lady with a walking stick.

isode in the Fourth Symphony, but even there I must say that
I find the return of the trio much too punctual. And the first
movement is altogether too rectangular (the trombone theme
at measures 178, 182, 186, 190), and the *Romanza*, especially
the embroidering violin triplets, is almost too faded even for
dinner music in a Swiss hotel.

R.C.: And are you still enthusiastic about Gounod, Messager,
and Lecocq? How do you compare Gounod and Bizet?

I.S.: Please, please. I had a certain taste for Lecocq at the
time of *Mavra* and I wrote a *souvenir* of him into a flute melody in *Jeu de cartes*. He was a *musiquette* composer of gifts
and originality. I own his autographed score of *Giroflé, Girofla*,
and I still have a score of *La Coeur à la main*. Messager was
less highly endowed, but he was a charming man, very kind
and encouraging to me in my first years in Paris. He was to
have conducted the first performance of *Le Rossignol*, but he
backed out in favor of Monteux. As for Gounod, I was once
greatly attracted by his melodic gifts, but I did not mean to
condone his insipidity. Gounod blinded me to Bizet in my Russian years, and I could see nothing in the author of *Carmen*
except an intelligent eclecticism. In the cold war of Tchaikovsky vs. Rimsky, *Carmen* was admired more by the Muscovite
than by the Petersburg school. A case for plagiarism could be
made against *Pique-Dame*—compare Lisa's aria in the second
act and the Lisa-German duet in the third act with *Carmen's*
card scene, and the summer Garden chorus with the first scene
in *Carmen*—but the plaintiff would have to admire Tchaikovsky's taste even as a thief. The card aria is the centerpiece of
Carmen and, with the G-flat major smugglers' ensemble, the
Quintet, and José's last scene, its best music, a jewel, in fact,
surrounded by semiprecious stones. The card aria is made with
the simplest means, and embellished with a few masterful
touches like the oboe and trombone octaves and the string
appoggiaturas in the coda. I did not much admire *Carmen*
until recent years. Micaëla bored me, and so did that absurd
Flower Song, and all the prix de Rome modulations. But these

were period prejudices. *Carmen* was madly *démodé* by the time I became a composer. The vogue for the exotic, the foreign, the sham Spanish, was over, and the Broadway show-type opera—add a number, cut a number—in other words *Carmen*, was not yet *à la mode*. I considered it good cabaret music, but no more (which, indeed, some of it is; the *"bel officier"* is pure Piaf, and Dancairo and Remendado in their duet *"Carmen, mon amour tu viendras"* are like two saxophones out of Guy Lombardo). The last *Carmen* I saw in Russia had some novel staging. A Red Cross ambulance was the only object in view at the end of the opera. It stood just outside the bull ring. The *metteur en scène* must have been a vegetarian.

PROGRAM NOTES

OCTUOR

R.C.: Would you describe the circumstances attending the composition of the *Octuor?*

I.S.: The *Octuor* began with a dream in which I saw myself in a small room surrounded by a small group of instrumentalists playing some very attractive music. I did not recognize the music, though I strained to hear it, and I could not recall any feature of it the next day, but I do remember my curiosity —in the dream—to know how many the musicians were.[14] I remember too that after I had counted them to the number eight, I looked again and saw that they were playing bassoons, trombones, trumpets, a flute, and a clarinet. I awoke from this little concert in a state of great delight and anticipation and the next morning began to compose the *Octuor,* which I had had no thought of the day before, though for some time I had wanted to write an ensemble piece—not incidental music like the *Histoire du soldat,* but an instrumental sonata.

[14] This confession exposes me to Minkowski's analysis of the counting mania as a time frustration, i.e., of the compulsion to count as a wish to force future time, while the succubi at one's back push one into a false imagination. But time-dreams and counting-dreams are common with me, and so are dreams in which people shout, but inaudibly, like a cinema when the sound track fails, or talk out of hearing in the distance. I dream regularly now, too, that I am able to walk without a cane, as I could five years ago.

The *Octuor* was quickly composed (in 1922). The first movement came first and was followed immediately by the waltz in the second movement. I derived the *tema* of the second movement from the waltz, which is to say that only after I had written the waltz did I discover it as a good subject for variations. I then wrote the "ribbons of scales" variation as a prelude to each of the other variations.

The final, culminating variation, the *fugato*, is my favorite episode in the *Octuor*. The plan of it was to present the theme in rotation by the instrumental pairs—flute-clarinet, bassoons, trumpets, trombones—which is the idea of instrumental combination at the root of the *Octuor* and of my dream. The third movement grew out of the *fugato*, and was intended as a contrast to that high point of harmonic tension. Bach's two-part Inventions were somewhere in the remote back of my mind while composing this movement, as they were during the composition of the last movement of the Piano Sonata. The terseness and lucidity of the inventions were an ideal of mine at that time, in any case, and I sought to keep those qualities uppermost in my own composition. What could be more terse than the punctuation of the final chord, in which the first inversion suffices to indicate *finis* and at the same time gives more flavor than the flat-footed tonic?

My appetite was whetted by my rediscovery of sonata form and by my pleasure in working with new instrumental combinations. I like the instrumental games in the *Octuor* and I can add that I achieved in it exactly what I set out to do. (If I were to compile a textbook of instrumental usages, they would have to be chosen from my own works only, for the reason that I could never be certain of the exact intentions of any other composer and therefore of the degree of his success or failure.)

I conducted the first performance in spite of a bad case of *trac*, owing, I think, to the occasion: it was the first concert work of mine which I myself introduced. The stage of the Paris Opéra seemed a large frame for only eight players, but the group was set off by screens, and the sound was well balanced. The *Octuor* was composed for and is dedicated to Vera de Bosset.

FOUR-HAND PIANO MUSIC

R.C.: What attracted you to the medium of four-hand and two-piano music, and what were the circumstances of composition and performance in the case of the Eight Easy Pieces, the Sonata, and the Concerto?

I.S.: The Eight Easy Pieces were composed in Morges—the Polka, March, and Valse just before *Renard*, in 1915, the others after the completion of that burlesque. I wrote the Polka first, as a caricature of Diaghilev, whom I saw as a circus animal-trainer cracking a long whip. The idea of the four-hand duet was an aspect of the caricature also, because Diaghilev was very fond of four-hand piano playing which he had done with his lifelong friend Walter Nouvel[15] for as long as I had known him. The simplicities of one of the parts were designed in order not to embarrass the small range of Diaghilev's technique. I played the Polka to Diaghilev and Alfredo Casella in a hotel room in Milan in 1915, and I remember how amazed both men were that the composer of *Le Sacre du printemps* should have produced such a piece of popcorn. For Casella a new path had been indicated, however, and he was not slow to follow it; so-called neoclassicism of a sort was born in that moment. But Casella was so genuinely enthusiastic about the Polka that I promised to write a little piece for him, too. This, the March, was composed immediately on my return to Morges. A little later I added the ice cream wagon Valse in homage to Erik Satie, a souvenir of a visit with him in Paris. Satie, a very touching and attractive personality suddenly had become old and white, though not less witty and gay. I tried to portray something of his *esprit* in the Valse. I orchestrated

---

15 Nouvel had been a composer in his youth, one of the Petersburg *avant-garde* whose modernist tendencies irritated Rimsky-Korsakov. Another of Nouvel's piano-duet partners was the poet Kusmin, whom I first met with Diaghilev at Nouvel's St. Petersburg home.

the Valse for seven solo instruments after composing it, and at the same time prepared a version of the Polka for cimbalom and small ensemble and of the March for eight solo players, but the March and Polka never have been published in this form. The other five pieces were composed as music lessons for my children Theodore and Mika. I wished to cultivate their love of music and to disguise my piano pedagogy by composing very easy parts for them to play, reserving the more difficult parts for the teacher, in this case myself, hoping thereby to give them a real sense of performance participation. The Española was joined to the album after a trip to Spain, the Napolitana after a trip to Naples. Two of the Russian souvenirs, the Balalaika, which I like best of all the eight pieces, and the Galop, were added at a later date, and the third, the Andante, like most preludes, was tacked on last. The Galop is a caricature of the St. Petersburg version of the Folies Bergères, which I had watched in the Tumpakov, a demi-respectable night club in the Astrava (the islands of the Neva on one of which my wife Vera was born). Ravel, hearing me conduct the Galop in the orchestral version, advised me to play it at a faster—the fastest possible—tempo, but I think that was because he mistook it for a cancan. The first concert performance of the Eight Easy Pieces was sponsored by Werner Reinhardt, in Lausanne. My co-pianist was the young José Iturbi.

I cannot discuss the Sonata and the Concerto now, for they require analysis and professional talk of a very different kind, and what, dear program annotator, can one *say* about a modulation or a plan of harmonic structure?

Both works were written for the love of "pure art"—which is not only to say that they were not commissioned—and the geneses of the two were very different. The Sonata began as a piece for one performer, but was redesigned for two pianos when I saw that four hands were required to voice the four lines clearly.

I began the Sonata before and completed it after the *Scènes de ballet*. I have played it publicly only once, at a Mills College students' concert with Nadia Boulanger as my partner. I was staying with Darius Milhaud then, and the Sonata reminds me of an incident concerning the plumbing in the Milhaud house. One morning the lavatory drains stopped functioning. A plumber came, but we soon found that an archaeologist would have been more appropriate. Trenches had to be dug; the Milhauds had been emptying coffee grounds into the sink for years, and the pipe from their house to the street was silted solid with them.

The Concerto is symphonic both in volumes and proportions, and I think I could have composed it, especially the variation movement, as an orchestral work. But my purpose was otherwise. I needed a solo work for myself and my son, and I wished to incorporate the orchestra and do away with it. The Concerto was intended as a vehicle for concert tours in orchestra-less cities.

I began the composition in Voreppe and completed the first movement there immediately after finishing the Violin Concerto. I did not continue the composition, however, because I could not *hear* the second piano. All my life I have tried out my music as I have composed it, orchestral as well as any other kind, four hands at one keyboard. That way I am able to test it as I cannot when the other player is seated at another piano. When I took up the Concerto again, after finishing the *Duo Concertante* and *Perséphone*, I asked the Pleyel company to build me a double piano, in the form of a small box of two tightly-wedged triangles. I then completed the Concerto in my Pleyel studio, test-hearing it measure by measure with my son Soulima at the other keyboard.

The variations—originally the second movement—were separated from the *con moto* movement by three years and much change of musical focus. I started composing them as soon as *Perséphone* was completed, but I was interrupted again, this time, alas, by an appendectomy. My son Theodore had had a burst appendix and an emergency removal, and as the operation fascinated me, I decided to have my own appendix removed, however unlikely the danger of peritonitis in my own case. I forced the operation on my other children, also, and on Vera de Bosset and many of my friends—or, rather, to put myself in a better light, I recommended it highly. This surgical spree took place shortly after the premiere of *Perséphone* and just before I became a French citizen on June 10, 1934. I was still wobbly when I went to London at the end of that month to record *Les Noces*.

I had steeped myself in the variations of Beethoven and Brahms while composing the Concerto, and in Beethoven's fugues. I am very fond of my fugue, and especially of the after-fugue or fugue consequent, but then, the Concerto is perhaps my "favorite" among my purely instrumental pieces. The second movement, the *Notturno*, is not so much night music as after-dinner music, in fact, a digestive to the largest movements.

The first performance of the Concerto was sponsored by L'Université des Annales, a literary lecture society. I introduced the music with a fifteen-minute talk (which I would not now care to see reprinted), and I read this little discourse before many of my later performances of the work, as well. The concert, in the Salle Gaveau, was a matinée, which we repeated the same evening for a different audience. I performed the Concerto many times with my son in Europe and in South America (Buenos Aires, Rosario), sometimes preceding it with the Mozart C-minor fugue. After playing it in Baden-Baden in 1938, we made a commercial disc (for French Columbia) that was never released because of the War. I also performed the Concerto several times in the United States during the War, with the American pianist Adele Marcus. Once—in Worcester, Massachusetts, of all places—I introduced our performance of it with my old French lecture.

SYMPHONY OF PSALMS

R.C.: Do you recall what determined your choice of texts in the Symphony of Psalms? What do you mean when you refer to the symbolism of the fugues? What was your first musical idea? Why did you employ a predominantly wind-instrument orchestra? What were the circumstances of the commission?

I.S.: The commissioning of the Symphony of Psalms began with the publisher's routine suggestion that I write something popular. I took the word, not in the publisher's meaning of "adapting to the understanding of the people," but in the sense of "something universally admired," and I even chose Psalm 150 in part for its popularity, though another and equally compelling reason was my eagerness to counter the many composers who had abused these magisterial verses as pegs for their own lyrico-sentimental "feelings." The Psalms are poems of exaltation, but also of anger and judgment, and even of curses. Although I regarded Psalm 150 as a song to be danced, as David danced before the Ark, I knew that I would have to treat it in an imperative way. My publisher had requested an orchestral piece without chorus, but I had had the psalm symphony idea in mind for some time, and that is what I insisted on composing. All of the music was written in Nice and in my summer home at Echarvines. I began with Psalm 150 and my first notation was the figure

that bears such a close family resemblance to Jocasta's "*Oracula, oracula.*" After finishing the fast-tempo sections of the Psalm, I went back to compose the first and second movements. The Allelujah and the slow music at the beginning of Psalm 150, which is an answer to the question in Psalm 40, were written last.

I was much concerned, in setting the Psalm verses, with problems of tempo. To me, the relation of tempo and meaning is a primary question of musical order, and until I am certain that I have found the right tempo, I cannot compose. Superficially, the texts suggested a variety of speeds, but this variety was without shape. At first, and until I understood that

God must not be praised in fast, *forte* music, no matter how often the text specifies "loud," I thought of the final hymn in a too-rapid pulsation. This is the manner question again, of course. Can one say the same thing in several ways? *I* cannot, in any case, and to me the only possible way could not be more clearly indicated among all the choices if it were painted blue. I also cannot say whether a succession of choices results in a "style," but my own description of style is tact-in-action, and I prefer to talk about the action of a musical sentence than to talk about its style.

The first movement, "Hear my prayer, O Lord," was composed in a state of religious and musical ebullience. The sequences of two minor thirds joined by a major third, the root idea of the whole work, were derived from the trumpet-harp motive at the beginning of the *allegro* in Psalm 150. I was not aware of Phrygian modes, Gregorian chants, Byzantinisms, or anything of the sort, while composing this music, though, of course, influences said to be denoted by such scriptwriters' baggage-stickers may very well have been operative. Byzantium was a source of Russian culture, after all, and according to current indexing I am classifiable as a Russian, but the little I know about Byzantine music was learned from Wellesz long after I had composed the Symphony of Psalms. I did start to compose the Psalms in Slavonic, though, and only after coming a certain distance did I switch to Latin (just as I worked with English at the same time as Hebrew in *Abraham and Isaac*).

The "Waiting for the Lord" Psalm makes the most overt use of musical symbolism in any of my music before *The Flood*. An upside-down pyramid of fugues, it begins with a purely instrumental fugue of limited compass and employs only solo instruments. The restriction to treble range was the novelty of this initial fugue, but the limitation to flutes and oboes proved its most difficult compositional problem. The subject was developed from the sequence of thirds used as an ostinato in the first movement. The next and higher stage of the upside-down pyramid is the human fugue, which does not begin without instrumental help for the reason that I modified the structure as I composed and decided to overlap instruments and voices to give the material more development, but the human choir is heard *a cappella* after that. The human fugue also represents a higher level in the architectural symbolism by the fact that it expands into the bass register. The third stage, the upside-down foundation, unites the two fugues.

Though I chose Psalm 150 first, and though my first musical idea was the already-quoted rhythmic figure in that movement, I could not compose the beginning of it until I had written the second movement. Psalm 40 is a prayer that a new canticle may be put into our mouths. The Allelujah is that canticle. (The word allelujah still reminds me of the Hebrew galosh-merchant Gurian who lived in the apartment below ours in St. Petersburg, and who on High Holy Days would erect a prayer tent in his living room and dress himself in an Ephod. The hammering sounds as he built this tent and the idea of a cosmopolitan merchant in a St. Petersburg apartment simulating the prayers of his forefathers in the desert impressed my imagination almost as profoundly as any direct religious experience of my own.) The rest of the slow-tempo introduction, the *Laudate Dominum*, was originally composed to the words of the *Gospodi Pomiluy*. This section is a prayer to the Russian image of the infant Christ with orb and scepter. I decided to end the work with this music, too, as an apotheosis of the sort that had become a pattern in my music since the epithalamium at the end of *Les Noces*. The *allegro* in Psalm 150 was inspired by a vision of Elijah's chariot climbing the Heavens; never before had I written anything quite so literal as the triplets for horns and piano to suggest the horses and chariot. The final hymn of praise must be thought of as issuing from the skies, and agitation is followed by "the calm of praise," but such statements embarrass me. What I can say is that in setting the words of this final hymn, I cared above all for the *sounds* of the syllables, and I have indulged my besetting pleasure of regulating prosody in my own way. I really do tire of people pointing out that *Dominum* is one word and that its meaning is obscured the way I respirate it, like the Allelujah in the *Sermon*, which has reminded everybody of the *Psalms*. Do such people know nothing about word-splitting in early polyphonic music? One hopes to worship God with a little art if one has any, and if one hasn't, and cannot recognize it in others, then one can at least burn a little incense.

My first sound-image was of an all-male chorus and *orchestre d'harmonie*. I thought, for a moment, of the organ, but I dislike the organ's *legato sostenuto* and its mess of octaves, as well as the fact that the monster never breathes. The breathing of wind instruments is one of their primary attractions for me. I obtained a satisfactory all-male chorus only once, to my recollection, and that was in Barcelona with the *Orfeo Català*, whose two hundred little boys, with their mamas and relatives, almost filled the hall. I was careful to keep the treble parts within the powers of child choristers.

VIOLIN CONCERTO

R.C.: Would you say something about your Violin Concerto, the background, the genre, the later career of the piece as a ballet?

I.S.: The Concerto was commissioned for Samuel Dushkin by his patron, the American gentleman Blair Fairchild. Fairchild had discovered Dushkin and his talent for the violin, at an early age, and had sponsored his education and career thereafter. The publisher Willy Strecker also helped in persuading me to accept the commission, and Strecker was a friend of Dushkin, too. Dushkin conferred with me often during the composition, and thus began a close friendship that is now more than thirty years old.

The first two movements of the Concerto and part of the third movement were composed in Nice, but the score was completed at La Vironnière, a château near Voreppe which I rented from a country lawyer who looked like Flaubert. I was very fond of this house, and especially of my attic workroom, which had a fine view of the Val d'Isère, but the inconveniences of country life and the need to drive to Grenoble for provisions were too much for me and I eventually had to move.

The Violin Concerto was not inspired by or modeled on any example. I did not find that the standard violin concertos—Mozart's, Beethoven's, Mendelssohn's, or even Brahms's—were among their composers' best work. (The Schoenberg Concerto is an exception, but that is hardly standard yet.) The subtitles of my Concerto—Toccata, Aria, Capriccio—may suggest Bach, though, and so, in a superficial way, might the musical substance. I am very fond of the Bach Concerto for Two Violins, as the duet of the soloist with a violin from the orchestra in the last movement of my own Concerto possibly may show. But my Concerto employs other duet combinations, too, and the texture is almost always more characteristic of chamber music than of orchestral music. I did not compose a cadenza, not because I did not care about exploiting violin virtuosity, but because the violin in combination was my real interest. But virtuosity for its own sake has only a small role in my Concerto, and the technical demands of the piece are relatively tame.

Balustrade (1940), the ballet that George Balanchine and Pavel Tchelitchev made of the Violin Concerto, was one of the most satisfactory visualizations of any of my works. Balanchine composed the choreography as he listened to my recording, and I could actually observe him conceiving gesture, movement, combination, composition. The result was a series of dialogues perfectly complimentary to and co-ordinated with the dialogues of the music.[16] The *corps de ballet* was small, and the second Aria was a solo piece for Tamara Toumanova. *Balustrade* was produced by Sol Hurok, that savant of the box office, and it must have been his first and last misjudgment in that sense. The set exposed a white balustrade on a dark stage, and the costumes were sinuous patterns in black and white.

---

[16] Hofmannsthal to Strauss: "Ballet is perhaps the only form of art which permits real, intimate collaboration between two people gifted with visual imagination."

I first knew the late Pavel Tchelitchev in Berlin in 1922, during the time I spent there waiting to meet my mother, who was leaving Russia. I considered him more gifted as theatrical designer than as easel painter, but that is probably because he decorated my own ballets—*Apollo* as well as *Balustrade*—so extremely well. I was especially fond of his costumes for Giraudoux's *Ondine*, also, and I had a good opportunity to watch him work then, as they were executed for him by my niece Ira Belline. Tchelitchev had a queer and difficult character, for though lively and very attractive as a person, he was also morbidly superstitious, and he would wear a mysterious red thread around his wrist or talk hieratically about the Golden Section, the true meaning of Horapollo, etc.

SCÈNES DE BALLET

R.C.: Did you have a narrative or choreographic scheme in mind composing the *Scènes de Ballet*, and did the fact of the commission for a Broadway extravaganza influence the musical substance and style? What is your present view of this music?

I.S.: When Billy Rose telephoned me one spring day in 1944 with an offer of five thousand dollars for a fifteen-minute ballet suite, he said that my solo dancers would be Alicia Markova and Anton Dolin and that Dolin would compose the choreography. But in spite of Dolin, the choreography was my own, in the sense that I conceived the sequence, character, and proportions of the pieces myself and visualized the dance construction of this plotless, "abstract" ballet as I wrote the music. In fact, no other score of mine prescribes a choreographic plan so closely.

The orchestral introduction exposes two identifying devices, the "blues" chords, and the melodic-pull idea:

When the curtain opens (at No. 5) the *corps de ballet* is discovered dancing in groups. The melodic-pull music is played by four violas and danced by four ballerinas. At No. 9 the groups join together, and at No. 40 they exit as the ballerina enters, *sola*. The idea of the Pantomime was that different groups of dancers should enter from different positions, each group in co-ordination with one of the arpeggiated figures in the music. The *Andantino* is a solo dance for the ballerina. When I first played it to Markova and Dolin, in my house in Hollywood, they said the flute cascades suggested falling stars, but I am unaware whether any such pictorial nonsense was realized in the performance, or even whether this part of the piece was performed at all. My only scenic idea was that the ballerina should wear a black tutu with diamond sequins, her partner a classical gilet.

The music from Nos. 60 to 69 is a dance for the *corps de ballet*. The trumpet solo in the *pas de deux* is associated with the male dancer, the horn with the female. The frilled phrase-endings in the ballerina's *Allegretto* were conceived as possibilities for pirouettes. The recapitulation of the *pas de deux* with the full orchestra now sounds to me like—pardon the pleonasm—bad movie music: the happy homesteaders, having massacred the Indians, begin to plant their CORN. In the last two measures of this number the solo dancers disappear at opposite sides of the stage, and the second Pantomime is an ensemble for the *corps de ballet*. The orchestral *tutti* that follows is the male dancer's solo variation, and the cello duet is the ballerina's solo. The final Pantomime unites the solo dancers, and the rest of the score—from the jazz movement in 3/8 time to the Apotheosis—assembles the whole company. I envisaged, for the finale, a stage full of groups twirling and mounting "*delirando*."

The story of the first performance of *Scènes de Ballet* (I did not know that Glazunov had used this title when I chose mine) is very worldly indeed. Page by page as I completed the orchestra score, my friend Ingolf Dahl arranged it for piano. Mr. Rose professed to like the music in this piano version, or so I was told, but he was dismayed by my orchestral cellophane. The music was cut to a fraction of its original length when *The Seven Lively Arts*, the show for which it was composed, opened in New York. After the first night of the Philadelphia preview run I received a telegram: YOUR MUSIC GREAT SUCCESS STOP COULD BE SENSATIONAL SUCCESS IF YOU WOULD AUTHORIZE ROBERT RUSSELL BENNETT RETOUCH ORCHESTRATION STOP BENNETT ORCHESTRATES EVEN THE WORKS OF COLE PORTER. I telegraphed back: SATISFIED WITH GREAT SUCCESS.

Scènes de Ballet is a period piece, a portrait of Broadway in the last years of the War. It is featherweight and sugared —my sweet tooth was not yet carious, then—but I will not deprecate it, not even the second Pantomime, and all of it is at least well made. I like the Apotheosis best of all and, especially, the voicing of the chords in the introduction to it, with the repetition of the upper line in canon and in different harmonic contexts. The Apotheosis was composed on the day of the liberation of Paris. I remember that I interrupted my work every few minutes to listen to the radio reports. I think my jubilation is in the music.

SYMPHONY IN THREE MOVEMENTS

R.C.: You have at times referred to your Symphony in Three Movements as a "war symphony." In what way is the music marked by the impression of world events?

I.S.: I can say little more than that it was written under the sign of them. It both does and does not "express my feelings" about them, but I prefer to say only that, without participation of what I think of as my will, they excited my musical imagination. And the events that thus activated me were not general, or ideological, but specific: each episode in the Symphony is linked in my imagination with a concrete impression, very often cinematographic in origin, of the war.

The third movement actually contains the genesis of a war plot, though I recognized it as such only after completing the composition. The beginning of that movement is partly, and in some—to me wholly inexplicable—way, a musical reaction to the newsreels and documentaries that I had seen of goose-stepping soldiers. The square march-beat, the brass-band in-strumentation, the grotesque *crescendo* in the tuba—these are all related to those repellent pictures.

Though my visual impressions of world events were derived largely from films, they also were rooted in personal experi-ence. One day in Munich, in 1932, I saw a squad of Brown Shirts enter the street below the balcony of my room in the Bayerische Hof and assault a group of civilians. The civilians tried to protect themselves behind sidewalk benches, but soon were crushed beneath these clumsy shields. The police arrived, eventually, but by then the attackers had dispersed. That same night I dined with Vera de Bosset and the photographer Eric Schall in a small Allee restaurant. Three men wearing swastika armbands entered the room, and one of them began to talk insultingly about Jews and to aim his remarks in our direction. With the afternoon street fight still in our eyes, we hurried to leave, but the now shouting Nazi and his myrmidons followed, cursing and threatening us the while. Schall protested, and at that they began to kick and hit him. Miss de Bosset ran to a corner, found a policeman, and told him that a man was being killed, but this piece of intelligence did not rouse him to any action. We were then rescued by a timely taxi, and though Schall was battered and bloody, we went directly to a police court where, however, the magistrate was as little perturbed with our story as the policeman had been. "In Germany today, such things happen every minute," was all he said.

But let us return to the plot of the movement. In spite of contrasting episodes, such as the canon for bassoons, the march music is predominant until the fugue, which is the stasis and the turning point. The immobility at the beginning of the fugue is comic, I think—and so, to me, was the over-turned arrogance of the Germans when their machine failed. The exposition of the fugue and the end of the Symphony are associated in my plot with the rise of the Allies, and perhaps the final, albeit rather too commercial, D-flat sixth chord—instead of the expected C—tokens my extra exuberance in the

Allied triumph. The figure

was developed from the rumba in the timpani part in the
introduction to the first movement. It was somehow associated
in my imagination with the movements of war machines.

The first movement was likewise inspired by a war film, this
time a documentary of scorched-earth tactics in China. The
middle part of the movement—the music for clarinet, piano,
and strings, which mounts in intensity and volume until the
explosion of the three chords at No. 69—was conceived as a
series of instrumental conversations to accompany a cinematographic scene showing the Chinese people scratching and
digging in their fields.

The formal substance of the Symphony—perhaps Three
Symphonic Movements would be a more exact title—exploits
the idea of counterplay among several types of contrasting
elements. One such contrast, the most obvious, is that of harp
and piano, the principal instrumental protagonists. Each has a
large *obbligato* role and a whole movement to itself and only
at the turning-point fugue, the *queue de poisson* of the Nazi
machine, are the two heard together and alone.

But enough of this. In spite of what I have said, the Symphony is not programmatic. Composers combine notes. That is
all. How and in what form the things of this world are impressed upon their music is not for them to say.

JAZZ COMMERCIALS

R.C.: What were the origins of your pieces for so-called jazz
and other popular band ensembles—the *Circus Polka, Scherzo
à la russe, Ebony Concerto, Ragtime* for eleven instruments—
and how do you regard this music today?

I.S.: With the exception of the *Ragtime*, these were all jour-
neyman jobs, commissions I was forced to accept because the
war in Europe had so drastically reduced the income from
my compositions. The idea of the *Circus Polka* was George

Balanchine's. He wanted a short piece for a ballet of elephants, one of whom was to carry Vera Zorina, who was at that time Balanchine's wife. The *Marche militaire* quotation came to me as an absolutely natural thing, which I say to circumvent the inevitable German professor who is going to call my use of it a parody. The music was first performed in someone else's arrangement for the Ringling Brothers' Circus Band. After conducting my orchestral original, in Boston in 1944, I received a congratulatory telegram from Bessie, the young pachyderm who had carried the *bella ballerina* and who had heard my broadcast in winter quarters of the circus at Sarasota. I never saw the ballet, but I met Bessie in Los Angeles once and shook her foot.

The *Scherzo à la russe* was commissioned by Paul Whiteman for a special radio broadcast. I wrote it originally to exact specifications of his ensemble, then rewrote it for standard orchestra—which gave me some trouble, as the volume of mandolin and guitar in the Trio canon was so much lighter than that of harp and piano. Whiteman conducted the first performance himself, much too rapidly. He and others professed to hear reminiscences of *Petroushka* in it.

The *Ebony Concerto* was also written for a prescribed instrumentation, to which I added a French horn. Mr. Woody Herman wanted the piece for a concert that already was scheduled, and I had to compose it in a hurry. My plan was to write a jazz *concerto grosso* with a blues slow movement. I studied recordings of the Herman band, enlisted a saxophonist to demonstrate fingerings. "Ebony" does not mean "clarinet," incidentally, but "African." The only jazz I had heard in the United States was in Harlem, and by Negro bands in Chicago and New Orleans, and the jazz performers I most admired at that time were Art Tatum, Charlie Parker, and the guitarist Charles Christian. And "blues" meant African culture to me.

I conducted, not the premiere performance, but the recording in Los Angeles some weeks later. What I remember most clearly was the smoke in the recording studio. When the musicians did not blow horns they blew smoke, and of such tangi-

bility that the atmosphere looked like Pernod clouded by water. Their instrumental mastery was astonishing, but so was
their lack of *solfeggio*. Of the four pieces you name I like the
Ebony Concerto best, though it is remote from me now and
rather like the work of a sympathetic colleague I once knew
well.

Jazz—blanket term—has exerted a time-to-time influence on
my music since 1918, and traces of blues and boogie-woogie
can be found even in my most "serious" pieces, as, for example,
in the *Bransle de Poitou* and the *Bransle simple* from *Agon*
and in the *pas d'action* and *pas de deux* (middle section)
from *Orpheus*. In 1918 Ernest Ansermet, returning from an
American tour, brought me a bundle of ragtime music in the
form of piano reductions and instrumental parts, which I copied out in score. With these pieces before me, I composed the
Ragtime in *Histoire du soldat*, and, after completing *Histoire*,
the *Ragtime* for eleven instruments. The *Histoire* ragtime is a
concert portrait, or snapshot of the genre—in the sense that
Chopin's *Valses* are not dance waltzes, but portraits of waltzes.
The snapshot has faded, I fear, and it must always have
seemed to Americans like very alien corn. If my subsequent
essays in jazz portraiture were more successful, that is because they showed awareness of the idea of improvisation, for
by 1919 I had heard live bands and discovered that jazz performance is more interesting than jazz composition. I am referring to my non-metrical pieces for piano solo and clarinet
solo, which are not real improvisations, of course, but written-
out portraits of improvisation.

I began the *Ragtime* for eleven instruments in October
1918 and finished it on the morning of the Armistice. I remember how, sitting at the cimbalom in my garret in Morges,
like *Gretchen am Spinnrade*, I was aware of a buzzing in my
ears that increased until I was afraid I had been stricken like
Robert Schumann. I went down to the street and was told that
everyone was hearing the same noise and that it was from
cannon along the French frontier announcing the end of the
war.

I composed the *Ragtime* on the cimbalom, and the whole ensemble is grouped around the whorehouse-piano sonority of that instrument. I continued to play the cimbalom every day in my Pleyel[17] Studio in Paris between the wars, though I wrote no more music for it because of the difficulty of finding good players. Nevertheless, some of the piano writing in my *Capriccio* is cimbalomist in style, especially the cadenza in the second movement, which is a kind of Romanian restaurant music.

When the composition was completed, I asked Picasso to design a cover. I watched him draw six figures, each from a single, uninterrupted line. He chose the published one himself.

[17] The Pleyel company constructed new pedals that I designed for the instrument, and they tuned it regularly.

WORKING NOTES for *The Flood*

Stravinsky and Balanchine
Hollywood, March 15–16 and April 11–12, 1962

(1) Vacuum. Black scrim. The Prelude music is associated with Chaos, and at the end of the work with Sin. The 12/4 measure is a musical Jacob's Ladder. As we follow it upward the black velvet ceiling opens up. Movements of clouds. Angels' wings fill the screen. The angels are Seraphim, Russian-style, and we are aware of their wings rather than of bodies or faces. The camera pulls downward and we discover that they are framed like icons, and that together they form a triangular altar. *I.S.*: "This iconostasis should resemble a real Byzantine altar with the Chiasma or X symbol on top. The piece begins and ends in the Church." The revelation of the iconostasis must be synchronized with the unfolding of the *Noces*-like Te Deum which is (*I.S.*) "not Gregorian but Igorian chant." The voices should sound at measure 8 as though heralding from a great distance, and from there to measure 46, the musical climax, they should gradually move closer. At measure 46 the screen is filled with a "celestial effulgence" that washes out all detail.

I.S.: "To me the Noah story is symbolic, and I think of Noah as an Old Testament Christ figure, like Melchizedek. The subject of *The Flood* is not the Noah story, however, but Sin. Whereas the music of *Petroushka* attempted to create resemblances, *The Flood* music is, structurally speaking, all symbolic."

(2) The fade-out from the iconostasis begins at measure 60. *I.S.*: "The two chords are a kind of approval of what the chorus has been singing." The Genesis recitative could be accompanied by a montage of pictures symbolizing the Creation. For instance, at the words "Let the dry earth appear" we might see photographs of the moon, of the sea, of deserts. *I.S.*: "This is the place for animation and graphic arts, except that I would rather stay away from the surface of the screen." *G.B.* has an idea for a hand ballet of rubber sheets and plastic water bags manipulated to suggest shapes and forms. "But we might also show structures of roots and bones, *à la* Tchelitchew, and of hands sprouting grass from the fingers."

(3) The recitative becomes an *arioso* at measure 68. This should be danced by one or perhaps several people representing not humans, but non-associated movements, or exploratory movements, or the flexing movements of any living creature's discovery of its body. This section should be thought of as choreographic relief to the purely pictorial recitative.

(4) God, at His first vocal entrance, is represented by unbounded space and crystalline light. The divine rays could be plastic tubing. *G.B.*: "A shower of gold dust might fall on the screen every time God sings, but God is the most difficult visualization of all since He is still an object of some curiosity. We might see two ellipses, a parallel to the two voices, breathing or pulsating—the halved ellipses is the divine ideogram, after all—or we might be shown an eye, embryo, or vortex." *I.S.*: "God's music is sometimes reminiscent of Shadow's music in *The Rake*, which should prove, if proof were needed, that musical identities are purely circumstantial." The audience

must think that it is looking up every time God sings. The introductory bass drum notes are a signal for the screen ceiling to open and reveal the divine rays (i.e., plastic tubing).

The Creation of Man. Two shapes, recognizably human though covered, are seen from above. The substance of their chrysalis is peeled from them like two onions, and they stand statuesquely still until the Exile from Eden, at which time they lose their God-like postures. The two shapes are seen in profile only, or only from behind, though (*G.B.*) "profiles are unclear in TV and space is as undefined as soup."

(5) At first, and as God names him, Lucifer, too, stands statuesquely still. He is perched at a great eminence, and our view is from below. His face is jeweled, and gold wires crop from his head. His costume, glittering with reflective metals, is set off by a baffle of sequins. *G.B.*: "Perhaps we should see a mirror of him, or hall of mirrors with prismatic effects, rather than himself full face."

(6) With the recitative "Lucifer was vain," the Lucifer dancer begins to move. He jumps to a higher rock with each chord, but misses the last one, and at measure 130, the *arioso*, is at floor level dancing a lithe, athletic "twist." *G.B.*: "The floor is everything in television—backgrounds are comparatively unimportant—and if the floor is wrong, a small-scale hop may look as high as the Eiffel Tower."

Lucifer's transformation begins at measure 146. Photographically speaking, Satan is Lucifer's negative polarity. What was white becomes black, and the lips turn dark "red." The mask shrinks to skull size and becomes a corruption of its former features. The wings grow hideously veined, like a bat's. A short pause at the end of measure 151 will suffice for camera tricks to create sensations of pinwheeling, of falling and turning upside down. If this were a Cocteau film, Satan would do a parachute jump. The Fall might also be symbolized pictorially, for example, by photographing the tracings on a plate when two atoms collide. Each word of the phrase "Out, out, horror, helpless, hot, hot, hot" could be projected from a greater distance, and echoed and spiraled by tape reverberation. *I.S.*: "Though The Fall is instantaneous, theologically speaking, we must allow enough clock time for the audience to feel the heat."

(7) Satan's is a sibilant-sweet voice wholly different from the trumpeting Lucifer. *I.S.*: "The audience should be able to locate HEAVEN/EARTH/HELL by established camera levels, and recurrent visual clues, as well as by musical distance, which is to say that the music associated with these three spheres ought to be recorded to fixed and recognizably differentiated distances." Satan's aria "God made the world for love" is to be sung moderately *forte*, but the parenthetical words with the rhythm from "The Maidens Came" must be performed *sotto voce*, and the singer should pant and hiss for breath after each dotted quarter-note. The Satan dancer could sit during this aria, and stand at "to Paradise," which, incidentally, may be spoken by the narrator if the stage director prefers. We see Satan next in a transparent moth-bag serpent reticulated with wicker rings. *I.S.*: "The vermicular disguise must have an excremental shape, and Satan must appear unchanged and plainly visible inside." The next narration begins before the music, and the Pantomime, for musical continuity, could come between the first two phrases of horn music. *I.S.*: "The Tarnhelm music for two muted horns is likely to be my first and last attempt to compose a belly dance."

(8) Instead of showing the serpent in the tree or coiled about the trunk of the tree, we might see the tree itself turn into serpentine limbs that embrace Eve and Adam. The tree should be light in color at first, and artistically "beautiful"—*G.B.* thinks it should look like a willow, in spite of the fame of its fruit— but as the fruit is plucked, the tree withers and becomes sinister. Eve need not actually pick fruit, of course, but some brief symbolic pantomime—the music allows only a few seconds— should be synchronized with the narrated description. The first "cursed" should be timed to occur just before the brass chord at measure 177, and the second to just before the second

brass chord. With the first note of the contrabassoon, Adam and Eve start to cover themselves with black leaves from the now blackened tree and to walk in shame from Eden. *I.S.*: "The allegory of Eden, the curse of Original Sin, in this single measure of music, the largest and most complete-in-itself I have ever composed, is the dramatic climax of the whole work."

I.S.: "After Evil, God. At measure 179, the return to the Jacob's Ladder music, the purifying sky leads us to primal light. Air, clouds, distance. I have allotted but fifteen seconds of music for this change from the lowest to the highest, but the music should be able to accomplish it. Music is a non-temporal magic carpet."

In the God/Noah scene, God's voice may be indentified with abstract patterns of light. During God's aria, the camera discovers a black mote far below. We spiral down to it and discover Noah, who must seem to be very small and humble, even at earth level. He wears a patriarch's toga and a tulle cape that rises behind him magically and flickers with light during the tremolos accompanying his speeches to God. The dancing members of his family wear white leotards, and all of them are masked larger than life in slant-eyed masks seen in profile rather than full-face. *G.B.*: "We must avoid the question of style, of Biblical, Medieval, Renaissance, Byzantine, or anything else. We know only that we are trying to do something new and without a name."

God, or—as we do not actually see Him—His Master's Voice, is a Person, but a Person free of what talent scouts call personality. He is, in fact, a divine bore. Lucifer/Satan, on the other hand, is not a Person, so he abounds in personality. Lucifer/Satan is different each time he sings. In private life he might be an orchestra conductor, a *coryphée*, a high-diving champion, a film star, and ex-astronaut.

(9) *G.B.*: "The God-Noah dialogue could be seen like a tennis game, back and forth from the earth-level view of Noah to the light of the iconostasis, which is the visual anchor throughout *The Flood*. Generally speaking, the audience's view up to

this point has been from above, but we now see Noah from, as nearly as possible, his own position. I would like to elevate the dancers to audience eye level by means of a platform, not only because dancers should not be shown from above, but also because the audience should identify itself with the Noah family. Up to this point *The Flood* may seem to have been a spatial fantasy, a myth, a limbo of symbols. Now it is brought down to humanly tilled earth."

(10) Until the actual Building of the Ark, Noah is alone. He talks to God like a man on a desert island, bows before him, shields himself from His light. The drum roll will allow time for each visual switch to God, whose Light is immediate, but Noah's speeches begin slowly and falteringly, and his voice is that of an old man. The *ponticello* effect identified with God's radiance also could be used to follow a trajectory of light between God and Noah.

(11) After God's speech, and before measure 247, Noah prostrates himself, hugging the ground. *I.S.*: "As all Biblical Hebrews were, so must he have been frightened of the sea. The Flood was a more terrible form of catastrophe to a Hebrew farmer, in any case, than it would have been to a Homeric Greek." At measure 247 we see the legs of his approaching bairns. The legs kneel to him, and we know that he has been lifted up. In the following two measures the dancers stand like an assembly line.

The Building of the Ark. G.B.: "The dancers' movements must be as mechanical as a watch, and the builders' arms should work like semaphores." Noah reappears in the coda, measures 328–334, to survey the completed work. The builders stand by to inspect the Ark, verify its solidity, pinch it to see if it is "pukka." *I.S.*: "We should not be shown anything of the object itself except, perhaps, a shadow. The Ark is as unreal as the Trojan Horse."

(12) *The Catalogue of the Animals.* During the loading, Noah's sons stand by like longshoremen. Noah speaks slowly, and be-

fore the music begins, but the narrator reads his verse as fast
as he is able. The narrator could have a comb-and-tissue-
paper timbre and an American accent, like a square-dance
caller or a tobacco auctioneer. *G.B.*: "The animals could be
shown skiagraphically, as ominously large background silhou-
ettes, but this probably requires animation. Or toy animals and
wooden miniatures could be shown looming toward the audience on three conveyor belts (left, right, center overhead),
and if not toy animals, then photographs of real ones, or representative stylized parts, tusks, humps, splayed or padded
feet, zebras' stripes, tails, manes, trunks, wings, though this,
too, implies the participation of graphic arts. Rapid changes
in camera angles might be exploited also, thus suddenly showing the animals from above or below, or about to tread on us
full-face. The birds wing aboard lightly and last, for they can
fly to their roosts when we already are flooded. *G.B.*: "Another
notion to consider is that if the animals are miniatures, Noah's
sons could stand by the conveyor belts, pick them up and
throw them into the Ark—the surface of the screen, the audience's lap—like children heaping toys in a basket."

(13) *The Comedy.* Noah's wife could be characterized as a
Xantippe with a bottle. She has disregarded the Ark when it
was building, and she is on her way to a pub when the flood
begins. At the last minute her sons—vocally represented by the
chorus speaking in unison, or by the narrator—hoist their kicking mother and carry her into the Ark.

(14) *I.S.* thinks the music for Noah's "the earth is overflowed
with flood" might be supplemented by an electronic effect suggesting "atmospheric disturbances, or by a pure noise, like a
sinus tone."

(15) The flood is framed at both ends by "lightning." Measure
427, the musical turn-around, should mark the climax of the
storm visually, but the music is without climax. *I.S.*: "The music imitates not waves and winds, but time. The interruptions
in the violin/flute line say: "No, it isn't over." As the skin of

the sun is fire, so here the violins and flutes are the skin drawn over the body of the sound. This '*La Mer*' has no '*de l'aube à midi*' but only a time experience of something that is terrible and that lasts."

G.B.: "I imagine a floor covered with a shiny bitumen-like material, a deliquescent black surface bubbling like an oil field. Underneath this black tent the male dancers bob up and down from their knees, here and there and all over the camera area, like furuncles. The movements of the dancers might also be synchronized with countervailing explosions of black rubber tubes, balloons, bubble gum. The female dancers move among the mounting and bursting blobs of black. The men are the waves and the women the people drowning in them. The men fling and twirl the women, then swallow them in the folds of their black substance. The audience should feel that *it* is drowning. The audience is definitely *not* on the Ark."

(16) *The Covenant of the Rainbow.* The color change in God's music must be compounded with a change in visual "color." *G.B.*: "The rainbow could be formed by the dancers, of course, but the result might look like an advertisement for Radio City. Their costumes can help to suggest an arc or a bridge." At the end of the rainbow stands Noah, bowed in gratitude. Then, directly in front of him, unpleasant black objects (the viewer suspects that he has the DT's) inch out of the ground. They are the wing tips of Satan, another and unexpected survivor of the flood. The mayhem music of the Prelude is repeated to accompany this vision.[18] *I.S.*: "As Satan's falsetto aria with flutes is a prolepsis of Christianity, Satan must now be shown as Anti-Christ." *G.B.*: "If Satan is represented as a human-shaped spider in a web when he sings his 'God made the world for love,' he should be shown here as a creature with no face, or a face with lips but no other features." Adam and Eve

[18] This was George Balanchine's idea. It is the second instance in which the choreographer has affected the final shape of a work by Stravinsky: Balanchine induced the composer to extend the return of the F-major string music in the *pas de deux* from *Orpheus*. (R.C.)

appear again, fleetingly, in the background or in shadow. During the narrator's last speech, the camera dissolves from the allegorical tableau. Satan's final gesture toward Adam and Eve means that "the affair" is continual and that the end of it is also a beginning. The camera dollies to the iconostasis.

I.S.: "Satan's postdiluvian voice exposes a new temperament. Quieter now and very sure of himself, he is inclined to take his position for granted, which is why true Christians may overcome him. In short, he seems only to be as ineradicable as the music critic to whose position in the theology of Creation he may be compared. His threat is pedantic and the words are a turgid tirade, but the meaning of the piece is in them. At the end he skips across the stage, far below or out of sight, like the Duke at the end of *Rigoletto*." The camera fades from the angelic choir, and as the music returns to the Jacob's Ladder of the Prelude, "eternal radiance"—which is different from ordinary TV static—suffuses the screen.

I.S.: "Television should someday succeed in sponsoring a new, in the sense of more concentrated, musicodramatic form (not 'instant music drama,' which it already has, and which is obtained by pouring water on real composers' ideas). Visually it offers every advantage over stage opera, but the saving of musical time interests me more than anything visual. This new musical economy was the one specific of the medium which guided my conception of *The Flood*. Because the succession of visualizations can be instantaneous, the composer may dispense with the afflatus of overtures, connecting episodes, curtain music. I have used only one or two notes to punctuate each stage in The Creation, for example, and so far, I have not been able to imagine the work on the operatic stage because the musical speed is so uniquely cinematographic.

"Other than the possible development of a new musicodramatic form, the musical life of television does not interest me. A televised concert is a great bore. One sees conductors who look like English sheep dogs. One sees the timpani and the trombone and the oboe individually. One watches the players breathe, and moisten their embouchures. But seeing individual musicians play, in this way, distracts one from listening to the whole ensemble.

"The so-called underscoring of a TV drama could interest only that composer whose ambition is to design musical wall-paper. In Tahiti, recently, a fair native who had never heard European music asked me what my music was 'like.' Did it resemble Tahitian music—drums—or the jukebox bands in Tahitian night clubs? Our only common ground should have been the music of films we had both seen, but the fair *taïtienne* had never noticed any music in any film. And that should be the underscorers' motto: keep the film viewer from noticing the music, and in the event that he does notice it, help him to forget it as soon as possible.

"As to the question of mass media, I can only say that 'the intellectual elite'—if one exists, and I hope it does, history being a cemetery of aristocracies, as Pareto said—the elite is probably not opposed to mass media, but only to those who seek to determine what is suitable for mass media.

"The question of the parity between visual and musical experience is not altered by television, but nevertheless, if I live to write another opera, I suspect that it will be for the electronic glass tube and the Idiot Box, rather than for the early Baroque stages of the world's present-day opera houses."

Toronto, January 1962–Santa Fe, July 1962

APPENDIX A

Menzies Hotel
Melbourne
November 27, 1961

Editor
The Observer
22 Tudor Street
London

Sir:

Peter Heyworth's *Schnabel the Creator* (*The Observer*, November 10, 1961) quotes a remark by Glazunov printed in a book of Schnabel's writings I have not read: "Of all the 2,000 pupils I taught at the Conservatory in St. Petersburg, Stravinsky had the worst ear." I was never Glazunov's pupil, never a student in the St. Petersburg Conservatory, and Glazunov's only opportunity to judge my ear was through my music, a test *he* failed.

Glazunov was almost as much of an idol to me in my fifteenth year as Rimsky himself, that is, until I transcribed one of his string quartets for piano and impulsively took the score to his house to show him. Though I had never been presented to him, he knew my father, in spite of which he received me ungraciously, perfunctorily flipping through my manuscript and pronouncing my work unmusical. I went away thoroughly discouraged. Now though his later dislike was clearly due to the fact that I had not come to him for instruction but had gone directly to Rimsky, I cannot explain this early incident. As for Rimsky's own opinion of Glazunov, I can say only that the success of any pupil made him proud, and Glazunov was his most apparent success. To an academically minded man like Rimsky, Glazunov must also have seemed the safest of the younger composers, in the sense that the only rule he could ever undermine would be the rule of imagination.

A short time later, when I began to wonder at myself for having been interested in Glazunov in the past (the whiteness pilled from my eyes, as the translator of Tobit says) I continued to see him at conservatory concerts, often in company with that other reckless academician, Tcherepnin. He was always rude to me but I think that was because my remark that he was only a Carl Philipp Emanuel Rimsky-Korsakov had been repeated to him. After the first performance of my Symphony in E flat he told me that he thought it "rather heavy instrumentation for such empty music." He was also present at the performance of my instrumentations of Beethoven's and Mussorgsky's "Flea" songs for a Goethe-in-music concert conducted by Siloti, and at the premiere of my *Fireworks*. This time his comment was repeated to me: "*Kein talent, nur Dissonanz.*"

I have told elsewhere how in 1935 Maria Kuznetzov's son came to my studio in the Salle Pleyel and begged me to greet my "old St. Petersburg colleague" during intermission of a rehearsal of his music downstairs. I accompanied Kuznetzov to Glazunov's green room, but was greeted with as little sympathy—he extended two fingers and said nothing—as I had received thirty-eight years before.

All that this has to do with Schnabel, of course, is to say that our experiences of Glazunov were different. (Schnabel found him charming.) My encounters with Schnabel in Berlin in the

1920s and in New York during the 1939 war were pleasant enough, and I always had the greatest respect for Schnabel as a pedagogue. (I even tried to persuade him to take my younger son as a pupil.) But my encounters with his music were another matter. All the examples I have met with were timeless in the wrong sense (Schoenberg is reported to have told him that "rests are also permitted in twelve-tone music"), and one of them, a solo cello sonata, was probably the unloveliest lucubration I have ever heard. To me, "Schnabel the Creator" is a tenuous proposition and in the old word-association game, his masterpiece, the *Duodecimet*, would only make me say "ulcers."

Yours, etc.

IGOR STRAVINSKY

APPENDIX B

Soon after the publication of V. Yastrebtzev's *Recollections of Rimsky-Korsakov* Volume II (Moscow, 1962) scholars began to ask me for comment on the book's references to myself. I remember nothing about Yastrebtzev beyond the name, however, and when I try to associate that with my memory of faces in Rimsky's group, I confuse it with the librettist Belsky. The book is an accurate picture of Rimsky and his circle, though, and I am certain that it is a reliable chronicle.

Yastrebtzev first mentions me under the date February 28, 1903, merely identifying me as a young musician. Most of the other fifty-three references to me occur in memos of conversations at Rimsky's weekly gatherings, the *jours fixes* at which compositions by his pupils were performed and discussed.

Yastrebtzev notes that on March 6, 1903, I played my *plaisanteries musicales* at Rimsky's, but I have no recollection of these bagatelles. On February 17, 1904, he writes that I played my *chanson comique* and that Nicolas Richter horrified Rimsky's wife by playing a cakewalk. He adds that "Mitussov and Stravinsky amusingly demonstrated how it should be danced." Paws up, like circus poodles, or boop-boop-a-doop?

The entry of March 6, 1904, states: "During dinner the

young Rimsky-Korsakovs, with Stravinsky at their head, performed a charming cantata which Stravinsky had composed and dedicated to Nicolai Andreitch. The cantata was repeated by audience request." I have no recollection of this *Tafelmusik*.

The notes for August 22 and 23, 1904, written in Vehchasha, near Lzy,[19] state that Rimsky was "forcing" me to work at the orchestration, for winds, of the Polonaise from *Pan Voyevoda*.

I will quote Yastrebtzev directly for a few other entries that may be of interest:

February 9, 1905. Before tea, N. Richter played the F-sharp minor sonata, dedicated to him, by Stravinsky.

March 6, 1906. At the beginning of the musical program, Igor Stravinsky played his *Conductor in Tarantula*. (I think this was a piano piece inspired by *Koosma Prootkov*.—I.S.)[20]

February 27, 1907. Stravinsky's romances were sung.

April 18, 1907. Among those present was I. F. Stravinsky, to whom Nicolai Andreitch presented the orchestra score of the *Tableau of Tsar Tsaltan*. (Rimsky gave me this manuscript to commemorate the first performance of my Symphony in E flat. —I.S.)

October 31, 1907. After tea, Stravinsky and Steinberg played Stravinsky's *Pastorale* twice, singing on the vowel A. Stravinsky then presented his *Novice*, on the 3 first words—the bell sounds—of Gorodetsky's poem. The middle of the piece is beautiful, but the beginning is strange. Is it music or is it "on purpose"?

November 4, 1907. In the opinion of Rimsky-Korsakov, the talent of Igor Stravinsky has not yet taken clear shape. Rimsky thinks that the fourth part of his Symphony imitates Glazunov too much, and Rimsky himself. And he considers that in the new romances on words of Gorodetsky, Igor Feodorovitch puts himself too much on the side of *modernism*.

[19] See *Expositions and Developments*.
[20] See *Memories and Commentaries*.

December 25, 1907. After the performance of Stravinsky's *Pastorale* and *Spring*, Rimsky said: "I keep to my opinion of the *Spring*. What pleasure can anyone have in composing music to the words of such false Russian folk language? For me, all this 'lyrical impressionism' is contemporary decadence. It is full of mist and fog, but meager in content of ideas."

January 15, 1908. Talk about the Symphony by Igor Stravinsky. The orchestration of the first part is too heavy, but there are handsome harmonic and instrumental episodes. The Symphony will be performed by the Court Orchestra on the 22d January —Tuesday. (Gossip after a rehearsal, evidently.—I.S.)

February 16, 1908. Everyone was at the Belaiev concert yesterday, conducted by F. Blumenfeld. Stravinsky's Suite *Le Faune et la bergère*.

PART 2

A Diary

". . . They went quietly down into the roaring streets, inseparable and blessed; and as they passed along in sunshine and shade, the noisy and the eager, and the froward and the vain, fretted and chafed, and made their usual uproar."

LITTLE DORRIT

My "conversations with Stravinsky" were originally recorded in the logbooks of concert tours, Stravinsky being more inclined to talk about himself and his work while abroad performing music than when at home composing it. But the residual log books contained table talk and obiter dicta that could not be presented in question and answer form or separated from the circumstances of their utterance in my callow catalogue of things seen. These more casual remarks expose a different aspect of the man, I think, and one that should help to light a different piece of his portrait.

R.C.
New York, November 1962

1951

ITALY

August 15. Naples. The balcony of I.S.'s room at the Excelsior. Soft blues of bay and sky, Sorrento and Castellammare, the rocky island lumps, Vesuvio. But in spite of these views, our eyes are fixed on the street below. The *Constitution* has docked an hour before and the waterfront is an arena of strolling Americans and the touts who prey upon them with fountain pens, black market rates of exchange, offers of the favors of their female relatives. These salesmen lean against the seawall pretending to be absorbed in the view, then pounce around and harrow the victim at close quarters until eventually he buys something "just to get rid of the nuisance."

The shores are crowded with bathers, and the bay is white with sails. Beneath the balcony to the left are the docks of the Capri excursion boats. Here, every hour or so, a small steamer leaves or lands low in the water with tourists. On the right side of the hotel is a restaurant, the Transatlantico, and the Castle of Lucullus, now a jail. Another restaurant, the Zi Teresa, faces these incongruous buildings across a small inlet, and at night the rival names are spelled out in the brightest Neapolitan neon. Chinese lanterns festoon the façades of each dining establishment, and from each we hear the same music:

guitars, violins, soulful tenors. Now, in the morning, table laundry flutters from both their porches. This morning, too, I.S. is nearly recovered from an intestinal instability, the result of a visit to one of them.

Dinner at the Pappagallo with Auden and Kallman. Auden (last seen sprawled on the floor of his New York apartment, surrounded by open volumes of Saintsbury's prosody and the O.E.D.) looks outstandingly non-aboriginal in these surroundings. His hair is sun-hennaed, his skin is raw with sunburn, and the once-white Panama suit is not much help as a disguise. A gang of gamins single out and pursue him as we walk to the restaurant. He shouts *"Basta"* at them, but the foreign ring of the word only increases his plight. His right hand flaps circularly as he talks, and when the subject is serious the movement becomes more forceful and the static between words increases. His arguments are always categorical: "There are actually just two points: a) . . . and b) . . ." Another characteristic is his contempt of ill health. "Bad weather cannot exist if it is ignored," he will say, and on the strength of this philosophy, eschew a coat and catch cold. Puzzle games, quizzes, quests, hypotheses, delight him. Tonight at dinner, for example, he contends that "Italian and English are the languages of Heaven, and 'Frog' the language of Hell." I am supposed to follow this by inventing other Celestial/Infernal usages, but I can think of none and, anyway, Auden is already developing the idea that "The 'Frogs' were expelled from Heaven in the first place because they annoyed God by calling Him *cher maître*." (This is because of some French visitors who have annoyed Auden by calling I.S. the same thing.) He has a prodigious repertory of unintentionally funny C. of E. hymns and opera prima donna anecdotes; and though he is very proper, even a Puritan, delicately risqué stories amuse him, like the one about my German friend who when ill in Paris swallowed a suppository thinking it some strange kind of French pill. He has brilliant brown eyes set in a rumpled face (I.S.: "Soon we will have to smooth him out to see who it is"), but his eyesight is poor, and without spectacles he may fail to apprehend furniture, or wade through glass doors. When, drinking *grappa* in the Galleria, I.S. yawns, Auden quotes Joyce on "the apathy of the 'stars,'" but Auden himself is able to stay awake only long enough to swallow his sleeping pills. He tips the table over as we leave, having forgot that it was there.

August 26. To Milan. The train, a *rapido*, is wobbly, sooty, and two hours late. I.S.: "Italians will not believe without exaggeration. Thus, an expression like '*una cosa tremenda*' probably applies to something of no great moment, and words like '*stupendo*,' '*brutissimo*,' '*repelente*' are used to refer to very minor inconveniences. As you see, the slowest and least punctual trains are called '*espresso*,' '*rapido*,' or '*accelerato*.'"

A film star's reception for I.S. at the Duomo Hotel. The street is blocked off, and the entrance is protected by ropes.

September 5. Milan to Venice, the cast, chorus, and orchestra of the *Rake* in three reserved cars. Noontime, in the restaurant car, from a table across the aisle as we leave Brescia:

AMERICAN TOURIST NO. 1: "What town was that we just passed?"
AMERICAN TOURIST NO. 2: "I think it's called '*Uomini*.'"

As we pass Verona:

AMERICAN TOURIST NO. 1: "Say, didn't Shakespeare live here?"
AUDEN, INTERRUPTING: "But surely it was Bacon."

Venice. I.S.'s piano arrives. Trussed in canvas and hawsers, it is pulleyed from the canal to his second-floor room like a horse up the side of a ship. Faint sounds escape through his door thereafter, the same notes over and over, like piano-tuning. V. remarks that the hotel staff seem much relieved. They had evidently expected him to compose as Liszt and Chopin have been made to do in films, that is, with cascades of sound and stormy "passages." (He says, later, that his brothers always called him "the piano tuner, because I repeated a note that I liked.")

The Piazza. Pigeon love. The male treads and turns, blinks, treads again, chases. I.S. says that the bands playing on either side of the Piazza, "sound together like Milhaud."

A *Rake* rehearsal at La Fenice in the evening. No syllable of the La Scala chorus sounds English. And a midnight gondola ride with Auden, drunk and full of song—*Die Walküre*. I.S. says that Colette sang Wagner to him once, too, when they were drunk together on the Paris-Nice train. A large rat runs along the molding of a wall two feet from our boat. "The DT's," Auden says.

September 11. The premiere. A damp day. Auden, very out of patience with the stage director, proposes that we drink a bottle of champagne to his demise, and he threatens to change the line "A scene like this is better than a sale" to "A scene like this is slower than a snail." I.S.: "Auden is like an expectant aunt." But the opera survives its performance including a dozen disastrous entrances, and is very moving in spite of mistakes. Each loge is crowned with a bouquet of roses, and the audience is the *ne plus ultra* of elegance. At the Taverna, afterward, a tune detection game of citing resemblances to other operas. V. thinks the *mourning chorus* begins like the *Volga Boat Song*. Auden says the beginning of Act III, and especially the woodwind trill with the *fermata* reminds him of the dance of the apprentices in *Die Meistersinger*, and he says the "they are rebuked" in Bedlam is "an unexpected venture into Richard Strauss." The Terzetto, he says, is "Tchaikovskyan," and the Epilogue is modeled on *Don Giovanni*. Here I.S., who does not recognize or admit to any of the attributions, objects. "The Epilogue is a vaudeville or pasquinade, the *Seraglio* or *L'Heure espagnole*. In fact, some of the *Rake* is close to Broadway, Baba's music especially."

1958

ITALY

September 17. Venice. Leaving a concert at night, we collide in a side street with Auden. He is wearing an open-necked shirt, and espadrilles cut to accommodate his corns. Excited and in a great hurry, he tells us he must rush home, "Because I've just learned that Leopardi wasn't born in the south."

September 19. Auden for lunch. He fusses obsessively about punctuality, and when I.S. is five minutes late asserts: "The Russians won't win the war because they won't be there on time. *'Dieses warten,'* as Tristan says." Auden is in a German period, and later, telling us he intends to translate one of Goethe's prose works, he promises to "make him sound like a limey yet." Auden is less bothered by untidiness than by unpunctuality, and he seems to suggest that the Augean cleaning was a great mistake. When I.S. does arrive, Auden is openly contemptuous of the pill bottles arranged in front of his plate, and he whispers to me that "the steadiest business in the world would be a pharmacy next door to Stravinsky." Then,

AUDEN: "A true creator is always ashamed of most of his past work. Are you ashamed?"

I.S.: "No, I would do many things differently but I am not ashamed."

Auden believes that Tolstoy had a sense of humor: "I'm sure that even in his dreary late years if you had said to him, 'Now come off that old plow,' he would have laughed." I.S. disagrees and is certain he would have died of apoplexy. Talking about "*l'esprit de con* in literature," Auden calls the work of a famous male writer "a *connerie bien élégante*," but says that certain female writers, Virginia Woolf for example, lacked this *esprit*. When I.S. wants to know what the "female" difference is Auden calls it a "*vas deferens*." Auden tells us that he uses as a literary criterion, "People one would like to be with at dinner. No character in Dostoievsky would have made an amusing dinner companion, whereas most of Dickens' characters, including many who were evil, would have fascinated me at table." Proposing a new category of literary criticism, "Great classics of boredom," he nominates Dostoievsky as "a major bore. He always wants to talk about his soul. I cannot stand the Russians' total lack of reticence." He says the O.E.D. missed "unkiss," a word he found in Aubrey, and he shows us his new poem, *Farewell to Mezzogiorno*, which explains the remark the other day about Leopardi. When I.S. complains of intestinal unrest and says he has swallowed so much bismuth he feels like a weir, Auden starts to sing the Methodist hymn:

> ". . . *every bowel of our God*
> *with soft compassion rolls*."

Auden's fists are milk-white, pudgy, and hairless, but the fingers are stained with nicotine, and the nails are nibbled halfway to the moons.

We attend a concert together at night. At intermission, in a café, Auden engages I.S. in a discussion about a certain opera and suggests, "One should study it." I.S.: "No, I would just steal from it." When I.S. observes that in two minutes the second half should begin, Auden replies that "Cyril [Connolly] would say, 'Just time to eat a lobster.'" Back in the theater, Auden remarks that the women's chorus "looks like a bed of petunias."

With Paul Hindemith,
Wiesbaden, 1931.

With Giorgio de Chirico,
Venice, 1957.

3. With Carlos Chávez,
Mexico, 1940.

4. With H. D. F. Kitto,
Bath, 1957.

5. With Aldous Huxley
at a recording session,
Hollywood, October 1954.

6. With Edgar Varèse, New York, 1961.

7. With Vera de Bosset and
Blaise Cendrars,
Paris, 1925.

8. Venice, at the time of the *Threni* premiere, 1958.

9. With Mrs. Stravinsky, Venice, 1958.

ENGLAND

December 8. London. Dinner with the T. S. Eliots in their Kensington Gardens ground floor flat. The name does not appear on the tenants' roster, but the T.S.E.'s are waiting in the open door when we arrive, and holding hands. The walls of the apartment are bare except for bookshelves, and these are mainly in the dining room. According to Eliot, that is where arguments come up, "which is why dictionaries and reference books must be kept there." He produces a Liddell and Scott, in fact, when I.S. talks about the origins of "paraclete," but gives as much information himself, before opening it. Eliot is silent, generally, and his speech is slow and *diminuendo*. He harrumphs a great deal—"hm," "hmm," "hmmm," with extra significance in each 'm'—breathes heavily, wheezes. His fingers, which he is constantly folding and unfolding or touching tips to tips, are long and fidgety, but the life of the man is all in his clear gray eyes. (I.S.'s hands are remarkable for the large knuckles and the large spread between, and they are the least nervous I have ever seen.) Table talk—I.S.'s anyway—is concerned more with taxes than with literary gossip, and I.S. is disconsolate to learn that tonight's dinner is not tax-deductible. But literary gossip there is when Eliot describes the behavior of another poet as "iniquitous." I.S. calls the same person a "sincere liar." And Eliot says that "Cocteau was very brilliant when I saw him last, but he made me feel it was a rehearsal for a more important occasion." He is not kinder about another colleague—"Oh, I don't read him, I'm much too fond of him for that"—but his stories are generally self-effacing: "When we stopped at Gander on my last flight I was aware of a young woman hovering near me. I invited her for coffee but she only wanted my recollections of Virginia Woolf. . . . One day in a New York taxi with Djuna Barnes I noticed that the driver had become engrossed in our conversation. After Miss Barnes left the driver questioned me: 'Say, Mister, is that *woman* a writer?'" Eliot says that for him the most interesting part of our book was that concerning Dylan Thomas: "Thomas could have written a great comic libretto. I think he had the richest gifts of humor of any contemporary poet." I.S.: "And he was such a dear dumpling." Eliot claims he cannot remember his own poetry, "because it was rewritten so many times I forget which version was final."

He drinks sherry before, claret during, whisky after dinner, and he carves and serves the meat himself, walking around the table to fill our glasses. His laugh is a half-Bloomsbury "ha-ha," with a pause after each aspirate. After dinner he brings a scrapbook bulging with photographs and clippings, inviting I.S. to compose something for it, and saying that he writes in it himself every night. V.:

> "'A time for the evening under lamplight
> (The evening with the photograph album).'"

Eliot supplies quick translations of the foreign phrases that occur regularly in I.S.'s conversation, but insists he is no linguist and only "pretended to be one to get a job in a bank."

Eliot is slower and more bent than I.S., and he looks the elder. Through most of the evening I.S. manages to refrain from medical talk, but when he says his blood is too thick, Eliot recalls that in 1911 a doctor in Munich told him *his* blood was too thin. I.S., later, in the taxi: "He is not the most exuberant man I have ever known, but I feel I have been with someone very pure."

UNITED STATES

December 28. New York. Auden for dinner. He drinks martinis before, wine during, whisky after. When I.S. tells him we hope to see *The Seven Deadly Sins*—he and Chester Kallman have composed the lyrics for the English version—Auden says, "Better hurry and get tickets or you will never get in. *Vanessa* is on at the 'Met' that night."

December 29. I.S., telephoning the G. Wittenberg Surgical Company: "This is Mr. Stravinsky, S-T-R-A . . ." He spells it loudly and deliberately, as though dictating a telegram. "You fitted me with a truss three years ago and I want an appointment to have it repaired." He has a wrong number, however, and the other party has had to hear the entire speech without being able to interrupt. I.S. ill-humoredly replaces the receiver, then carefully dials again. "This is Mr. Stravinsky, S-T . . . You made a truss . . ." The same person answers, this time angrily. I.S., angry too, checks the number in his address book, finds it correct, is still convinced he must have misdialed, tries again. "This is Mr. . . ." but the man on the other end, no doubt believing himself the victim of a raving lunatic, slams the receiver. At this point V. examines the telephone directory and discovers that I.S. has miscopied the number. (The foregoing is a typical I.S. "scene." At least two such occur daily.)

1959

THE PHILIPPINES

March 28. Honolulu to Manila, crossing the International Date Line in late afternoon. After nine hours of empty ocean, Wake Island is, as V. says, "an existence philosophy in itself." We watch the sunset from the shore of the shadowless solarium, then scuff through pink coral dust to the canteen. Another plane, eastbound, has landed, meanwhile, and one of its passengers, a Swiss, introduces himself to me with: "I want to thank you for your Webern records." On Wake Island! Filipino natives gather by the gates to watch our takeoff. They are charcoal black, like figures in an underexposed negative.

Guam. Midnight. A large moon. Warm wind rustling the palm trees.

March 30. Manila Airport, 5 AM. The I.S.'s count their baggage—*ras, dva, tri, chetiry*—over and over, like rosary beads. The U.S. Cultural Attaché, a Mr. Morris, accompanies us to the Manila Hotel, where a dozen eager porters pack us into our rooms. Old Manila is black and grim, except for pretty lattices and grilles, and the translucent mother-of-pearl "*capiz*," or clamshell windows. The shores of the Bay are lined with hundreds of "night clubs," in reality, tiny two-customer booths and simple Coca-Cola carts. They are a squalid sight now, at daybreak, but after we have seen the labyrinth of orange-crate dwellings inside the old walls, they seem almost gay. Drive to Taytay and Lake Taal, stopping at the Church of Las Piñas, on the way, to hear a bamboo organ. Built by a Spanish friar who had no metal, the organ—keys, pedals, seven hundred and fourteen pipes—is entirely bamboo. A young monk plays Gounod's *Ave Maria* for our alms. The sound is like a choir of recorders: sweet, weak in volume, badly out of tune.

The road leaving Manila crosses salt flats, and the shoulders of the highway are heaped with bags marked ASIN, the dialect word for salt. One other common sign is SARI-SARI, the Chinese for sundries, but all directions and most billboards are in English, because the eight major Filipino dialects have made no progress toward consolidation. Beyond the flats, at the edge of the jungle, a police roadblock warns us of banditry in the neighborhood. This both alarms and encourages the I.S.'s. The road is hemmed in at first, by thick canebrakes, and at times it is entirely canopied by liana. The only signs of habitation— bamboo huts on stilts—are in the coconut and banana groves, but we see only two people, men carrying red-shakoed cocks. Halfway to Taytay a carabao herd crosses the road.

Taytay is high and treeless, and the natives carry black umbrellas against the torrid sun. A bus with all its passengers asleep is parked along the roadside. They are merely observing the siesta, of course, but they look as though enveloped by poison gas. All other Taytayans clamor to be photographed and to sell us fruit. A few say "Happy New Year," but the only other "English" syllables they know are "Coca-Cola," which product appears to be the economic index of the whole community, judging by the monuments of empty cases. We eat at the Taal View Lodge, with a panorama of the volcanic lake a thousand feet below.

Dinner at the U.S. Embassy with the Bohlens, who obviously enjoy exercising their Russian, which they speak with an attractive American drawl. We spend most of the evening looking at photographs taken during their Russian term, but they also show colorslides of the Banaue country in northern Luzon. Two geologists were decapitated in this region a week ago, probably because of suspicious questioning, and in one frightening photograph a Banaue warrior charges toward the camera brandishing a spear, though *his* intention, says the Ambassador, was not to throw the spear, but to sell it. We ask the Bohlens about José Rizal, the Philippine "Washington" and "Goethe," whose statues fill Manila's parks and whose biography fills its bookstores, but the Ambassador considers Rizal's *Noli Me Tangere* to be "competent literature, no more." The Bohlens say that dog meat is a delicacy in the islands, edible even in high society, and that markets exist where the buyer may select his canine still in the quick. The Bohlens have had to hide their poodle since its arrival in the country, so great is the native appetite and the danger from dognappers. During dinner, the Ambassador opens the screen doors for more ventilation, and a large rat leaps inside. It is not found by the time we leave.

We try to sleep with our lights on, hoping they might discourage the musical geckos on the wall—"chirp, chirp"—and the cockroaches and other monsters on the floor from joining us in our beds.

March 31. The great rice fields of Antipolo and Morong are burned out and brown, and the whole island world is waiting for the rains. A checkers contest is playing in the middle of the street in one town, and billiard tables stand by the roadside. We watch a water carrier trotting along the road in a swinging caracole. He holds his shoulder balance with the right hand, and balances himself with the other, like a football player running interference. Planting has begun in irrigated paddies near Morong, and we come upon a circle of women pounding the rice with flails. The church at Morong, a crossbreed of baroque and pagoda, is inhabited solely by pigs, and the town is draped from end to end with fishing nets.

HONG KONG

April 1. Hong Kong. The airport. A travel agent conducts us to the Kowloon ferry and, across the water, in Hong Kong, to the Repulse Bay Hotel. As the boat moves, a BBC voice on a loudspeaker warns us not to smoke. The warning, repeated in Chinese, lasts ten times as long and swoops up and down a whole xylophone of inflection. Among the foot passengers are coolies who slough their shoulder poles and baskets to the deck, and boys who go from car to car peddling Wrigley's gum.

The Repulse Bay Hotel might have been built by the Canadian Pacific Railroad for a Chinese settlement in Saskatchewan. We sit by a stained-glass peacock, in the restaurant, then move to a terrace with a view of the jade sea, the purple sampans, and the sugar-loaf islands. The food is deliberately British, and the waiters are obliged to inquire three times whether we want "fiss" before we realize they mean fish: "You want eat egg first or fiss?" According to I.S., the *salon du thé* orchestra has "made a Rossini overture sound like 'Chopsticks.'"

April 2. At William McGee's in Gloucester Road, fifteen tailors take turns speaking to us through the English of one young boy. The McGees are Shanghai Chinese, he says, and they do not understand the Mandarin and Cantonese dialects that are most common in Hong Kong. He also says that though few boys of his age are able to do brush calligraphy, the older generation has not relaxed its contempt of penmanship. But, according to him, the majority of Hong Kong Chinese cannot write at all or remember enough characters to be able to read a newspaper. Being unable to pronounce an R, he says "foul dollas," but he means "four dollars," not "filthy lucre." I.S. wonders why his English is so monotone, "since he singsongs his own language." I.S. asks him the Chinese for good-bye, and he says, "'Bye-bye' is all we know." As the tailors measure and fit us, he translates a stream of excited questions about life on "stateside."

We hail three rickshas from a queue and bump alongside buses, trolleys, cars, people—Chinese, Indians, British civil servants, tourists, beggars, porters with yokes, women with head loads. Our runners are barefoot, and they carry towels in their belts to mop perspiration. From a pier, we watch a junk unload crates marked "Made in Japan." A man, woman, and seven children live on this small vessel, and it is an ark of domestic animals as well. Hong Kong at sunset is concealed in mist. We go to bed with the hoot of harboring boats in our ears.

April 4. At the resettlement buildings in Kowloon—concrete barracks housing half a million refugees—children swarm around us but turn superstitiously from V.'s camera. We are detained in the principal street first by a funeral and then by a wedding, the former with white, the latter with red flowers. Through the glass windows of the silver-plated hearse, six men can be seen sitting around the coffin. They wear American-style business suits but Chinese headdress. We drive to Shatin at noon and eat on a terrace overlooking the valley of the Kowloon-Canton railroad.

Farther inland are pagodas, temples, walled cities. Today is Chinese All Souls' Day, and the road is filled with processions. According to Buddhist ritual, the dead are exhumed after seven years—*les beaux restes*—and reburied in blue urns. Their first place of burial is then marked by something that looks like a concrete armchair, and a large former burial ground is a whole assembly of armchair cenotaphs. They—the *beaux restes* —are then reburied in blue urns. At Taipo, the driver promises to show us a "model poetry farm." I.S. says he expects to see "a group of aspiring Chinese poets attending a lecture by Stephen Spender," but the driver was simply unable to pronounce the "L" in poultry. At the border of the People's Republic, old women come to be photographed, demanding "one Melican dolla, please" for the service. They wear loose black trousers, high-collared jackets slit at the sides, lampshade hats. One of them has a bicycle with a pig in a cage fixed to the handlebars. We return to Kowloon by way of Castle Peak, where black-sailed junks fill the bay.

JAPAN

April 5. Tokyo. Preparations for the Royal Wedding. Railings have been raised around the moats of the Imperial Palace to keep the crowds from falling in, and throughout the city colored balloons trail messages of felicitation.[1] Cherry blossom season is over, but celluloid and paper imitations have been fixed to streetpoles and trees.

A press conference. I.S. to me: "I wonder how they are going to say 'neoclassic' in Japanese." The interpreter is Hans Pringsheim, a nephew of Thomas Mann, who has lived in Tokyo for twenty-five years. His translations are generally rapid though an occasional short phrase of I.S.'s—"No, I don't like it"—sometimes takes two minutes in Japanese. Cameras grind throughout the hour-long interview, but the faces behind them show no interest in the target, and the questions, too, are generally wide of the mark.

April 6. Kamakura. The sea is the gray of Whistler's *Pacific* in the Frick Museum, and the beaches are black. We eat in a Chinese restaurant sitting cross-legged (numbing, this) around a revolving table and pointing on the English side of the menu to shrimps in scrambled eggs and Peking duck. This is our first meal to be negotiated entirely with chopsticks.

The Great Buddha appears smaller at three yards than at three hundred, and from a distance the eyes seem to be closed. I.S.: "It is full of electricity. I would not dare to touch it." People wait to kneel before it, quickly, and clap their hands as they rise. At the nearby toy-stalls, the crowds are equally rapt, though some of the toys, magnetic cylinders and so forth, seem to us like mechanical aptitude tests.

[1] In my erroneous imagination. The messages were business-as-usual advertisements.

I.S., on the return to Tokyo, complains of intestinal spasms. "Why has no one written a book about toilets and travel, with chapter headings like 'W.C.'s in Greece,' 'Spain from the bathroom window,' etc. The subject is extensive, and a two-volume compendium is required. Intestines regulate our travels, and they are the principal worry, and anal anxiety the profoundest emotion, of all those people you see at Persepolis, or the Parthenon, or Cuzco, or anywhere else. But travel books never mention the subject, and of the major authors only Voltaire gave due importance to '*la chaise percée.*'"

April 7. Dinner at the Fukudaya, a seventeenth-century farmhouse converted to a private-room restaurant. Shoes are exchanged for slippers in what was once a stall for massaging steers—to distribute the fat evenly, a practice still encouraged by serious gourmets. Inside, we sit around a low table, suspending our legs over a brazier deep in the floor beneath. Hot sake is then brought by geishas who kneel at our elbows and replenish our cups after each sip. Tonight's special *hors d'oeuvre* is a spoon-size tennis racket made of fried kelp, to honor the fact that the Prince and Princess-to-be met on a tennis court. Successive courses—*tempura, unagi* (eel), and too many other seafoods to remember or eat—are served in a larger room in which we squat around an open fire-pit. After dinner, geishas accompanied by a gramophone do some very boring folk dances.

April 8. The Kabukiza. Arriving in an interval between plays, we are taken to see costume rooms, prop rooms, the offstage music room, and the revolving-stage mechanism invented by the Japanese four centuries ago. And we are introduced to an eleven-year-old actor, swordcarrier to Togashi, the Keeper of the Barrier Gate in *Kanjincho*, the next play. An even younger actor is being prepared behind the curtain for official presentation to the audience, a formal initiation rite or Thespian Bar-Mitzvah. Both children glisten with greasepaint.

Back in the foyer we buy boxes of *sushi* (rice) and *magura* (raw, red tuna) to eat during the play. A clapping of wooden blocks announces the end of the interval and we reach our places as an attendant runs across the wide stage front pulling the curtain open with him. Six elderly actors and the child debutant march on stage and kneel on mats facing the audience. Bows are proffered almost incessantly as one of them speaks, and the ceremony is at least as theatrical as *Kanjincho* itself.

The actors are accomplished musically as well as plastically, which is to say that they are also singers and experts in *Sprechstimme*. In fact, *Kanjincho* is a *Sprechstimme* opera, with *Sprechstimme* arias, ensembles, recitatives, dialogues. And the musical element is primary. The vocal noises, the grunts, groans, strangulated falsettos, are a delight to I.S., who tells me excitedly that the unity of sound and gesture is absolute, and that he has not been affected by an orchestra in a long time as much as by the *glissando* of the hour-glass drum and the sound of the lone Kabuki flute.

When Benkei, the hero, prevents Togashi from seeing that the scroll he has pretended to be reading is blank, and when, later, Benkei crosses his eyes to indicate extreme tension—this is called the *Mie*—the audience shouts. Shouting occurs again as Benkei, escaping Togashi's suspicion, performs the series of leaps known as Tobiroppo. We learn afterward that these shouts are words of advice: Take your time . . . Do it well . . . *Olé*.

A late visit to a loud, crowded night club, the Benibasha. "Ladies and gentlemen, winter is over," the menu reads. "Spring is of most comfortable climate, and every creature begins. We should be happy if you are able to smell Real Japanese Nation." This is to introduce some deodorized folk dances. The clientele is largely American, and the announcements are in American; in fact, the only non-American aspect is that of the forty or fifty women standing behind a grille, a sad, overly made-up harem-for-hire.

April 9. Classical Japanese pornographic art is antiseptic to Western sensibilities—to our sensibilities, at any rate; a collection of impolite prints is surreptitiously offered to us in a bookshop. Instead of voluptuous movements of naked bodies, we see only inert people, often in groups, and fully and elaborately clothed. In many of the illustrations the point is obscure and the picture a puzzle, but in others the viewer may be confronted with gross and exaggerated sexual organs. Like the best European erotica, this is mostly eighteenth-century.

Japan is more beautiful in the rain, especially in the country, where one may still see the kind of straw raincoat worn by a Hokusai farmer. The spectacle of bicyclists balancing umbrellas is a pretty one, too, though not for I.S., who finds it "too acrobatic." (Every Japanese owns one or more umbrellas, and an umbrella is part of the equipment of most hotel rooms.) We drive to Hakone, but stop at a hotel in Miyanoshita, because of the violence of the thunderstorms. Concrete fortifications, unwelcome reminders of 1945, are still mounted along the beaches south of Kamakura, but a more formidable obstacle to an invading army are the roads, and one wonders how a highly industrialized country can afford such winding, narrow, and imperfectly paved highways. Near Miyanoshita we overtake a funeral procession, its colored paper wreaths wilting in the torrent.

I.S. counts seven major traffic accidents on the return to Tokyo. "Kamikaze drivers," says "Slim"-san, *our* driver. "They will even come down the wrong side of the road hoping to bluff countertraffic into the ditch." Motorcycles outnumber automobiles, and are even more reckless and aggressive. Most motorcyclists—and many pedestrians—wear bandages over their mouths, like operating surgeons.

April 10. The Royal Wedding Day is proclaimed at 6 AM by cannon volleys that startle us out of bed. We watch the parade on television, having been warned not to brave the crowds. The horse guards gallop almost into the screen, and the *banzai*-shouting mobs are shown at close range, but the Prince and Princess are kept in the far distance.

From V.'s notebook on the Japanese: "Their eyesight is not so bad—spectacles are not so endemic—as wartime caricatures have led us to expect, but their teeth are far worse." And: "The men and women are different races. The Japanese pursue a cult of ideal femininity—high, hushed voices; shy manners; doll-like makeup—which they contrast with a loud and bellicose masculinity, but this exaggeration of sexual characteristics is in no sense chivalric. In fact, the Japanese woman is the servant of her knight." Another of V.'s entries claims that "the Japanese say 'yes' even when they don't understand, hoping you will forget." And: "The women giggle without provocation, but fail to appreciate any situation we would call humorous." I.S. is enjoying himself more than V., partly, I think, because of his Japanese height. Standard-size installations fit him exactly. Whereas my head is a foot above the mirror when I shave, and my knees press against the wall of the W.C., these utilities are comfortably tailored to I.S. But according to I.S., his favorite luxury in Japan is the absence of tipping, "of the fumbling for money and the personal embarrassment we suffer at arrivals and departures nearly everywhere else in the world."

April 12. On the station platform for the early train to Kyoto: young women with puffy faces and flat profiles, carrying their babies on their backs; old men with white, wispy beards; old women in kerchiefs, smocks, boots, accompanied by children dressed like Eskimos. In spite of the crush, everyone queues up calmly when the train arrives. Seats are found for us in the caboose by officials from the Osaka Festival, who say, it seems in response to no matter what we do, "Thank you very muts," and "If you pease, if you pease." Our fellow passengers are camera fanatics, who while away the journey photographing exits of tunnels. This so-called observation car is equipped with a bar—"Scotch" whisky, Japanese or imported—and two W.C.'s, marked respectively "Western Style Lavatory" and "Japanese

Style Lavatory." The latter, a hole in the floor, testifies to the superior strength and mobility of Japanese knees. Waiters canvass the train for luncheon orders hours in advance, that the meal may be served at appointed times and without delay, but at noontime the smell of *sushi* being eaten out of wooden boxes in the third-class carriages makes us regret not having ordered the Japanese meal ourselves. Division of labor is so minute in the European-style *wagon-restaurant* that different boys set the table with, respectively, knives, forks, and spoons. Hot hand towels are brought before the food, as in all Japanese restaurants.

A densely industrial landscape as far as Atami, where we reach the sea, and after that, inlets, rivers, and rounded rows of tea bushes, the flat land growing rice. At Kyoto we are met by geishas, who clack along on high wooden shoes and in full costume. They are as shy and embarrassed as we are, I think, but faces under so much white flour betray nothing.

April 13. The temple of Sanjusangen-do is a forest of 1001 figures of Kwannon, Goddess of Mercy, life-size wood-and-goldleaf images, each with eleven faces and a prodigious number of hands; the long, straight ranks of this graven audience occupy what is said to be the largest room in Japan. But the temple is a repository of other wood sculptures, too, diabolical figures, demons, demiurges, and winged Beelzebubs mostly, though a few ascetics and contemplatives can be found, and especially two gentle Sivas playing cymbals and a lute. The proliferation of the Kwannons, the literalness of the multiplication, has horrified I.S., however, and he can think of nothing else. "The repetition is arrogant. I will have 1001 sleepless nights."

We drive to Osaka in the afternoon, to hear *Figaro* by the Vienna State Opera. The long street approaching the city is choked by rivulets of alleys debouching a dense and perpetual traffic, and the driver cannot find the Grand Hotel. He asks directions of taxi drivers, policemen, pedestrians, but it is a

long time before anyone is able to help. I.S.: "How did they
ever manage to find Pearl Harbor?"

At the *Figaro*, in the Osaka Festival Hall, the Japanese orchestra is good enough, though never quite in tune, but the
play is disappointing: we want more Kabuki. A Japanese musician approaches I.S. at intermission, addressing him in, or so
we think, English, but I.S. says later that this person sounded
to him "exactly like Donald Duck." Dinner in the Alaska Restaurant, ten flights up, from which elevation Osaka is trans-
formed by myriad neon abstractions.

April 14. Kyoto is rectilinear, like a Chinese city, in spite of
which it is difficult for the visitor to find his way. Kyoto is a
city of black houses with black slate roofs; of crowds in gray
and black kimonos; of black-robed, smooth-shaven monks and
priests; of swarming bicycles; of bamboo TV antennas; of tourists, especially Japanese, who pour out on temples and shrines
as though from Aeolus' bag. Kyoto is not conspicuously clean,
except in the residential districts, where tidy stacks of firewood stand against each immaculately proper house. I.S. notes
that "the survival of a wooden city like Kyoto is due to miracles—sudden rains—or fire departments."

The Ryuan-ji lake is girdled by red camellias and a carpet
of moss. And the trees are as holy as the temples. Never destroyed and apparently never even pruned, many of the
limbs have to be supported by Dali-like systems of crutches.
The spiky ginkgo trees are tied with strips of white cloth representing *ex voto* messages. They look like women in curlers.
We rest on the temple porch, looking at, but I am afraid not
contemplating, the furrowed sand and its islands of rock.

The temple of Ishiyama-Tera. The twin images of the Deva
kings, under the eaves of the outer gate, are worm-browsed
and white with bird droppings. Beyond the gate, novices and
lay brethren gently whisk the grass with besoms. The principal temple is half hidden by tall cryptomerias. As we enter,
on an open porch hung with paper lanterns, a priest is kneel-

ing to an altar piled with oranges and bread. He makes a guttural noise as he rises, and performs a ceremonious hand flourish.

According to a tradition, the *Tale of Genji* was written in the adytum's "Murasaki Room," and the rent was paid with a copy of a sutra in Murasaki's hand. It is now preserved here along with two scroll portraits: *Murasaki Looking at the Moon* and *Murasaki at Her Writing Table*. In the first, Murasaki stands gazing out of a window, her long hair covering her shoulders and back. The hair is braided in the second, and a magnificent pleated kimono billows behind her like a tent.

April 15. At the Shugakuin Palace we are followed by a guide, a great nuisance, and his translations are not always enlightening; only hours later, for example, do we realize that "pray house" means "play house." The treasure of the Middle Tea House is a fragment of painting, a fish escaping through a torn net, but Shugakuin is more famous for its gardens, which are the tidiest imaginable, thanks to old women in white smocks and caps who tiptoe about dusting the moss. The late cherry blossoms look like popped popcorn.

To Kozan-ji to see the eleventh-century animal cartoon scrolls by the priest Kakuyu. The houses in the region have moss-thatched roofs held down at the gable ends by sawhorse braces. The temple is at the edge of a ravine. A priest and his wife welcome us with low bows and bring green tea, meringues, candy butterflies, and candy blades of grass. According to V., temple tea cannot be sipped or gulped, but must be swallowed over the meringues in three draughts. We note in the guestbook that our signatures are the first in a Western script.

At the Kyoto Geisha review, we marvel most at the instant changes of scenery. Every prop turns upside down or inside out, and the winter scene becomes the cherry blossom scene in two seconds flat. The show is a caricature, not always intentional, of the posturing Kabuki actors. The final scene is a sunrise over the rocky Japanese coast, a tawdry but breathtaking spectacle that wins prolonged applause. I.S.: *"C'est très Mikado."*

April 16. The Katsura Detached Palace. V. has heard too many expressions of rapture about it and is disappointed, but our visit is also spoiled by showers that muddy the paths, and by the guide to whom we are leashed and who lectures us on "modular co-ordination." I.S. compares the paperbox rooms to "Mondrians in three dimensions" and says that he likes the idea—the formality—of the "Moon-Viewing Platform."

Sambo-in. The temple walls are covered with paintings of golden clouds, bamboo and pine branches, gold-flecked chrysanthemums, willows lightly trembling in the wind. (Auden: "One knows from the Japanese what a leaf must feel.") A procession of horsemen winds through one series of the panels. Their black hats alone are a Zen picture. In the last pavilion, a fat Buddha statue gazes without appetite at a tray of apples.

The gardens of Byodo-in are red, white, and mauve, from magnolia, plum blossom, wistaria. A bell booms as we enter the temple, which is in the middle of a small lake, and which has a bronze phoenix on top, like a weathercock. The Amida-Butsu, inside, is attended by *putti* who play zithers and shepherds' pipes and who dance for joy, each on a private cloud.

We stop at a roadside restaurant in Uji to drink sake and eat candied fish, but the proprietor is reluctant to leave his television long enough to serve us. An old man stands by the door selling cinnamon cakes from a cart harnessed to three monkeys.

Nicolas Nabokov arrives from Tokyo, and we go together, before dinner, for a massage, an hour of steel-fingered female muscles, without a moment's pause, and at a cost of only 300 yen. We then walk in the paper-lantern district of the Gion, which I.S. likens to "a dainty Broadway." N.N. is whiter and shaggier since we saw him last, and he looks more than ever like Turgenev; or like a big lapdog, for he is constantly smooching and hugging the I.S.'s in canine fashion. The cor-

ners of his mouth have turned down, too, I.S. thinks because
he has so often imitated American speech out of the sides of
it that he is now beginning to talk that way normally. N.N.'s
culture- and sex-talk are so amusing that the I.S.'s are able to
forget all about Kyoto. And N.N.'s impersonations are brilliant.
Once he has been heard in set pieces like "The American Ful-
bright Student in Florence" or "Stephen Spender and the
Sanskrit Poet Reciting Their Verses to Each Other," as well
as in on-the-spot improvisations—he is currently doing a hi-
larious "Noh" play—the butt of the mimicry can never again
be seen in the same, pre-N.N., way.

April 17. I.S. receives a letter this morning from the people who
have commissioned his *Movements* for piano. After reading it
he says, "I think I will have to add another minute or two of
music." V.: "So much for 'all-encompassing conceptions of
form.' The artist simply makes it up as he goes along."

Beyond the moats and great stone walls of Nijo Castle are
rooms with life-size mannequins posed and costumed to illus-
trate scenes from the Shogun's court. The floorboards outside
the Shogun's bedroom chirp like nightingales when walked
upon—on purpose, it is said, to betray a would-be assassin.

The paintings of Nanzen-ji: a hunter dressed as a decoy in
deerskin and antlers; a fantasy picture with a man on a crane's
back, high in the sky; a jungle full of brightly burning tigers.
I.S. is attracted by a collection of percussion instruments, and
especially by the *mokugyo,* a fish-shaped woodblock—*gyo*
means fish—with a flat mouth. Struck by a sponge mallet, it
emits a long, low moan, like the sea.

April 18. The temple of Konju-ji smells too sweetly of sandal-
wood, and the young Buddha in the half-lotus position, his dais
strewn with lilies, is overrefined. On the other hand, the Buddhas with several sets of arms look disturbingly crustacean.
Our guide, a young monk, is annoyed with us and with his
job. He Baedekerizes in Japanese with no care as to whether
we understand, and he seems to imply that we are wasting our

time. We film a game of ring-around-the-rosy in front of the temple. Children come running from all directions to be in the picture, and they bow to us gratefully afterward.

April 19. To Osaka. We pass two Buddhist pilgrims on the road. They wear white robes, white hats, and white leggings, and carry wooden staves.

The Osaka Noh Theater is a square room half filled by an elevated stage and a long wide ramp called the *hanamichi.* The audience—there are seats for about two hundred—faces the acting areas from two sides, but during the whole of the five hours we are present, not more than half the seats are occupied, and about two-thirds of the occupying half are always asleep, in rotation, like the election system of the United States Congress. The audience eats continually, and the knitting of chopsticks forms a steady accompaniment to the play. A few stalwarts, all elderly men, follow the plays in score books, from back to front, like rabbis reading the Bible.

The first play is a riddle, and the actors are three white-faced ghosts. A chorus of eight men in gray-blue aprons and black cassocks chants somberly for a *mauvais quart d'heure,* we have no idea what about. The next piece, *Futari-Daimyo,* is an *entr'acte* in which a peasant boy outwits two pompous samurai, defeating them in a duel and stripping them of their finery. It is a type of *Don Quixote* satire, probably for the amusement of a decadent age. The dueling is the high point of the play, which is without musical accompaniment, and the ballet of dueling fans is so exciting, comparatively, that half of the audience actually wakes up to watch it.

In the third piece, the back row of the chorus chants while the front row, one performer at a time, dances. The dancers brandish their fans as though for momentous action, but nothing happens and the play is inhumanly slow and boring. From time to time a foot is poised in the air, and after it has been forgotten, is stomped down suddenly, with a great racket. The actors wear *tabi,* the two-compartmented white foot gloves, and they walk by sliding their feet and raising the toes first.

The solo dancers chant, too, alone at first, and then in dialogue with the chorus. The chant rises a diminished fifth toward the end of the play, a comparatively exciting effect that reminds the I.S.'s of the Russian Church.

Hanagatami, the next item, is an oriental *opera seria*, slower than *Parsifal*. Five musicians and eight choristers enter the stage like burglars, through a half-height butler's pantry window in the right rear corner. The choristers carry their fans in front of them during this infiltration, but conceal them in the sleeves of their surplices during the play. The drama seems to be concerned with a maiden who wishes to present a basket of flowers to a prince, but who presents them improperly and is rebuked. The first two hours are a lesson in floral presentations to princes, at any rate, though at the end of the play when the maiden again offers her bouquets and this time they are accepted, we see no difference in method. The prince, a child of eight or nine, wears an orange costume with white pants, and a black *kammuri* hat with a tail. He does not speak, and his only action is to exit, but he wiggles and looks worried all the time he is onstage, as though he had neglected to relieve his bladder.

Near the beginning of the play an old man enters carrying a flower basket. He is followed by a girl dressed like Pocahontas, also with a basket of flowers. The "girl" is a masked man, of course, but the mask is small, and a man's gullet wobbles beneath its chin. The "girl's" voice is deeper than any of the men's, too, and the mask distorts "her" words acoustically, though we have no cause to complain about that. During the first thirty minutes the old man and the flower girl stand motionless while a low dim chant is mumbled by the chorus. Then Pocahontas finally exits, and for a moment the end seems near, but the music grows more dramatic—a duet of wolf cries with clicks and taps in the drums—and she reappears with a twin sister for whose benefit the whole lesson is repeated. I.S.: "It is insanely boring."

The musical element is always paramount, from the ritual

untying of the cords around the percussion instruments at the beginning to the last note of the offstage flute. The prince is heralded by a fanfare for flute and drum, and this is the only time when the drummer is not continually licking his thumb and moistening the drum head. The vocal noises—gravel-filled gargles, slow slurs in falsetto—are even more astringent than the instrumental. (Abé, who wrote a classic book about Noh, was a pupil of Schoenberg in Berlin before *Pierrot lunaire*, and one wonders if Schoenberg had heard anything about Japanese *Sprechstimme* arts from him.)

Hanagatami is followed by an offstage concert of flute and drum, and by another chant-play in which each member of the chorus performs a solo dance that is, in effect, a walk punctuated by loud stomping. This time the dances conclude with some comparatively spectacular leaps.

The final play is named for the god of fencing, whose abode is Mount Matengu. The God, Kuramatengu, appears in the latter part of the play, and his entrance, with the *hanamichi* curtain raised straight out and up, like a canopy—and not, as ordinarily, rolled or drawn—is its most impressive moment. Five- and seven-syllable verse patterns are easy to distinguish because of the higher pitch of what we assume to be the first syllables, but the drum also measures the beat of the verse, and is, as I.S. says, "the pulse of the play." The story concerns the young Prince Yoshitsune's education in swordsmanship. The first part of the play exposes his lack of skill in that art, at any rate, for which reason the old god is summoned. Kuramatengu's coat is a gorgeous purple, white, and gold, and to show that he is a god, his mask is several times larger than the masks of the humans. He moves in strange leapfrog fashion, too, one supposes to indicate the eccentricity of a god as imagined by earthly characters.

April 20. Osaka. The Bunraku Theater startles us at first: the puppets are much larger than we expect, and the stage is a hundred times the size of European marionette booths. Of the four puppeteers manipulating a single doll, one is barefaced and three are black-hooded like executioners or Elizabethan stage-keepers. Because of an optical deception, the black figures appear to be following the puppets; their three pairs of black legs are unpleasantly spider-like. This crew is so apparent at first that a sustained effort is required to focus our attention away from them, and though we are more able to disregard the controlling machinery as the play unfolds, we never give ourselves entirely to the reality of the dolls. The puppeteers move in waist-deep trenches, except in duels, battles, or other crowd scenes, at which times they emerge full-height on the open stage. With characteristic Japanese fidelity to scale, the child puppets are manipulated by children.

The musical element, the *joruri*, is more interesting (to us) and the performance of the narrators, who read, sing and ventriloquize for as long as an hour at a time, is a *tour de force*. The vocal gesticulation is wider in range than that of Kabuki or Noh, but this is natural, given the demand for realism. Today's play is a talky tear-jerker, full of murders and kidnappings, and the narrative style is a corresponding swagger and exaggerated pathos. The narratives are accompanied by a single samisen. Today's audience is made up largely of old women, and it is a noisier and hungrier audience than at Kabuki or Noh: the theater smells nauseatingly of *sushi* and hard-boiled eggs. Each act is heralded by the offstage clapping of two wooden blocks—*tsuke-uchi*—and by accelerating beats of an offstage drum. Drum rolls separate the scenes, too, exactly as they do in *Petroushka*. Before the curtain is parted, the musicians are swung in on a revolving shelf, from the stage left. They kneel rigidly behind a row of lecterns, the narrators at the audience end of the row, the samisen players toward the stage. The narrators hold their books to their heads, in both hands, before beginning to read. At the end of the play they drop their heads to the lectern, woodenly, like puppets, and they remain in this position until the musicians' platform is revolved out of sight. The audience never watches the readers, as we do most of the time. Today's plot seems to glorify a

peasant woman's sacrifice of her son so that the son of a noble-
man might live. We follow it vaguely through three brief, ac-
tion-filled scenes, but the fourth scene goes on for nearly three
hours and is all narration.

April 21. We dine in Kobe with the Muriyamas, who are pa-
trons of the Osaka Festival, and examine their silk-screen portraits of *haiku* poets, a famous collection. The meal, eaten in
the garden, is barbecued American style, but served orientally:
men first. Madame Muriyama listens acutely to I.S.'s every
word, and at one point she questions him about his use of "conservative." I.S.: "I dislike the idea of conserving, of keeping in
cans, but the conservative positively bores me only when he
tries to stop new things from growing, whereas the radical
bores me as soon as he begins to shout, 'Look here, see how
radical I am!'"

April 22. Nara. The scarecrows in the rice fields are equipped
with noisemakers that clap loudly in the wind, but the ruse is
unsuccessful and flocks are feasting everywhere. Horyu-ji, the
oldest temple in Japan, is rejuvenated continually, board by
board, and by expert architectural geriatricians. Its great pagoda whistles with sparrows like a colossal wooden flute. In the
museums: a kind of Neptune, with a trident, riding a frog's
back (Amanojako); a black horse with white glass eyes; a
portable shrine with Buddha dolls inside. The forest of the
Kasuga Shrine is full of overfed but still greedy deer, and the
Great Buddha is the largest, but also the ugliest and dustiest
image in the world. Women in a long line wait to touch another, smaller Buddha, an action said to guarantee protection
from baldness.

April 24. Tokyo. Gagaku dances at the Imperial Palace. According to the program, the first piece, *Etenraku,* "has been
source of inspiration for creation of Japanese folk songs as well
as having been set for Western symphony orchestra." The
choreography, for male dancers, is without event or interest

and to us the attraction is confined strictly to the music. The stage is a boxing ring set in a gravel court. The musicians sit on the far side of the court between two twenty-five-feet-tall drums called the *taiko*, played by men on ladders. The instruments are mouth organs, kotos, flutes, small cymbals, deep, thudding theorbos, and the *hichiniki*, which are a kind of shawm. The mouth organs are held like periscopes, pipes pointing up. They sustain harmonic clusters, and in many of the pieces they are the first and last instruments to sound. But the *hichiniki* is more curious still. It produces a slow, sloping sound, like a siren; a wail with intermediate scale-step pitch entirely dissolved. I.S.: "We cannot describe sound, but we cannot forget it either." The instrument is a handspread long, with a large double-reed mouthpiece. The player appears to breathe in as he blows out as though performing some kind of Yoga exercise. One of the dances tells the story of Ch'ang Kung of the Ch'i Dynasty, a prince so fair of face that he had to wear a grotesque mask in battle. The music is alternately monophonic and polyphonic, but it is more attractive as sonority than as composition. Ch'ang's mask is the head of a mythical beast.

A call on Suma-san, to see his collection of Chinese art. Suma-san himself greets us at his garden gate in kimono and wooden shoes, which surprises us because we have seen him heretofore only in American business suits. His treasures include Wei Buddhas, steles, Middle Chou bronzes, Han terracottas, porcelains, jades, screen paintings, and scrolls. He introduces each object with the same phrase: "A very singular piece, don't you think?" But though this is invariably true, the most singular piece is Suma-san himself. Bronzed, bald, barrel-chested, he is at once a Buddha and an ex-wrestler. His English is fluent and so are his several other European languages: he has served widely in the diplomatic corps, last and least fortunately as Ambassador to China during the Japanese occupation. He is vainglorious, and he can hardly finish a statement without complimenting himself: "My watercolors are very attractive, very well done, don't you think?" As the

Crown Princess is his niece, the Royal Wedding has puffed
him up even more. His account is interrupted by Madame
Suma's summons to tea. Later, as we prepare to leave, the great
connoisseur endears himself to us by corralling twenty to thirty
children and grandchildren with whom we line up to be photographed.

Dinner in a geisha restaurant by the Tokyo River: whole
—undecapitated—cold fish; fried bees; tentacle soup. The
geishas are pretty but incommunicative. After undressing us,
and helping us into kimonos, they kneel at our elbows throughout the meal, like guards.

April 25. A private concert for I.S., at University House. A flut-
ist demonstrates a throat trill, and a slow *portamento*, like that
of the *hichiniki*; and a koto-ist demonstrates the uses of his instrument in a variety of music from sixteenth-century polyph-
ony to twentieth-century Hawaiian-guitar. The koto-ist has
clawlike picks attached to his right thumb and first two fingers.
When our host remarks that the new koto music is "at least
sincere," I.S. replies that "sincerity must never be used as an
excuse." When the hostess says she finds it beautiful, I.S.
agrees: "Yes, it *is* beautiful, but like the organ in Radio City."
After the concert a young composer asks I.S. whether he
should change the order of a series if he comes to a place
where he "hears" it in a different order. I.S.: "Certainly not.
Find a way to hear the notes in serial order." I.S., in reply to
another question, about melody: "What a silly word that is ap-
plied outside of a small range of music. What is the *melody*
in a piece of sixteenth-century koto music, or in a *virelai* by
Machaut? You may speak of melodic contour, of course, or
melodic silhouette, but not of melody in your sense."

May 3. In Yokohama with Kaoru K., a windy night. Kaoru
suddenly complains of a particle blown in her eye, and I take
her in a taxi to a hospital. I ring the emergency night bell for
twenty minutes before a nurse appears, and, inside, we wait
another twenty minutes for a doctor. Cockroaches swarm over

the floor, which fact would bother me a lot less had we not been obliged to leave our shoes at the entrance. The doctor, when he comes, does not appear to notice them—he certainly *sees* them. Without washing his hands, he lifts Kaoru's eyelid between bare thumb and finger. No mote is found and no remedy prescribed. We pay 100 yen, and depart. Kaoru is not relieved.

May 5. A final visit to the Kabukiza, to see a play about an emperor who is remembered for having treated his human subjects less kindly than his animals. It is remarkable chiefly for the acting of three "dogs" and for a ballet of demons.

We fly at night to Anchorage.

ENGLAND

September 6. London. Dinner with the Eliots at Claridge's. T.S.E. looks younger and acts livelier than last year, but his talk indicates that he thinks of himself as a hoary ancient with little time left. He complains a great deal about social obligations: "I cannot accept lectures because the people who pay for them expect me to attend cocktail parties at which I am inevitably caught between someone asking me what I think of existentialism and someone wanting to know what I *really* meant by such and such a line." When a certain prominent critic is mentioned, Eliot refers to him as a brain-picker. "I know because he once tried to get me drunk and to pick mine. He is insanely jealous of all creative writers. Incidentally, his own only good line must have happened to him or been told to him by someone else. In one of his novels a man strokes a woman's back remarking how soft it is, and the woman says, 'What the Hell did you expect, scales?'"

Eliot on Pound's new *Cantos*: "There are more Chinese characters than ever. Pound is becoming the best Chinese poet in English." When I.S. talks about the Japanese theater, Eliot says that though he has never seen a Noh play, he did watch a Noh dancer in one of Yeats's plays and was moved by it: "One really could believe the dancer had become a bird. And what do the Japanese like in Western theater? Ionesco, I suppose, and Tennessee Williams?" Eliot says that "*Wozzeck* is too simple for a play and just simple enough for an opera."

This time, Eliot drinks a gin and tonic before, claret during, whisky after dinner. He eats a partridge, and though, after a final moment of indecision, he does not actually choose a cheese, he enjoys sniffing the cheese platter. His eyes fix on each of us in rotation, with a longer fix and an affectionate smile for his wife every time around. "Aldous was pessimistic when I saw him last; too many people in the world, and more all the time," he says. But one looks for special twists of import or irony in everything the man says, and even in the simplest phrase: "I should think so, indeed, indeed," the echoed "indeed" seems to ring with extra significance. He likes to chat about the weather—"Isn't it unusual? Why last year at this time . . ." And he talks about plans to visit his birthplace near St. Louis: "The house doesn't really exist anymore. If ever a plaque is erected for me, it will surely go to one of the neighbors."

1960

MEXICO

August 1. In the airplane to Mexico, I.S., after hours of watching the desert landscape: "The moon must be like this, but with more face powder." I.S. talks about the possibility of an opera on the subject of Maximilian and Juárez, which he thinks would have been ideal for Verdi in his *Don Carlos* period. "Imagine the scene of Carlotta going mad in the Vatican, and the finale with Maximilian tipping the soldiers who are preparing to shoot him." These speculations are interrupted by an announcement from the steward: "Men and women may use the lavatory indistinctly."

I.S. is applauded at the airport by a committee of composers, professional autograph-collectors, a detachment of soldiers, schoolchildren. We take a taxi called a "crocodile," no doubt because of the black sawtooth necklace painted around its perimeter, but the taxi's tactics are even more jagged and perilous than the emblem suggests. It contests the road with buses whose destinations are long Aztec words complicated with knots of tl's, tz's, and xt's—Ixtaccihuatl, Tlalnepantla, Azcapotzalco.

August 2. Rehearsal on the stage of the Bellas Artes. A student approaches I.S., saying, "We are too many to meet you and I

have been chosen to shake your hand for all." I.S. thanks the student audience *en masse* for the, as he calls it, delegated handshake. I.S., after I have rehearsed excerpts from *Lulu*: "Berg is a thematic composer, and how he loves to caress his themes, to turn them this way and that. But the vibraphone, Lulu's doorbell, goes on urinating in the ear a little too long."
I.S.'s friends the Bal y Gays are at the rehearsal. The Bal y Gays are refugees from Spain who keep a small gallery on the Paseo de la Reforma and who in forty years of marriage have grown as alike as twins. When I am introduced to them, I try to make conversation in a gabble of Italian Spanish, and they let me go on and on before saying, in English, that they do not understand a word. We laugh over this and are instant friends. I.S.'s friend E.J. has also turned up at the rehearsal. In his new goatee, he looks like a "beatnik de luxe," as I.S. says. E.J. has a mad laugh, like a hornbill in the jungle.

At Guadalupe, the two main buildings stand at a radical tilt from each other, and from the front portal of either the toppling of the other seems imminent. A score or so of Indians are lurching toward the church on their knees. They move forward slowly, sometimes with minutes between each motion, like birds changing position on a beach, but with evident difficulty and pain. One of them, a young woman, grasps the shoulder of her son, a child who is on his knees, also, and who is carrying a baby in his arms.

I.S. is impressed by the visit—and deeply offended by a mock prayer of E.J.'s: "Dear God, forgive us our outlets." He has knelt before the Image of the Virgin, touched his forehead to its glass case, burned a candle at Her shrine.

A press conference. Guadalupe has not increased I.S.'s store of charity. He is rather sharp about "*Les Six*," calling them "Six Characters in Search of an Author," and referring to an opera by one of them as "*Les Mamelles de ma tante.*" He describes one well-known composer as "a first-rate impersonator," and he calls a certain New York critic a "crab; he even walks sideways." Britten's *A Midsummer Night's Dream* fares no bet-

ter: "Well, you know, I prefer the play." But he speaks warmly
of his late friend the Mexican poet Alfonso Reyes. "Reyes was
a tiny man with a large wife. He looked like Burl Ives facially,
but his wife looked more like the rest of Ives. In spite of his
size, Reyes tried to follow an ancient custom, an abduction
rite, and carry his bride over the doorstep. I did not actually
see him do this, of course, but I will remember him doing it
as long as I remember him at all."

August 3. A "Museum of the Revolution" is under construction
in Chapultepec Park. The workmen pass buckets of cement
hand to hand, like an eighteenth-century fire brigade.

We drive from Chapultepec to Tenayuca, to see the astro-
nomical pyramid, but our chauffeur has only a vague idea
where it may be. He stops every few minutes for fresh supplies
of information, always turning afterward in a radically different direction. In the town of Tenayuca, women are the only
creatures (including mules) actually at work. Grandmothers
carry heavy bags past staglines of idle young, and great-grand-
mothers collect the laundry from the limbs of cactus plants.
The pyramid is small, disproportionately smaller than the
stone serpents, weighing several tons each, coiled in its yard.
I.S. compares it to a "*paskha,*" the Russian Easter cake, but it
is flatter than that and blurred, as though it had been under
water for a considerable time. We scale the walls and burrow
through a catacomb at the base.

V. on early Mexican cultures: "They were cruel, slave-state
societies, priest-ridden and god-ridden, and serpents were favorite gods. Even the greatest heroes were not immune from
the possibility that their hearts might be torn out. Suicides
were allowed to go directly to heaven, however, and that is
the Mexican mystery: why the civilization did not disappear
by its own hand."

August 4. The concert in the Bellas Artes, a silk-and-feather
audience. V. is with the President's wife, and Don Gorostiza,

the director of the theater. The orchestra plays the *"Viva Méx-ico"* at the end, and the *"diana,"* which is the salute to the bravest matador.

COLOMBIA

August 8. 8 AM. The airport. A wrangle with an immigration official who insists that I.S.'s first name must be George. The man next to me crosses himself frantically as we speed down the runway, but then sits calmly back and reads *El Universal.* Beyond Antigua we fly over volcanoes, some red-lipped and steaming, others filled with pools or sealed and muted with vegetation. At San José the terminal is full of progressive fres-coes and reactionary guards. We land again, two hours later, at Panamá, with a view of both oceans. A delegation of Pana-manian musicians awaits us as we leave the plane bathed in clouds of steam heat. One of them makes a speech, presents I.S. with a native embroidery, and proudly announces that he is an "electronic composer." (I.S., later: "An electronic folk-lorist, no doubt.") Cameramen appear and as we make our way to the Bogotá plane, joined by a Panamanian woman in a feather shako, the scene is filmed. The jet roars, flexes, and rises like a rocket over the bay and canal and into the sudden, equatorial night. Bright orange fires are burning on the lower Andean slopes. At Bogotá, which is cold enough for heavy coats, the path to the terminal is thick with dead *cucarones—* beetles.

August 9. We awake breathless and light-headed. I.S. com-plains of vertigo and fluttering heart, and the hotel manager brings him an oxygen mask, which he clasps to his nose for periodic ten-minute inhalations.

The eaves of houses on the hillsides project over and almost cover the narrow streets. The Indian women wear black hats and long black braids and they are as burdened as the mules; in the marketplace they carry trays of pineapple the size of card tables on their heads. The mules do not distinguish be-tween street and sidewalk.

The furnishings of the Teatro Colón were brought from Europe a century ago by boat and mule, a journey of many weeks. And more than half of the orchestra is European, too; I.S. switches from Italian to French to German to Russian, but is always understood by at least one faction. The theater is cold, and many of the musicians wear ponchos throughout the rehearsal. We still do not know whether our second concert is to take place the day after tomorrow or not until Saturday, but I.S. says this is *mañana*-ism and we must adjust to it.

A late-afternoon taxi tour. The driver thanks us for hiring him and vigorously shakes hands with us as we enter his cab. The city is the usual mixture of ugly-new-international and pretty-old-local (green balconies and white walls—usually with *"Cuba sí, gringo no"*). For some reason the driver thinks we should see a cemetery above the city, a desolate neighborhood, where cows pasture in the streets and buzzards bank overhead like airplanes looking for landings. He then says that his daughter is buried there, after having been "killed in a hospital." An Indian family is kneeling by the cemetery gate. They hold lighted candles and look like a Holy Family by Georges de la Tour. Back at the Tequendama, more gratitude, handshakes, and *"muchas gracias,"* as we leave the taxi.

The Tequendama restaurant. (Problems of Spanish pronunciation: I.S. asks for a side order of ham and he receives jam.) A party of *"norteamericanos"* arrives at the table next to us, the men pushing the women to the table like mowing machines. Compared to the Colombians, the *"norteamericanos"* talk too much, laugh too much, open their mouths too widely (and masticate too conspicuously). The dinner music begins with "A Song of India," which I.S. says makes him feel very old. "I remember the day Rimsky composed that piece. How surprised he would be to know that the opera is remembered by it alone." A *bogotano* dinner guest asks I.S. if he ever met Albert Schweitzer. I.S.: "He came to a concert of mine in Strasbourg in the mid-nineteen-thirties and we dined together afterward. He wore a frock coat and a wing collar and he looked like Maxim Gorky or a provincial pastor. One could see that he possessed *"charisma"* (Max Weber's sense), and whoever has talked with him will believe stories of the sort I heard at Aspen after his visit there—that animals came out of the woods to him; but already then, that night in Strasbourg, the poor man attracted too much adulation."

The collection of pre-Columbian gold in the Banco de la República is the richest in the world, and the gleam of it is so great that the basement cache requires little other light. Some of it is alloyed with copper and platinum, but most is pure and bright yellow, and though the whole Andean region is represented, objects of Chibcha culture preponderate. We see disc-shaped diadems, doughnut-size earrings, heart-shaped pectorals, crescent-shaped crowns; golden breastplates, golden armlets, golden horims, golden greaves; and goldfoil bangles, ear spools, lip pendants, nose ornaments like epaulettes of Napoleon III. Laminated funeral masks and other death raiment, including burial charms and talismans, account for a large part of the trove. The gold funerary urns are shaped like whisky flasks. The boudoir—gold tweezers for eyebrow depilation, gold hairpins and safety pins—is largely masculine, as are all body ornaments. There are gold canes and cane finials, gold scepters, gold aspergillums, gold flutes, a gold *bocca marina*, gold fishhooks, gold animal figures—sad-eyed frogs, alligators, abstract snakes

—and gold-wire Klee-like cacique figures

strung on necklaces like paper cutouts.

The bookstores of Bogotá are well stocked and the reputation of Bogotá as a literary city is borne out by all of the people we meet. According to our new friend Edgardo Salazar de Santo Columma, *bogotanos* read because they "have no place to go and nothing else to do." The principal newspaper, *El*

Espectador, publishes book reviews of the caliber of *Les Arts* or *The Observer*, he says. During a visit to a bookstore, the I.S.'s see a hunchback. They would like to touch the hump for good luck—a Russian superstition—and though I ridicule the idea and protest the indignity to the afflicted man, they are perfectly serious, and obviously disappointed when he leaves before they have time to get near him.

A reception at the United States Embassy. Mustached *señores* and large, bosomy *señoras*—"plump, florid viragos," V. says, remembering Hazlitt. We learn that a language congress is currently in session in Bogotá with the object of eliminating silent letters from written Spanish and of expunging anti-Semitic definitions from the dictionary of the Spanish Academy.

Visit to an emerald dealer, where we learn that the deep green and perfectly homogeneous stones are the most valuable, rather than the pale ones with gardens inside. And a souvenir shop: blankets and ponchos; skins of boa constrictors, ocelots, alligators; stuffed alligators and live baby alligators, puffing and glaucous-eyed. The proprietor names a tribe of jungle Indians who keep tamable but poisonous snakes to protect their small children; baby-sitter reptiles who guard the hearth from animals and even from other snakes and who do not, as a rule, sting their keepers.

From V.'s memo book on *bogotano* habits: "*Bogotanos* drink large quantities of postprandial coffee, then retire for long siestas; *bogotanos* say 'gracias' and 'con mucho gusto' about a thousand times a day; *bogotanos* are long-winded, in spite of the altitude—judging from their press conferences; *bogotanos* are fascinated by politics, which, after literature, is their principal conversation; *bogotanos* (or Colombians) commit ca. two hundred murders a month."

August 12. I.S., or a part of him, is to be monumentalized. Three sculptresses come to make a cast of his left hand, which they place on a wet towel and cover with a gray plaster pudding. This takes twenty minutes to dry, after which one of the women cracks it with a hammer and piles the artifacts into a pail.

At the concert, I.S. reads Simenon when not conducting, but he tells me after my performance of the Bach-Schoenberg chorale preludes that "It is *farben* and *dynamik* music and so rich in both that one must hear it a dozen times to hear it all, but I regret the final harp arpeggio in '*Schmucke Dich*' and the last cymbal crash in '*Komm Gott.*'" At intermission he discovers a spider on the lavatory wall, reaches for a score, says, "We'll kill him with the *Firebird.*" On the way to bed, I.S., who is terrified of typhus and dysentery: "I get so bored brushing my teeth in ginger ale."

August 14. To the Salt Mine Cathedral at Zipaquirá, a pre-Columbian excavation now expanded and impregnated—like a ship in a bottle—with a church. Almost all the way there, a wall of rain pulses against the car like surf. At Chía, the muddy Río Bogotá is spanned by an early colonial-period bridge, but the architecture of the villages—and the windowsill geraniums —is Swiss. Today is a farmers' fair, and the people everywhere are drunk on *aguardiente.*

The salt-mine tunnel envelops the car closely, and after a hundred yards in the darkness and a few confusing turns, our claustrophobia is as great a threat as the nearly suffocating salinity. The sodium-chloride Lourdes is a quarter of a mile into the mountain. There one leaves one's car in a subterranean parking lot and treks to the eerie lead-and-blue church. Today being Sunday, it is full of Indians kneeling to clergymen in green robes, like Shinto priests. I.S.: "It might be an important heresy, Adamites or Albigensians—but an underground movement in any case." The church was hollowed supposedly for the convenience of the miners, and it is regarded by them and by Colombians generally as the eighth wonder of the world. At the inaugural service a few years ago, half of the congregation fainted in the thin, salt-flavored air. Fearing to do the same, we hasten our departure but the car lacks air, too, stalls, and has to be pushed.

We return to Bogotá and drive to Tequendama Falls and the "*tierra caliente*," a corkscrew descent of three thousand feet, at every downward coil of which the tangle of vines, fronds, and flowers is thicker and more tropical in color. Overcoats are peeled, then jackets and shirts. Only twenty miles from Bogotá the air is forty degrees warmer.

"Twice as high as Niagara," yells a souvenir-selling Indian at the precipice of the falls, and the view—no retaining wall—is giddying even though obscured halfway down by mist. A statue of the Madonna is the only deterrent to suicides, but we hear the story of a pregnant Indian who threw herself into the cataract only a few days ago, pulling her screaming son with her, in full view of a horrified crowd. The road from the falls to Santandercito, at the edge of the jungle, is a narrow, fenceless shelf overlooking a two-thousand-foot drop. It is unpaved, riddled with cavities, and often almost sealed off by fallen rocks. But though the possibility of a landslide is as chilling as the threat of the abyss, we cower close to the mountain and—on the theory that forward movement is less risky than a "U" turn—crawl ahead. Every few yards, a shrine or a cross commemorates a slip over the side, but does not seem to warn against new ones. Just as I am suffering a swooning, Icarus-like moment, a bus named Jesús María Pizarro roars past, its wheels bulging over the brink, its horn blaring contempt. (Colombian drivers will stop or pass anywhere without signaling, and they can never be trusted to obey traffic lights, for which reason the Bogotá police stand on lofty daises, under awnings of tinted glass, *au-dessus de la mêlée*.) Before starting back we stop in the Hostería de los Andes to eat a *fritanga* and drink a nerve-steadying herb tea.

PERU

August 15. The air route to Quito follows the Magdalena River to the Cauca River, the "*tierra adentro*" of the archaeologists, but it also follows the ups and downs of air pockets, and we buffet violently most of the way. The crust of Ecuador is cracked and brown, and the cities are composite squares or

rhomboids. The Quito terminal is a new building, newly
splashed with murals, newly filled with Indian wares. In the
street, other, non-franchised Indians sell the same things—silver buckles, blankets, shrunken heads, Panama hats—at fraction prices. On the takeoff, we skim adobe and red tile houses
and mountain shelves on which clouds droop like partly de-
flated balloons. At Guayaquil, a riverain city and quadruple
junction of sea, jungle, and desert, boats with white tails
of water skirt the bay; from our height they look like spiro-
chetes. We fly lower over the excavation sites of Trujillo and
Chan-Chan. Here the shoreline is empty and dead and the
waves in the desert—curious mounds that imprint the sand like
tents—are higher than the waves of the sea.

At Lima, where we drop through several layers of bad
weather, I.S. is received like a film star. The night is cold
and damp and so is the Country Club, a gloomy Manueline
hotel with rooms a lonely half-mile from the lobby. We flee
to the centrally located and no less palatial Gran Hotel Bolí-
var, which supplies three within-walking-distance rooms and
three portable heaters. Each of us tries a different fish for
dinner, corvina, liza, and pejerrey, all delicious.

August 16. 7 AM. Dizziness and "bends" from the loss of altitude and from the quantities of powerful black coffee taken
to be alert for an early rehearsal. The orchestra cannot keep a
tempo, the players forget immediately, they read slowly, and
their tuning seems to be vaguely Pythagorean. The rehearsal
is wearying, too, as each direction has to be repeated three
times and as the Indians do not, on principle, admit to mistakes. Their instruments were at fault, or the player wasn't
ready, or he hadn't understood where we were beginning, or
one of the *gringos* in the orchestra had said something to confuse him. I.S. shocks them deeply by saying, "Sorry, gentlemen, that was *my* mistake." But, according to the conductor,
the Indians are always dependable in the concerts where the
gringos are sometimes nervous and erratic.

The greater part of our time in the Museum of Anthropology

and Archaeology is spent looking at textiles, at laces from the necropolis of Paracas, above all. I.S.: "The life of an ancient Andean must have been a purgatory of weaving." But we also enjoy the Chimu ceramics—owls, turtles, monkeys, cats carrying litters, a vicuña giving birth. One room is dedicated to ceramic models of legless, armless, and otherwise mutilated people; to a complementary display of some two hundred pre-Columbian surgical instruments; of skeletons showing evidences of surgery—for example, of skulls with copper or bronze trepanning. The museum also exhibits cases of *repoussé* gold masks and carved nacre set with precious stones; a yard full of steles from Tiahuanaco the size of the sarsens of Stonehenge; a *sub rosa* collection of phallic objects (jugs with phallic spouts that whistle when poured); mummies. Some of the mummies are in flexed position, knees to chin, hands and feet bound by hemp-of-byssus. The bamboo tubes through which corpses were fed chicle from above the ground still are in their mouths, and the crowing roosters and cornucopia eternity symbols are still on their coffins. We drive from the museum to a corral of llamas and alpacas. I.S. finds them "less snooty than camels, but their spitting is more spiteful."

Marmosets are sold in the streets of Lima from cages that look like hand organs; but, then, everything can be bought in the street, from toy llamas to ten-course meals. In certain respects, Lima reminds us of Naples. When cars stop at traffic signals, boys jump on the fenders and wipe the windows for tips. The cafés, the street noises, and our favorite restaurant are Neapolitan too, but the resemblance game breaks down with the architecture, the statuary, and the thick gray sky. Driving in Lima is like driving in the Lincoln Tunnel; the visibility is about the same, and the lights are phosphorescent in both instances.

Drive to the ruins of Pachacámac on a thin road between the sea and dunes of pink-brown sand. The better road is in the disinterred city; it is as solidly paved as the Appian Way. The ruins are on a heap of mounds above the sea. In the distance is Pachacámac Island, white with guano, like a frosted cake. We climb the ruins in a stillness pierced by the cries of the guano birds and echoed by the moaning of the seaward wind. The dead city is severely geometrical, and so is the architecture of its afternoon shadows. Behind us are the Andes, vague, blue, illusory presences, perhaps not there at all, but known to be from maps.

A cocktail party by the Lima Music Club, in a home famous for its collection of Cuzco primitives and Colonial-period soap-stone carvings. The cocktail-party language is French, and everyone talks about common acquaintances in Paris. Another subject is servants. "Peru is the only country where good serv-ants are still inexpensive." But Lima *is* feudally class- and race-stratified and the only Indians at this party, or anywhere in "society," *are* servants.

Lima Cathedral. Pizarro's cadaver, a viscous, yellowish sack, lies in a glass case to the right of the door, but Kika, the Peruvian girl accompanying us, will not look at it. "That is the man who destroyed our culture," she says—after four hundred years! We drive to the Cemetery of the Presbyterian Master in an unsuccessful search for the grave of V.'s uncle, the Marquis Théodore de Bosset. The dead are stacked in long rows of granite filing cabinets.

August 19. Shortly before the concert we are summoned to meet Manuel Prado, the President of Peru. Señora Prado has seen I.S. "conduct something or other" in Venice in 1951, when she "went over for Carlos de Beistegui's ball." (*"Elle a du chien,"* V. says later, but I prefer to translate this classic ex-pression as "She's a bitch.") By the end of the interview I have formed a prejudice in favor of any future revolution in Peru, but satisfaction comes sooner than we expect. Hisses and boos from the dress circle and from the upper balconies even more scurrilous noises greet the President as he enters his loge, and this is nicely contrasted by the stomping, cheering, and bravo-ing that follow a minute later for I.S.

CHILE

August 20. To Antofagasta and Santiago. A slow ascent over roofless huts and the white-rimmed, beryl-green sea. Though the Antofagasta airfield is in the midst of a desolate and featureless desert, the Chilean police warn us that cameras are forbidden. We walk for an hour in a warm sun and a cold, dry wind. From Antofagasta to Santiago the desert is a spilled chemistry set—copper, cobalt, rufous, laterite, sodium, sulfur —and the Andes are an almond-white wall rising out of a sea of dirty cotton-wool clouds. Dry riverbeds coil down from the mountains and spread into dry alluvial fans. Santiago is hidden by clouds, and we turn above the airport for an hour before landing in a rainstorm. At the Carrera Hotel, we eat filet of *congrio*, and go early to bed.

August 21. At 7 AM, we are startled out of bed by a brass band playing the national anthem in the plaza across from the hotel. The soldiers at this flag-raising ceremony wear German-type uniforms and march in goosestep. Above them and behind, the cordillera, white and gleaming in the sun, is higher than anything in the world.

To Las Vertientes, ourselves and several Chilean musicians, in four automobiles. The purpose of this expedition is "tea and photography," as V. says, but we enjoy the ride and the occasion in spite of that. Mimosa and wild peach blossoms whiten the hills, and, after Peru, the trees—pines, poplars, willows—are refreshingly green and varied. The tea party proves to be a feast with meats, pies, cakes—especially a honey cake called *loukouma*. It is also a composers' press conference. The composers stare at I.S. in stricken wonder at first, and respond enthusiastically to remarks like "Yes, Bach is good." (But they do not know what to make of his "Palestrina was simply a great bureaucrat of counterpoint.") "Mr. Stravinsky, what do you think of South America?" "Oh, I like impossible-to-humanize landscapes." "And of Santiago?" "It is a used-car lot of statues and monuments. The smaller the national history, the larger the commemorating stones." "Mr. Stravinsky, what was C.-F. Ramuz like?" "Well, I hardly know, as we were drunk most of our time together." Slightly shocked pause, then, "Oh, yes, I am and always was a drunkard. I have been told this is my inferiority complex, and I am content with the explanation. At dinner parties I long to be in the kitchen with the servants rather than at table with the hosts, and I felt the same desire at home in my childhood. Drink is joy, and the word spirits is a good word. I would rather be full of spirits than be the sober prisoner of my dinner neighbor and her opinions." The dinner neighbors here do not know how to take this, but when I.S. poses for photographs with them, the remark is forgotten.

We drive back to Santiago in a light rain. Black ponchos appear everywhere. We watch a wet polo contest at the edge of the city.

August 22. Visitors: Delia del Carril, the former wife of Pablo Neruda and an old friend of the I.S.'s. Juanita Guandarillas, the wife of I.S.'s London friend, Tony Guandarillas. A sister of the Paulet Thévenaz who painted I.S.'s portrait in Leysin in 1914. Fabian Fedorov, who was a friend of V.'s father and who tells V. about his death and burial in Santiago twenty-five years ago.

I.S., at a conference for young composers: "I have a sense of my material weeks before I compose. As Hume said, 'It is impossible for us to think of anything which we have not antecedently felt.' But I am always surprised by the suddenness with which it comes to an end. I feel like a satisfied animal then." Someone asks about his borrowings from the eighteenth century. I.S.: "I was a kind of bird, and the eighteenth century was a kind of bird's nest in which I felt cozy for laying my eggs." And about what he calls his physical reaction to electronic music. "When I was a child in Russia, I knew a peasant who could make a horse urinate by soft whistling. That same whistling sound I have heard in several pieces of electronic music, and it makes me suffer the same micturition as the horse. But some electronic sounds have the effect of colonic irrigation also, on me at least." I.S. calls the music of a prominent Stockhausen-ite *"eau de Cologne."*

Before bed we eat *chirimoyas*, a sweet, white, mushy substance with black, almond-shaped pits. The fruit is scooped out of hard avocado-like shells.

August 24. The concert in the Teatro Astor. Webern's *Marcia funebre* goes smoothly, though the orchestra has no idea of attack, phrasing, anacrusis. I.S., after conducting the *Firebird*: "The horn came in on F instead of F sharp, like salt when you expect sugar."

ARGENTINA

August 25. To Buenos Aires. The cordillera turns to fire in the setting sun, and we are afraid of turning to the same thing as the plane bumps and drops between the mountains. We land at midnight, in what feels like a New York January. The arrival is televised, and though I.S. has a sore throat, he manages some affable remarks. A banner at the airport entrance: BIENVENIDA STRAVINSKY. The Plaza Hotel is an hour's ride away, at high speed. At 2 AM, the I.S.'s complain about their rooms, and we resettle on another floor.

August 26. Rehearsal at 8 AM. The Teatro Colón is a perfect sound box, and the *ponticello* whispers in the Webern are as clear as in a hall that has the help of a microphone. The musicians are a little arrogant, a little dour and unwilling to be corrected, but they are quicker and more capable than any other orchestra we have conducted on the tour (a very small compliment). German and Italian are the rehearsal languages; no one speaks any English. At the end of the *Firebird*, an elderly gentleman introduces himself as a pupil of Rimsky-Korsakov at the same time as I.S. (I.S. to me: "Not true, of course, but even if it were, what right does that give him to disturb me now?") He wishes to commission a dedication piece "of major proportions" for the opening of a new hall. I.S.:

"Why doesn't he ask one of the innumerable Elgars around who specialize in that sort of thing? 'Of major proportions' means, simply, pompous."

Buenos Aires is a city of beautiful trees—jacarandas, Japanese magnolias, hydra-headed ombús, aguaribays, rubber trees. And a city of absurd statues and monuments. I.S.: "A life-size statue of a man in a large open place is ridiculous. Size alone can suggest the heroic—Michelangelo's *David*—and why bother to carve the man next door." All complaints in Buenos Aires, whether of class hatreds or the hotel plumbing, are scapegoated to Perón, but the walls of buildings in the workers' neighborhoods are still defaced with slogans like *"Vuelve Perón"* and *"Obra de Perón."* According to our host at dinner the people are divided, bitter, without hope, and the true *obra de Perón* is that *"nous ne sommes pas des nouveaux riches mais des nouveaux pauvres."* We order beefsteaks in the restaurant of La Cabaña, Mendoza, but the photographs of prize steers on the walls inhibit our appetites.

August 29. A press conference. "Señor Stravinsky, what does South America mean to you?" I.S.: "Hotel rooms, first of all, some too old, some too new. And desert, and jungle wildernesses, with their extremes of climate. And people; some of the faces and profiles in the orchestras I've conducted must have been copied from Inca tombs. But nationalism, too: each country hates its neighbor. And racialism: I saw swastikas in Santiago, and I am told that they can be found here. South America is still culturally colonial to Europe, too, and so far as I have seen, cultural ties hardly exist with the United States. From here, Europe seems nearer in every way than the United States, and the Monroe Doctrine does look like a purely *yanqui* idea. You will not like this, but I will say anyway that in my general impression South America is a *triste* continent." Indeed, they do *not* like it but I.S. was never one to withhold his mind, and today he is furious because of the twenty-six percent service charge on his hotel bill.

Spend the day at San Isidro and Algarrobo, with Victoria

Ocampo and her sister Angelica. A book-filled house with a garden (giant philodendrons) overlooking the Río Plata. We eat *empanadas*, a kind of beef and raisin *pirochki*, and sit by a quebracho fire looking at photograph albums of former house guests: I.S., Tagore, Count Keyserling, Isherwood, Lawrence Durrell, St.-John Perse. At Algarrobo, where in 1818 San Martín y Pueyrredón planned the wars of Chilean and Peruvian liberation, Victoria is refused admission because she is wearing slacks. But when we are inside, after a resonant protest, she guides and instructs us, pulls and pushes us, until, suddenly bored and impatient, she walks out ahead and waits in the street. Victoria has a fresh, pink, young girl's complexion. And Victoria is very proud—the portraits of her grandparents in the living room were painted by Pueyrredón *père*—and contemptuous of her new Krupp and Thiessen neighbors, with their protective electric fences.

A meeting of Argentine composers with I.S. Questions discussed: the uses of analysis to the composer (no formulated conclusions); the problems of trying to teach an "integrated-traditional" as well as a "mathematical-experimental" study of musical composition (ditto); the fault of avant-gardism, which is its dependence upon a superficial aspect of competition—the need to outdo the other at all costs—and its ignorance of music in the pre-electronic era (no remedy); the function and value of international study committees (I.S.: "a UN committee for onanism in underdeveloped countries wouldn't surprise me at all"); the problem of "predetermined forms" (agreement: "form" is the thing, not "serial technique"). During the discussions, someone says something about Beethoven's "power," and I.S. jumps on this with, "I don't like that word because it has too much of the meaning 'use of power.' Say 'might,' rather." This exchange makes me realize how little our published colloquies show of I.S.'s cunning with words, his apprehension of them and his sensation of their weight and aptness. And I realize, also, that nowhere have I recorded his two most characteristic expressions: "Who needs it?" and "Very strange." The latter is used in response to events and situations no one else thinks at all odd, and the former is heard in a great variety of circumstances, but chiefly at concerts. Listening to a new string quartet by Professor Q, for example, I.S. will grow restless and start to mumble: "But who needs it?"

On the return to Buenos Aires, a Russian woman diverts us with a recitation, by heart, of *Old Possum's Book of Practical Cats*. Argentine night traffic is even more dangerous than Argentine day traffic. Signals do not exist at intersections, and on the long suburban avenues the law is every man for himself. Headlights are turned on only at the suspected approach of another car.

August 30. The concert. The audience is warm to Debussy's *Martyre* and polite to Webern's Six Pieces, but I.S. stops *Petroushka*, which is played chaotically, and after a fearful pause starts it over again. "Such are the humiliations of fame," he says later. "The notes must be articulated like *petits pois*, but they came out a pease porridge. And the public applauds all the same. What one does is no matter when one is only taken for what one is. Of the perils of old age—senile optimism, fame, therapeutic nihilism—fame is the most terrible."

August 31. Lunch with Jorge Luis Borges, a small, nervous man—his fingers fidget continually, re-aligning the napkins and silverware or rubbing his knees—shy as a ferret and nearly blind. He fixes his conversation partner with one eye, but says he cannot see anyway, and he compares himself to the captain in *The End of the Tether*. His spectacles are as thick as the glass casters under the legs of a piano. Borges teaches the Ph.D. course in English at the University of Buenos Aires. "A mere eight months were allotted for it formerly but the clever people who control the University have now reduced that to four." His range of reading not only in that, but also in five other languages leaves us far behind. We sit around a purple anemone centerpiece eating *dulce de leche*, which I.S. complains, later, has made him ill.

BRAZIL

September 4. 6:30 AM. The airport. The muddy river. The long
causeway at Buenos Aires. The view of both shores from the
middle. The pines, beaches, red roofs of Montevideo. The
whirlpool land patterns and dark green *fazendas* of Brazil.
The canyons shaped like streak lightning. We circle Rio de
Janeiro an hour before landing.

The Ouro Verde is a small Copacabana hotel on the wave-
patterned mosaic sidewalk. We sit on the terrace drinking
thimble-sized cups of sugary blue coffee, surrounded by bath-
ing suits, barefeet, beach muscles, and chocolate faces, *pousse-
café* faces, pale faces. The language is full of "bbzzs" and
"shzs." Suddenly a full, yellow moon, and dark-skinned girls
in tight pants and sweaters start to solicit every man on the
walk.

September 5. 6 AM. A canine chase on the beach, two terriers
running pell-mell to the water, and back again as fast as
possible. The earliest bather is a fat man who tries to exercise
with a fat rubber ball. By seven-thirty, watermelon carts appear, and boys carrying condor kites. An hour later, the beach
is crowded, whites and blacks in equal numbers—though an
American in the bar says that desegregation is "more apparent
than real, and even apparent only on the beach."

A drive through the city and by the sea. Old trams, open at
the sides; old buses and taxis; but the traffic, though fast and
reckless, is not as terrifying as in Buenos Aires. Iron balconies,
iron grilles, iron shutters. Trees; a well-shaded city. New building on stilts, old buildings made of stilts. Curvaceous wooden
churches. Street stands selling live crabs. The road up to the
Paneiras Corcovado is in places canopied with vines, like a
tunnel, and alternately washed away and covered by land-
slides, but we reach the top at moonrise. Rio at night is indeed
a *"Cidade Maravilhosa."*

Dinner at the Bec Fin, and conversation afterward with a

young Brazilian writer about Machado de Assis and *Othello*. The beach at midnight is littered with lovers.

September 6. A New Yorker in the hotel bar tells us that he lives by borrowing at six percent in the United States and lending at Twenty-eight percent here.

I.S., back from a stroll, boasts to us that he was propositioned by one of the *poules* patrolling the hotel area: "I was tempted by the suggestion—you could have dialed a telephone with her nipples—but I could see that she had a lot of mileage on her and I thought it best to decline."

September 7. Brasília, Port-of-Spain, New York. The pilot from Rio to Brasília is an I.S. "fan" who says he was rejected by the psychologist of another airline because in reply to the question "What is your favorite book and favorite piece of music?" he answered *Also sprach Zarathustra* and *Le Sacre du printemps*. We stand behind him in the cockpit for the take-off, and for an unscheduled aerial tour of the bay. Beyond Rio we fly over jagged mountains, eroded and sun-calcined plains, cities clinging narrowly to winding dirt roads. Beyond Belo Horizonte, a sprawling mass of new buildings, are clumps of jungle, dried-up water holes, black rivers with sand islands, like spotted snakes. Brasília is a large-scale map, with future streets traced in, circular perforations for trees, artificial lakes, clusters of tin-roofed workers' huts. The few lonely skyscrapers suggest Hiroshima, but look like a partly undenticulated comb. Three hours later we pass the Amazon at Santarem, where the fat brown river receives a transfusion from a clear blue lake and from many tributaries. From Santarem to the Orinoco, we see only the thick green mat and small cloud puffs indicating storm detonations. Trinidad seems exaggeratedly British, the pith helmets and shorts, the Crown insignia, the accents on the loudspeaker. In the waiting room, I.S. watches a baby trying to walk: "Just like me," he says, sadly. A whole village has come to see us take off, and from the air they are a quilt of color.

1961

MEXICO

March 31, Good Friday. Cuernavaca. The Las Mañanitas lawn is a bird paradise: black herons with golden combs; pigeons with shuttlecock fantails and feather leggings like the long-underwear tights of pugilists in the Nineties; parrots screeching in the surrounding plumbago bushes; peacocks horrendously crying "Help." I.S.: "The peacocks look like Ziegfeld girls."

On the difficulties and dangers of an Italian vocabulary in a Spanish-speaking land: I.S., at table, wanting butter, orders *"burro,"* but the waiter says, "Sorry, we do not serve mules." Later, when I.S. uses the word *"vergogna,"* intending to excuse himself, the Mexicans blush profusely. It means "Large lingam" to them.

At three o'clock, acolytes in white dalmatics enter the plaza and mark the death of the Saviour with wooden rattles and ratchet wheels.

Taxco. The Borda Hotel, overlooking the town. The moon, rising like an observation balloon, is a signal to the dogs on the adjacent hills to begin their nightlong barking. A candlelight procession weaves through the darkened city below, moving, in spreads and bunches, like an accordion or a worm. The women wear black kerchiefs, and the men dark *serapes* and

10. With Roger Sessions,
    Princeton, August 1959.

11. Conversation with Stravinsky,
    New York, 1959.

12. Conversation with Stravinsky, Kobe, April 1959.

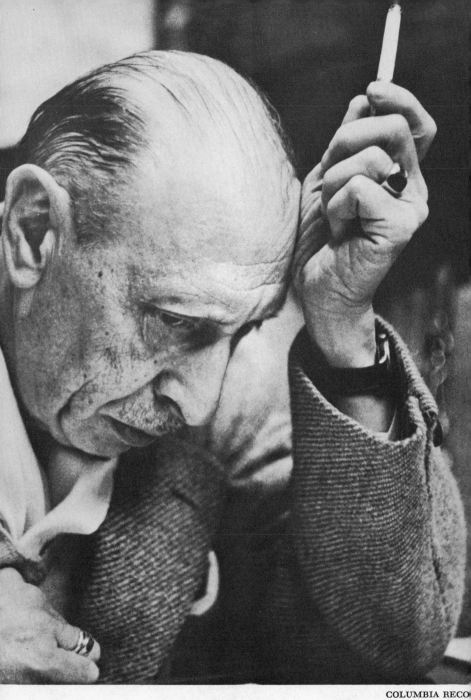

13. Listening to playbacks, New York, 1957.

14. Recording the *Movements* for piano and orchestra, Hollywood, 1961.

15. Linear interpretation of self-portrait drawn 1962.

16. With a koala bear, Sydney, 1961.

17. With President and Mrs. John F. Kennedy at the White House, January 18, 1962.

18. With Shostakovich, Mme. Khatchaturian, Aram Khatchaturian, Kiril Kondrashin, Kara Karayev, Mme. Furtseva (USSR Minister of Culture), Mrs. Stravinsky, and Tikhon Khrennikov, Moscow, October 1962.

sombreros, and everyone holds a candle with a colored card-board hilt.

Vicente, our driver, is a tall, powerfully-built man who might have had a highly successful career as a bandit. He accompanies us to Santa Prisca—"That is Santa Prisca, you see what I mean?"—but the church is empty of worshipers except for a few old Indian women who scorn the benches and say their orisons on the bare aisle stones. Small boys scrub and polish gold altar ornaments that look as though squeezed from tubes of gold paste, but signs warn us *"no tocar el dorado."* The non-gilt walls are galleries of *ex voto* pictures of lost pigs and cows. The Christ images are draped with purple.

Midnight. The convent of San Bernardino, a silent mass of people, inside and out. At the door is an unshrouded Christ with the silver wings of an angel and with a black cross roped to His lacerated back. At the end of the main room is a "hill of Calvary," with three life-size crosses. The center one is empty, except for strips of embalming linen that hang from it like curtains, and the tilted ladder of the deposition, but limp, dead "bodies" are nailed to the others. The room is packed with kneeling people, including children tottering on the edge of sleep, but every face in the room is transfixed. Suddenly a wail goes up from an organ, slow, somber, oriental. At this, a path is cleared from the door to the three crosses, and a boy enters, black-hooded and bare to the waist like a medieval executioner, with a heavy cactus cross on his back, and a lighted candle tied to each spread-eagled arm. He walks the length of the room in evident pain and, with help, kneels before the empty cross, beginning a long, slow chant as his knees touch the floor. No clerical vestment is seen in this most Catholic service and, for all outward sign, the officiating priests could be plain-clothes detectives.

I have rarely seen I.S. so moved. And it is not only because of the rites, as he says, but because the whole community has participated in them. "The whole community believes and the whole community belongs. And let us not call their celebration of the mystery of death primitive, either. It has the dignity of tragedy, for one thing, and for another, I believe that personal gods, whether or not they are the projection of a higher wish of humanity than abstract ones, are far less dangerous. And the Indians *do* have a naturalism, a man and woman *do* walk with their arms around each other in a natural, non-promiscuous way, unlike the flaunting, self-conscious movie-taught way of the American boy and girl by the hotel pool."

The streets afterward are no longer funereal, as Indian boys dressed in the tunics and helmets of Roman legionaries gather in the Plaza for a procession that will last until dawn. At 5 AM, sirens announce the end of their vigil and we go to bed under clouds like curdled milk.

April 1. To Iguala and Acapulco. As we leave the hotel, Vicente: "Have you enough bags?" (i.e., "Are more bags to come?") Outside Taxco, many roadside stones are whitewashed with the legend: "*Muero Apurto*" (Kill Apurto). Apurto is the governor of the province, Vicente says: "Mexicans funny people, *señor*. You see what I mean?" On the steep road *bajando* to the hot country, the precipitations of the careless or unlucky are marked by crosses, and one frightening turn is commemorated by a stone coffin as well. Indians squat by the roadside or ride donkeys—far back on the animal, not neckward as *gringos* ride; five small boys fill the deep-ridged back of a single mule. As we descend, the arid cactus *barrancas* are relieved by valleys of maize in which husks, cobs, and stalks are stored in trees, like birds' nests. Aviaries are common, and each hive-hut is a different color, like an advertisement for Pittsburgh Paints. Pigs and cows roam the road attended only by vigilant vultures. The farther *bajando*, the more fragmentary are the Indians' clothes. Vicente: "It is hot. You see what I mean?" Near Iguala, Indians swing pulque pots at us from the side of the road, like priests with censers, and other Iguala Indians try to sell us ceramics, baskets, guava, chicle, parrots, lovebirds. We stop at a roadstand and, surrounded by dark-eyed children, drink coconut milk spiked

with gin. An hour later the heat and the gin have put us to
sleep, but Vicente soon wakes us with: "There's Acapulco, you
see what I mean?"

April 8. Coyoacán. We buy "Virgin's milk cheese" in the market, and the sweet cheese of Oaxaca, which is peeled or un-
raveled from a white ball. And we watch a wedding in the
Convento de San Diego Churubusco, a rendition of "None but
the Lonely Heart" by a tenor, violin, and organ, in three different versions of unison. At the completion of the ceremony,
the priest extends the woman's veil over the man's head, and
anoints them from an ampulla. As we leave the church, a beggar pushes his cup to us. His face and beard are exactly the
same as the Christ image inside the door.

We drive to Tepotzotlán in the afternoon, to the Churrigue-
resque church which I.S. first saw in 1940 and has avowed to
be, for him, the most moving Christian building in the world.
And the rose-colored stone and glittering gold interiors *are* alluring, beyond I.S.'s account, as one comes to them from the
maguey desert. The aisle columns are red and the dome and
the angels are white—the angels are like ghosts in the frame of
so much color. The chapel of the Virgin of Loreto is full of
mirrors. I.S. says that this is because it is the "womb of the
Virgin, and wombs, like all places of love—like a brothel—are
always lined with mirrors." We look up through a hundred
feet of narrowing funnel to the Dove of the Eucharist which
reflects, in blinding whiteness, the older god of the sun.

FINLAND

September 9. Helsinki airport. Midnight. I.S. is tight from too
much schnapps on the plane, but he manages a short television
interview nevertheless; and though he says "ish" for "is," the
Finns can't have noticed as their own language sounds like a
continuous diphthong anyway. A ride through moonlit forests
to the city. The hotel is only one story of a building whose
other floors are offices. The Finnish for elevator is *hissi* and
the Swedish is *hiss.* Both words appear on the elevator door,

but without other translation, and this is the only Finnish we ever learn. Our rooms have a view of the gull-busy boat basin and the wooded islands in the bay. The I.S.'s are homesick for St. Petersburg.

September 10. A son-in-law of Sibelius, who is a conductor of the Helsinki Opera, and a second gentleman, a composer, take us to the Sibelius home at Jarvenpaa. A daughter of Sibelius, a white-haired lady, meets us at a pathway near the house, and walks with us to her father's woodland grave, a large granite nameplate on which I.S. places a bouquet. Each room of the Sibelius house is warmed by a tile stove, and the wooden floors are scrubbed white and smooth. It is the cozy home of a country composer and no aura of attempted "Beethovenization" hangs over the place—indeed, one has to look for the cabinet of recordings and the bound collection of Sibelius' works. I.S. says he had heard Sibelius' first or second symphony with Rimsky, whose comment was: "Well, I suppose that is also possible." I learn from this anecdote that I.S. was called "Guima" by Rimsky, "and by all those who loved me. My wife always called me Gui." I.S. says he is fond of the Sibelius *Canzonetta* for strings, "The first half of it, anyway. I like that kind of northern Italianate melodism—Tchaikovsky had it too—which was a part, and an attractive part, of St. Petersburg culture."

A thick fog has settled over the Helsinki harbor when we return, and we are kept awake all night by cries of lost boats.

September 12. The markets. Heaps of mushrooms, fish, berries, flowers. Mixture of languages, with much Russian. V. looks for a hotel she remembers from her childhood, but it was destroyed in the war. The center of the old city is a white square, with a statue of Alexander II. The new city is a mass of gray stone apartment buildings that could come from anywhere in the world. Rehearsal. A few of the musicians speak English or German, but translations are required for most. We are presented with large bouquets at the concert and, after the concert, at a dinner by the Finnish Composers' Union, with large, very kind speeches. The Finns are shy, grateful, hospitable.

SWEDEN

September 13. Stockholm. *The Rake's Progress—Rucklarens Väg*—at the Royal Opera. The stage apron has been extended over the orchestra pit, neutralizing the proscenium arch, and the fullest stage depth is exploited, as at the end of the brothel scene, when the actors freeze in a background silhouette. A Brechtian poster, *Rucklarens Väg*, replaces the curtain and is used as a between-scenes drop, which helps to emphasize each episode as a progress of pictures in the Hogarthian sense. The groupings are Hogarthian too, and so are the pictorializations, especially in the earlier episodes, in which Hogarth is openly imitated; the scene of Mother Goose, bottle in hand, falling backward on her couch, is a *tableau vivant* of the painting. Sets are changed before the audience's eyes, not furtively, in the dark, but as a co-ordinated element in the movement of the play. Thus, "London" is lowered from the sky at the beginning of the street scene, and is populated with tradesmen and townspeople during the C-minor prelude. This London scene is visually the most attractive, but it is the last that can be described as English in color and style of décor. After it, the costumes become more Swedish, and gray and black predominate over pink and orange, though, of course, this change to a more mute and somber palette also follows the tenor of the play.

I have never seen I.S. so moved by a performance of a work of his—in fact, one seldom sees him not angry—and this in spite of large cuts and legions of places in which the direction is at loggerheads with the book. I.S., later: "For the first time, Tom's decision to marry Baba was convincing. I wanted to thank Bergman for that, and for innumerable details. When Ann weeps as Tom leaves for London, Tom starts to come to her, but Truelove motions him back and goes to her himself. I cannot describe Truelove's motion, but I believed in it. And the

fact that Tom and Shadow sing from loges in the auction scene
does bolster the idea that they are at large. Such small things,
and a hundred more, create the credibility of the play." The
groupings, too, are always striking and—in the sense that they
do not infract the conventions of opera—natural. Arias are
sung to the audience, stage front, and so are actionless ensembles, such as the quartet and trio in the first scene. But
Bergman makes singers move their arms and eyes as they have
never moved them before.

The most novel aspect of the musical performance is the *sotto
voce* singing of the *secco* recitatives. And the most imaginative
is the playing of the graveyard scene as a *crescendo* on stage,
in contrast to the dynamically static harpsichord solo. The
harpsichord is elevated from the orchestra pit to slightly below stage level, and it is therefore, as it should be, closer to
the singers than to the orchestra.

September 14. The Royal Theater at Drottningholm is
equipped with twenty-odd eighteenth-century sets—back-
boards and drops, plus perspectival systems of sliding side-
scenery. The Intendant works the antique machinery for us,
displaying movements of clouds and waves, thunder from a
drop of rocks in a net, the ascent of a plaster god—a real *deus
ex machina.* The king and queen in official attendance sat on
red thrones in the front center of the audience, but when in-
cognito, with lovers, they were sequestered in latticed loges.
The other seats are still designated for *"cavalieri," "friseurs,"
"valets."* Surrounding the stage are forty actors' rooms, each
with fireplace, pewter *lavabo*, clothes block, wig dummy,
dressing table, mirror. The corridors are galleries of actors' portraits and of theater designs of the Bibiena period, including
the originals for Cesti's *Pomo d'oro*, of handbills for popular
plays such as Voltaire's *Tancrède*. The wallpaper is a hand-
sewn and hand-painted parchment.

September 16. Uppsala. Ocher and red buildings, windmills,
farmhouses roofed with sod. In the old church on the Royal

Ridge, once a temple to Odin, and the site of a circle of sacred trees before that, pews, pillars, pulpit, holy images, are worn like driftwood. A row of hourglasses stand on the preacher's rostrum, each with a fifteen-minute measure of sand, a guarantee against theological filibuster. The church was for professors and prebendaries, many of whom, including Anders Celsius, are buried in the floor. Outside the church and apart from it is the *klockstapel*, a wooden belfry laced from the waist up with round-edged shingles like a coat of mail.

In the new city we see the house of Linnaeus; the statue to V.'s distant cousin, the arctic explorer Finn Malmgren: the gold casket of St. Erik, and the tomb of Swedenborg, both in the cathedral; the eighteenth-century Theatrum Anatomicum; the Carolina Rediviva Library. Here we examine the part-books of Schütz's Christmas Oratorio; organ entablatures in Buxtehude's hand dated 1680 and signed *"Membra Jesu Nostri, Organista S. Maria Virgines, Lübeck"*; drawings by the Swedish kings of which the best, by Gustav IV, look vaguely like Goyas.

Evening at the country house of Set Svanholm, director of the Royal Opera, with Ingmar Bergman and his new wife (by no means the first), a beautiful Estonian. Bergman is tall, has a nose like a clasp, deep-set eyes, a mole on the right cheek. Contact is immediate, and as soon as he talks—fluent English— his hands become lively and expressive. His statements are well tailored and his ideas are clearly staged; in fact, nothing about the man is tentative. He says with passion that "the artist has only to discover what to do and with all his strength purify the doing"—and we all want to discover something and to rush out and do it. When I.S. asks what initially attracted him to *The Rake*, Bergman says "A bad performance" —which enables us to discuss *his* performance. I.S. says that the Bedlam and brothel scenes were overpopulated: "A few characters may be memorable, never a mass of them." Bergman agrees. "In fact, I invented a name for each person in the chorus and individually trained each singer to be that person, but my work was destroyed when the chorus had to be enlarged for musical reasons." He says that his first idea was "for a stage long enough and deep enough so that the actors could appear and disappear in the darkness, not through doors." And his second idea was that the opera should be divided into two acts of five and four scenes each, "principally because the second act, as published, does not have a strong beginning, middle, and end structure. I considered the play up to the unveiling of Baba's beard as one line, and not only the play but the music; this is the protasis, and the rest is the peripeteia. And I was more concerned with the line for the episodes than with rounded act-structures. I thought, too, that in this opera, perhaps more than in any other, the audience must not lose attention to the stage for a single moment, which accounts for—please forgive me—the cuts." Bergman has abbreviated the orchestral march before the brothel and excised Tom's aria at the beginning of Bedlam, two places where other directors have complained of I.S.'s misapplied musical thrift and where, customarily, pauses have been introduced because of insufficient musical time. "But another reason for the two-act division was that I could not break for an intermission after the bread machine and allow the audience to go out confused. This scene is the most difficult in the opera to stage, or to believe in." I.S. agrees, and adds: "The waltz music there is intended to be completely indifferent." Bergman claims to have dreamed that the machine had a lion's mouth. "I dream about everything I do. Dreams purify my ideas." I.S. says that he too dreams about every problem in his composition.

I.S. thinks that Bergman has made Baba believable, "and that is not easy. To reverse a remark of somebody in Henry James, 'She was perhaps a lady but never a woman.' Still, Baba recognizes Shadow for what he is. And though she enters the drama as a monstrosity from nowhere, she leaves it as a sympathetic personality." Bergman: "Baba cost me more thought than anyone else. She is the artist in all of us, and not merely the circus artist. This, incidentally, is why she is such a great advance over the idea of the Ugly Duchess. Her beard must be beautiful, not grotesque, and the audience must believe in the reality of what it sees, no matter how fantastic. And besides, the point of the marriage, at least by the time of the breakfast scene, is not its exoticism but its conventionality. Tom is bored with her because she is shallow." Bergman has expressed this on the stage in the way Baba and Tom lie apart on a ludicrously large bed at the beginning of the breakfast scene.

Bergman believes that the street scene, the confrontation of Tom, Baba, and Ann, is the climax of the opera. "That is where Shadow's work is shown in the open, and that is why I bring him onstage: he must watch this scene with satisfaction." I.S. says that the silent movement of people in the streets during the trumpet solo is "the most beautiful thing in the opera. You have a deep feeling for music." Bergman: "The question for the opera director should always be, 'How much does the music tell us already?' In the street scene it tells us exactly how those people feel. In fact, it tells us that they are not people but shadows."

I.S. thinks the second act was "more Swedish than the first, and more like a Bergman film. The freaks at the auction and in Bedlam, which was a medieval madhouse, Brueghel rather than Hogarth, were especially Bergmanesque, but so was the solitary dummy at the end of the brothel scene." Bergman's answer is that he had spent so much time on the first part of the opera that too little remained for the rest. "And I became wary of following Hogarth, who is dangerous because too attractive in himself." I.S. remarks that the Epilogue succeeded better than it has in any other production: "It did not come as a shock because the audience never lost track of the 'fable' aspect. This was managed in a way that suggested Brecht's *Verfremdungseffekt*, though your 'illusion of reality'—the cave-of-shadows reality—is the very thing Brecht tried to dispel." Bergman: "The Epilogue is simply a matter of preparation, which is why I begin with it also and make of it a frame for the whole work." He has staged a dumbshow during and even before the Prelude to Act One, and before Baba's inventory recitative, which is the overture to "his" Act Two, but these

are as much devices for fixing audience attention as preparations for the Epilogue. "What the Epilogue should mean is that
'now the play is over and you can go home and talk about the
singer's high C.'"

In Bergman's staging of the graveyard scene, Shadow both
enters and exits through the ground. I.S. thinks the appearance
weakens the effect of the disappearance, but he likes the way
Shadow sits on the tombstone at the beginning of the scene
"and the silhouette of the three Gothic steeples, which are
more and more strongly felt as the action develops." Bergman:
"At first the audience is aware of the three spires only as omi-
nous presences, but by the end of the scene it knows that they
are Golgotha and the meaning of the play."

I.S. says that Bergman's Bedlamites respond too quickly,
stand up too fast, after the first flute duet—"though I shouldn't
have repeated that flute lullaby *twice*"—and that Tom, after
Ann's exit, arises very suddenly too, for a dying man. Bergman: "Mistakes like these are part of the charm of opera, and
they are probably necessary, for they seduce us to try again."

September 21. A few days ago we have seen the first act of a
bad performance of *Rigoletto.* This morning, when I whistle
one of the *ballo* tunes:

I.S. asks me whether it is *Rigoletto* or *Traviata.* He is thinking
of:

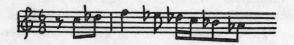

in *Traviata.* This is one of a thousand examples that he hears
intervallically rather than rhythmically, with the intervals as
connecting roots and the rhythms as elaboration.

September 25. More talk with Bergman about *The Rake.* I.S. asks why no clock was shown in the brothel. Bergman: "Because it is so obvious in the music. I prefer to see the eyes of the actors watching something that we hear unmistakably as a clock, and to make the real audience believe through the eyes of the stage audience." Bergman contends that Shadow, at his first entrance, "should seem to be a kind of lawyer—the *advocatus diaboli.* Of course, the critics, who only understand typecasting, said that my Devil was not demonic, and they complained that Tom pouts and mopes more than he roisters. But the progress of the Rake *is* well accounted for in the sets, don't you think, and he really does look a millionaire in the fourth scene." I. S. asks why the costume of the auction crowd is black. He says this struck him as Hyperborean, and reminded him of the black-robed oarsmen in toy, peasant-carved scullers. Bergman says that black is worn in the parish boat races in his native northern Sweden, but that he had not thought of this while staging the scene. "The only reason was that as I wanted to focus attention on Baba and Ann, I gave color only to them." The auctioneer has stood on a pedestal, but I. S. thinks he should be removed still farther from the bidders, who sit—and this is effective—with their backs to the audience.

Bergman says he would stage I.S.'s *Oedipus* without masks. "A mask may be beautiful, and it can be a useful façade for all sorts of things, but the price, which is the loss of contact, is too great." As we part, he asks me to keep contact.

GERMANY

September 29. Berlin. The barricades and land mines at the Brandenburger Tor are partly concealed with flowers. I.S. points toward what was once the Adlon Hotel, where he says he met Schoenberg in 1912. Between us and it are policemen with bloodhounds, binoculars, walkie-talkies, submachine guns at the ready. In the French sector, *"Die Mauer"* is low enough so that neighbors may converse or stare over it, and old place names survive, some of them now cruelly ironic: "Bellevuestrasse," which is one of the ugliest views, and "Dem

Deutschen Volk," a sign on a huge building still hideously gutted and cadaverous from the war. On the boundary sidewalk, crosses with wreaths and bouquets commemorate fatal East-to-West leaps, and all windows and doors on the line are bricked-up and boarded like a set for Sartre's *No Exit*. A sign, *"Wir sind alle Brüder,"* has been nailed to a blockaded church with a barbed-wired Crucifix on the door. Tank patrols make us keep safe distance from a not-yet-walled field in which old men and women labor at gunpoint. Several times during this heart-sickening tour we are obliged to close the windows of our car against the stench of death in buildings still rubbled and derelict from the carnage of 1945.

YUGOSLAVIA

September 30–October 7. Belgrade. Passports and currency declarations are collected before permission is given to leave the plane. A hot, windy night, the sidewalks packed with people. Our rooms at the Metropole face the Sava where it curves to meet the Danube. They are hardly luxurious to begin with, but in addition, the telephones have been disconnected, the lights are constantly failing, handles of doors and bureaus fall off at the slightest tug, and room service takes between two hours and never. A more serious problem still is the water, which is always scalding and which works for only a few unpredictable moments each day. We hoard it in our bathtubs, like rain-catchers, and construct runnels to try to flush the toilets, burning fingers and drenching clothes in the process.

Besides ourselves, the hotel is occupied by French, Italian, and American movie companies whose luminaries—the Americans are Gregory Peck, Mel Ferrer, Jeanne Crain, Akim Tamirov, John Barrymore, Jr.—almost never leave the bar, presumably because of language difficulties and the non-existence of indigenous entertainment.

Language. The maids, waiters, porters know a few words of German or Italian, but most officials we meet speak only the local language. The I.S.'s are able to follow the drift of this through words of common Slavonic origin, but they complain that these "etymological conversations" are tedious.

People. Bulky women, brunettes and blondes. The men—caps and dungarees—are large-boned and heavy-set, like Tito. Everyone to whom we are introduced—musicians, dancers, theater employees, culture officials—is extremely hospitable.

Politics. No United States or Western European publication is in evidence at any kiosk, and Italy, a short sea away, seems as remote as Nepal. But we are always aware of Russia. The principal hotel in the commercial district is called the Moscow, and the principal square is the Marx and Engels. As in other "Communist" countries, tips are said to be refused. They are not refused by hotel personnel. The local saying is that "tips are not given, but they are taken."

Money. 600 dinars to the dollar is the official exchange, but the U.S. Embassy gives us 750. Yugoslav currency is "soft"—worthless anywhere else.

Food. German and Italian dishes grossly cooked. Local wines and cheeses are good but coarse. We subsist principally on almonds, baklava, Turkish coffee, and a salty Serbian *chèvre*. Slivovitz, the plum liqueur, is imbibed everywhere and at all hours. It is the most enduring and endearing of Yugoslav institutions.

Music. The orchestra greatly enjoys its discovery of *Oedipus*, but the spectacle of such excellent musicians so completely unaware of contemporary music is pathetic. We attend a seedy performance of *Onegin* at the small non-ventilated National Theater. Here and, later, at our own *soirées*, we learn that the success of an event is gauged by the quantities of flowers hauled on stage afterward. The applause swells with each bouquet, as though the flowers themselves were the performers, and, naturally, the stage looks like a flower show for every artist who can afford it. The floral tributes are stored in the artists' large but weakly illuminated dressing rooms during the performance. When United States Ambassador George Kennan comes to greet us there before *Oedipus-Perséphone*,

I.S. tells him it is like "the visit of a high diplomatist at a state funeral."

In the Music Academy, Marshal Tito's photograph is on walls and desks in every room, but the only composer's likeness we see is Liszt's.

Architecture. All government buildings and the newer apartment houses follow a severely unornamented one-party style that is ugly to the point of comicality. As most churches and mosques are new, large, and ugly too, we probably overrate, in contrast, the attractiveness of the old, steep-gabled shops and houses around the marketplace. Belgrade is electrically bright (when the lights work), like Athens, and as in the Greek city, prettier at night with its Cyrillic neon.

The country. A late afternoon drive to Oplenac, the reconstructed "Byzantine" church and Escorial of the last Serbian kings. Poplars and plane trees, tobacco fields and vineyards, whitewashed farmhouses with thatched roofs. The women wear black shawls, and the men black hussars' hats, leggings, handlebar mustaches. Traffic is limited to bullock carts and canvas-covered gypsy wagons. The Oplenac mosaics, manufactured in Germany about forty years ago, represent the bad taste of our parents—which we say even though knowing that in a shorter time still the same will be said about our own works.

I.S. at the Belgrade airport, to a culture official who wants his summation of the visit: "*À la longue* we got rather bored with the hot water."

SWITZERLAND

October 12. Zurich. An exhibition of Hittite art in the Kunsthaus. Orthostat reliefs: a weather-god with hammer and tongs, a juggler, a lutenist, a hand-clapping dancer, a fierce griffin with an absurd pussycat mustache, a warrior with an Assyrian Katzenjammer beard. Ceramics: pitchers with pommel handles, rhytons, half-sieve strainers, fertility idols, some like matchsticks and all as abstract as Arp; curled-toe babouches exactly as though from the Turkey of the janissary period; figurines of dancing gods with stilts and horned caps, or tall, conical ones like those of medieval jesters. Hittite cuneiform, in clay writing tablets, looks like the beach tracks of a flock of birds. Hittite bronze and gold, in statuettes of steers, is dandelion yellow, sometimes with silver or electrum stripes.

The Nightingale at the Zurich Opera. I.S. thinks the costumes are more African than Chinese. "The 'Death' is an African liban rather than a Chinese shaman, and the Bonze is a Barbary Captain Kidd. But the palace of the Emperor of China looks like a coolie's cottage, and the Emperor of Japan's mechanical nightingale is a rather frightening pterodactyl. And why should the Japanese emissaries have green faces? A bad crossing? Too much tea?"

ENGLAND

October 16. London. Dinner with T. S. Eliot, who complains of having had to waste time refusing invitations to the Tagore Centenary. "I took the poetry out of the library to be certain I had not made a mistake, but I could make nothing of it. Difficult to tell that to the Indians, though, or, indeed, to admit that one does not rank Tagore with Shakespeare and Dante. Bill Yeats used to say he liked Tagore, but he was making a case for 'The East' at the time. I receive regular shipments of the works of new Indian poets, incidentally, together with letters inviting my comments. Once I replied, ripping the thing apart, and a few months later I found my by no means complimentary letter printed as a preface to the published poems! A Kashmir shawl was the reward for these criticisms, and when I returned that, another and much better shawl came with a note agreeing that the first one had not been worthy of me." This is all said quietly, flatly, diffidently, with a pause after each phrase as though the speaker were suffering from emphysema. (He is.)

Eliot's facial lines are sharper than ever, and I.S. remarks, later, that he looks like "one of those Hittite ceramic birds." His lips are purple and his ears are large and red. His head is hunched low, as if from a yoke, and he leans forward with his legs apart when he stands, as though he were skiing. He is almost painfully decorous, and though he knows we are coming directly from the airport, a last-minute note is sent to inquire whether by chance dinner is formal. In fact, it has been arranged to discuss a proposal that I.S. set to music two lyrical stanzas, as Eliot calls them, from *Little Gidding*, but Eliot quickly dampens the project by doubting that "they can be set." He has a habit of saying "yes" at each break in the other person's talk.

Eliot on his recent debate in the *Times Literary Supplement* concerning a mistranslation in the New English Bible: "I enjoy this sort of thing when I feel, as I do now, that I have the right end of the stick." And on Pound: "He was always a poor judge of people and, indeed, of most things except poetry. He really believed that his monetary ideas would change the world—we were all a bit tarred by that brush. But he had great gifts, and I owe more to him than to anyone. Which reminds me that I should send him a letter; hm, hm, difficult to know what to say." The only books mentioned all evening are *romans policiers* and plays of Voltaire that neither Eliot nor I.S. has read. Eliot says he bid for and won a complete Voltaire at an auction when he first came to England, but never appeared to pick it up. "That has been on my conscience ever since." The poet and the musician are both admirers of Simenon. Eliot: "I can read about Maigret when I can read nothing else." Other favorite sleuths are Nigel Strangeways and Perry Mason. Eliot: "Gardner certainly knows California law, but Chandler was a better writer." I.S.: "A detective story is like a fugue in that you must see the end in the beginning." Travel talk. Eliot pronounces Milan to rhyme with Dylan. When V. voices some criticisms of Switzerland, Eliot says, "I see what you mean, but I like it because it more resembles what it used to be than any other country."

October 20. Oxford. Isaiah Berlin's, with Robert Graves, who is tall and military in posture, large-eared, and, today anyway,

clean-shorn. Like Michelangelo, he has had a broken nose and
—probably like the sculptor too—his fingernails are rinded with
dirt. When I.S. inquires about his present work, Graves says
he is "disguised as a professor, implausibly." When Graves
asks I.S. the same question, I.S. describes "serial versification,"
to which Graves's comment is: "Poetry is less purely genial
than that and more demonstrably linked to moral questions."
Graves begins a story. "I started down the street this morning thinking of a woman when suddenly my breast pocket
burst into flame . . ." but whether the fire was actually in-
cendiary or merely allegorical we never find out. He tells of a
conversation with David Ben-Gurion in which Ben-Gurion tes-
tified that "Israelis are less good taxpayers than the citizens
of Protestant countries, but rather better than those of Catholic
countries." Isaiah Berlin calls this "an excellent beginning for
sociological speculation." Graves talks about "hallucinátory
psilocybin mushrooms" and claims that they "induce a state
of grace." And about Paul of Tarsus: "He was not a Jew, of
course, but a Syrian—you remember the Ebionite Epistle?"
And Plato: "He has done more harm than any one person
except Freud." And Aristotle: "A thoroughly unpleasant character." And, "Shall I tell you my idea about Alexander the
Great? It will take just three minutes"—he looks at his watch.
"That legend of the Priest's serpent at the Oasis of Siwa is
nonsense. Alexander decided to conquer the world out of the
jealous desire to surpass Dionysus. Like Dionysus, he declared
himself 'son of Zeus.'" Etc., but Isaiah Berlin thinks he con-
quered out of curiosity—to discover what was behind the next
hill.

I.S., composing a "tonal row" and accompanying words of
dedication for the Berlin guest book, asks for an English equivalent to the Russian "*kanitel.*" Isaiah says that literally the
word means a silver or gold skein, but, commonly, a long and
entangled argument, and someone quotes "or ever/the silver
cord be loosed." Graves puffs on his cheroot and jumps in—he
is the fastest man with words I have ever seen—"The Yiddish
for that is '*magillah*' and the Greek and Latin are . . ." etc.,

etc. I.S. to Isaiah, in Russian: "Do you suppose he is going to give the Etruscan, too?"

Watching Graves listen enviously as I.S. and Isaiah speak Russian, I ask him which of his languages he would most readily exchange for it. "German," he says, without hesitation. When Graves leaves to deliver his inaugural lecture as Professor of Poetry, Isaiah refers to him as "an Hibernian and an antinomian, and a would-be Pharisee if that would help depose Jesus and crown the White Goddess. But he is a true poet and a true wit."

Isaiah reads passages of the Bible to us in Hebrew, translating word for word: "El, Elim, Elohim. Elohim is used to denote the lords of the others, the Hammurabis, the 'after strange gods.'" He promises to produce a properly accented copy in Russian transliteration for I.S., if I.S. decides to set the Isaac and Abraham story. He suggests that I.S. consider using "the first and seventh days of the Creation, the two Holiest Days," but I.S. says that that would be "longer than a British weekend."

October 23. Dinner for I.S. by the Institute of Contemporary Arts, with E. H. Gombrich, Henry Moore, Herbert Read, etc. Gombrich—shining black eyes, long, blunt chin—talks measurement psychology, and when someone asks his opinion of a picture, says: "I don't know; I am a historian and therefore prefer sitting on fences." Henry Moore, small and soft-spoken, talks about the pigeon hazard and outdoor sculpture. I.S. tells him that what he remembers most clearly about Rodin's atelier was "the *démodé* furniture. It had absolutely no connection with what Rodin was doing."

October 27. Cambridge. Tea with E. M. Forster. We knock on the inner door—the outer has been opened to reveal the nameplate "Mr. Forster"—exactly as King's College clock strikes four, and Forster's pleasure in this punctuality is almost inordinate. Forster has a long cranial index, long nose, long fingers, long legs—too long for the torso, which may account for the light, floating walk. A glint lights his blue eyes, and a still clearer glint shines in everything he says. Hunched and down-looking, he watches the fireplace during most of the conversation, standing up from time to time to poke the briquettes. His voice is quiet, which leads us to believe that the reason he asks me to repeat several of my statements is not deafness, but my savage American accent—that or the excessive incredibility of what I say. A shock of gray-brown hair covers the crown of his head, and his mustache, which wiggles pleasantly during his toothy grins, is still tinged with the same color.

Bookshelves line much of the room, and random piles of books are everywhere. I also remember an upright piano, a table, old plates, old portraits, a Victorian divan on which Forster sits, soft armchairs on which we sit. He talks about the furniture and claims to have "few possessions, including heirlooms, I would mind losing. That mantelpiece, for instance, was made by my father, but I could certainly do without it." Next to the mantel is a framed embroidery of his mother's name, and we wonder if he would part with that as painlessly.

The conversation grinds to long agonizing stops, agonizing because while some people are silent out of appreciation, and others for the reason that they are truly dumb, Forster's silences are acutely critical. He artificially resuscitates the talk, making us feel the fault is ours, with questions like, "Did you come on the 2:36 train?" He mentions books: "I never reached the end of *Don Quixote*, did you?" We haven't, of course, but would we admit it if we had? "I liked *The Holy Sinner*, surprisingly enough. Mann always knew a great deal, but his other books were so *heavy*"—the last word stands out as though it had been picked up with forceps. On Tolkien: "I dislike whimsicality and I cannot bear good-and-evil on such a scale." But is this entirely true? Isn't good-and-evil Forster's main subject? (And isn't he, in fact, primarily a moralist whose deepest fear is moral snobbery?) We feel that he is judging us the whole time, in any case, like a supreme governess. When he brings a tray with sandwiches and cakes, and I choose a cake, I am instantly made to feel that probably I should have chosen a sandwich. Even the weather is a subject for judgment. When I ask if the rain has stopped he settles silver-rimmed spectacles on his nose, goes to the window, says, "I will try to decide."

A "Humanist" discussion, touched off by a remark of Forster's about a historian friend of his who has been "putting the Medici in their places." To the question why Humanists are intimidated by scientists, Forster replies: "We fear we cannot tell them anything and we are self-consciously aware of the non-technical nature of our language." He talks about India, about the fragments of an Indian diary he will soon publish ("I wish I had done more of it"), about a meeting with Tagore in 1910. He shows us a smooth white box with wires attached to the base, like a Jews harp. "The Uganda natives played these instruments as they worked on the roads —the 'strings' were obtained by cutting the telephone wires. Do you recognize the wood?" We don't, of course, and therefore immediately feel we have earned a bad mark. Forster talks and listens to talk about music with keen attention, and the comparative high point of his enthusiasm is the recollection of his lecture on music and the arts at Harvard: "I was delighted to be asked to do that because it meant that someone had seen from my work how much I cared. I accepted the invitation within the hour of receiving it." As we leave, he thanks us for the visit, and we feel for an almost thawing moment that he really may have been pleased. Later, in the train, our vindictive talk shows that we have been nicked by the razor-like intelligence under the decorum and old lace.

Dinner with Cyril Connolly. A disproportionately large head, like a Bacchus, a flat profile with a Pekinese nose, flat ears with sprigs of hair growing out of them—"earbrows," I.S. says. Fixing us with what he calls his gimlet glare, he proves himself a glittering *raconteur*, but other people's talk bores him and makes him restless. He tells us about a lunch today with the President of Senegal, with whom he discussed French wine for a great while, only to discover, when the meal was served, that the President was a strict Mohammedan. He tells us that many psychoanalysts now agree that "women want to go much further back than the womb; in fact, all the way back to father's penis."

EN ROUTE

November 8. Cairo. A forty-hour delay for engine repairs and fog, which a Quantas official hopes to excuse by the claim that "our planes are the safest in the world." (I.S.: "Naturally. They rarely leave the ground.") At Karachi a Sikh policeman comes aboard. Black jodhpurs, black feet (bare), black mustache (twirled), blue turban with a white feather. He reminds I.S. of the *Firebird*. At Calcutta, the maintenance squad is in loincloths, and here and in Bangkok they bring mosquitoes and heat with them. Violent bumping and shaking—"slight turbulence," the pilot says—over the Gulf of Siam, and a rough landing at Singapore, where blue-black Malays empty the ashtrays and primp the pillows.

November 9. Daybreak over Borneo and the South China Sea, and breakfast—gin and orange juice—at Darwin: a promontory, rivers and jungles, a landing strip on a platter of red earth. Then, after three more hours—of desert, black hills, and, finally red-roofed cottages on sand dunes—we land at Sydney, which, says I.S., "looks like impetigo."

NEW ZEALAND

November 11. Over the Tasman Sea to Auckland. I.S., to an airport official who has been explaining why he must pay overweight: "I quite understand the *logic* of it. What I am objecting to is the money." Field Marshal Lord Alexander is a fellow passenger, and we chat with him (about matters that interest none of us); he reads a Perry Mason during the flight, and is received in Auckland by hip-hip-hoorays from girl cheerleaders in Scottish kilts. New Zealand is a rim of sand between the light green vitreous sea and dark green hills. We stay in the Rodean, a boardinghouse with a view of the bay (and not much else).

November 12. Tour of the harbor. Ebbing tide, followed by mussel gatherers picking the pools and uncovered land. We watch a trawler dock a net spangled with shellfish. The Maori boatmen sound like cockneys. Englishness, too, in cricket fields, bowling lawns, church spires, tall oaks, Empire names like Khyber Pass Road, Constable subject matter in clouds, shadows, greens. Each house has its own "tidy plot" and its own flower and vegetable gardens. New Zealanders—this is their ultimate Englishness—are all gardeners. "That hedge'd take a bit of cutting," the driver says indignantly, though disclaiming at the same time that he is a "horticulturalist," and the sight of yellow gorse, "that noxious weed," puts him out of sorts altogether.

"Mauree," with the German 'au', is our hosts' pronunciation for Maori. Their "yöess" (yes) is an oddly Scandinavian sound (when they say it, for they prefer "righto" instead), and their "r" words are a combination of Boston and Dixie. We are driving an English cah in a land of pretty flowhs of which Wellington is the seat of the pahlamint. The accent of the Rodean waitress is more remote still. Breakfast consists of braid and eggs, unless one prefers scones (rhyme it with prawns). Small hills are hillies to her, and she translates our whisky orders to "nips"—and the furtiveness suggested by her word is appropriate to the restrictive conditions in which the article is acquired and consumed. But cockney expressions occur even in the language of the law, and signs on the roads warn motorists to TIP NO RUBBISH.

Conversation is dominated by pride in natural New Zealand, and little curiosity is evinced, however strongly it may be felt, about the wonders of other lands. The tone of this sometimes makes one suspect an appeal to prospective settlers, but the alluring argument of free public hospitals is offset, in my case, by the bachelor tax. Almost as apparent, in conversation,

is the rivalry with Australia. "Our horses are better racers . . .
We have better lobsters . . ." and so on. (For the Australian
attitude, I quote our baggage porter at Sydney airport: "Going to New Zealand for a few days? That'd be enough, I
should think.") The drive is accompanied by a steady discourse on N.Z. history and local lore, during which I.S., in the
back seat, falls asleep. He wakes, at length, exclaiming in a
startled voice, "the street." Our host, at that point talking
about the New Zealand Navy, asks, "What street?" and I.S.,
after a strenuous pause, manages to say, "What is the street of
our hotel?" He confesses later that he had been dreaming
about Paris and was directing a taxi to his old apartment
there.

Dinner of cockle fritters, steamed hapuka, and bread served
with about a pound of butter per person. V.: "Like many small
countries, New Zealand is folksy, friendly, homey, tidy, full of
flowhs, screamingly dull."

November 15. To Wellington. Volcanoes. Mt. Ruapehu,
smooth flanks covered with a snow mantle; and Ngauruhoe,
which is smoking. A bumpy landing in strong winds. But Wellington must be the windiest capital in the world, and we are
always wet with spindrift from the sea in what appears to be a
permanent gale. And Wellington seems to be even more Victorian than Auckland. Its prettier buildings, those with Gothic
windows, iron railings, and iron awnings over the sidewalks, are
that, in any case, but these the Wellingtonians are eager to
demolish. I.S., as we pass a statue of Victoria: "But she looks
exactly like a policeman."

Reception by United States Ambassador Akers. Two hundred hands to shake—those of other ambassadors, the New
Zealand Prime Minister, many members of pahlamint. Large
N.Z. lady: "Well, frankly, Mr. Stravinsky, I like the *Firebird* best of all your works." I.S.: "And what a charming hat
you have." Small N.Z. gent: "People here are fond of modern
music. We had half a program of your works once" (I.S.,
later: "My *Scheherazade*, no doubt") "and we've even heard

pieces by Shostakovich and Ache" (Egk). Wife of high N.Z. dignitary: "Do you like architecture, Mr. Stravinsky?" I.S.: "Let me think about it."

November 18. A drive along the straits. At the entrance to the harbor, a concrete igloo fort from 1942–45. Abundance and variety of flowhs: marigolds, foxglove, wild sweet peas and wild daisies, golden wattles, pale lupines, roses and geraniums the size of peonies.

Visit from Doris M., who has exchanged letters with one of my sisters since childhood, and who is now married to a sheep rancher in Parnassus, a railway junction in Samuel Butler country on the South Island. Doris has been to Wellington only once previously, and that twenty-two years ago, and never otherwise has she traveled beyond her home island. The journey here has been her first in an airplane. And, she has never seen an orchestra before. This is the most exciting weekend of her life—she says. But tomorrow is shearing day in Parnassus, and she must be back there by 4:30 AM; the musterers take to the hills at that time, before the cries of dawn birds can give the alarm to the sheep. She talks to us of sheep tending, the lambing, docking, dipping, the crutching of ewes, the eyeclipping of heavy fleeces, the care of the hoggets, the fate of the culls. Her hands are scarred, not from sheep but from crayfish, which she hunts in snorkel and fins but without gloves. Another of her seaside pastimes is the making of earrings from surf-polished marl. Doris says that once, driving slowly along the beach, she heard "a fat lady sobbing," but running to the edge of the water found a dolphin dying of a propeller wound. "Tears rolled from its eyes, and its crying was terribly human." She tells us about blue ducks and mutton birds (wedge-tailed shearwaters), which migrate from the south of South Island to Siberia, and which Maoris alone are licensed to hunt. Cold mutton bird is considered a delicacy by some, and by others the richest meat in the world, but indigestible.

No danger of our stomachs being put to the test in the St.

George Hotel. It maintains the poorest fare in the world and the most puritanical code. Visitors may call only at prescribed hours, as in a reformatory, and by suffering the same suspicion. Wine, available in no city restaurants, can be obtained in the hotel, but only by registered guests who are willing to be regarded as depraved. And the day is as rule-ridden as a boarding school. Coffee is not served at night, but only tea, and the other way around at noon. And unless a special placard is attached to one's door, one is inundated at daybreak with a clattering service of compulsory tea.

Fly to Sydney. Sunset in blue, red, and black layers like a flag, then a precipice of cold light. When the pilot asks how we feel, I.S. (tight) says, "Rather like a planet."

AUSTRALIA

November 21. Press conference. I.S. says he is struggling with his global body image. "I feel upside down and 'way down there.' We have a spiritual geography, too, and in it, a Great Barrier Reef of the soul." Someone asks whether he has had "any ideas" since his arrival in Australia. "Sir, I have 'ideas,' as you say, all my life, and neither more nor less in Australia than anywhere else."

Dinner—Australian oysters, the best in the world—at Lady Lloyd-Jones's, an 1840 plantation house with gardens and gazebos. Lady L.-J. is high-spirited—in fact, far less tame than her lions, who are, in this case, not only I.S. but also Patrick White, a rugged figure with a craggy jaw and a hard stare. White laments "the unofficial censorship in Australia, the provincialism that patronizes second-rate imports above first-rate locals, the intellectual deprivations" of life in the antipodes, but he prefers to talk about ballet, books, the music of Mahler. *When* he talks, that is, for he is a silent temperament—the only non-buoyant Australian so far—and a lonely and gawky writer who has probably groaned inside all evening. He promises to attend our concert, which is to take place, we have discovered at today's rehearsal, in a vast Victorian cavern with an opulent echo.

November 22. Reminders of Empire: the statue to Captain Cook, the Victorian brownstone, the names like Hotel Castlereagh, the zoning by trades—Macquarie Street is a surgeon's row like Harley Street. But England disappears with the first below-the-surface scratch. The physiognomy of Sydney is not graceless, and it is not without good architecture—as well as amusing: the tiny cottages with tall steeples, and the pretty polychrome houses with valentine-lace ironwork. The most attractive buildings, those with broad verandahs and white columns, are the work of Francis Greenway, the convict architect whom the free settlers continued to ostracize even after he had built the best of their city.

The Taronga Zoo. The Malayan otters have Edwardian whiskers and kind faces, and they squeal like pinched schoolgirls. Kangaroos and wallabies look less happy, at least in the mass. They limp like cripples and their stockades suggest hospital wards in which the patients are all busy picking each other's fleas. Koalas are marsupials, too, but nocturnal, and when a keeper plucks one from the bole of a tree and plumps it in my arms, it turns sleepily from the light. "Cute," says I.S., but V. thinks that "by adding a cigar it would pass for a banker." As we pass the nearby gorilla cage, the yellow-eyed tenant flings a handful of sawdust at us.

Birds, gorgeous and noisy. Except the kiwi, which is apteryx and, apparently, suffers from agoraphobia—it seldom leaves its hut as if, aware that extinction is near, it wished to hurry the process. Red-headed lorikeets, red-eyed manucodes, gaudy macaws, cassowaries, "satin birds" who fill their nests with bits of anything blue. Birds of Paradise, some with opal eyes and scissortails five times the length of the chassis, some black velvet, with even longer antennae. (I.S.: "Their lovers must be very jaded.") The kookaburras have hearty, knowing laughs, and recessive lower mandibles; they look and sound terribly complacent.

November 25. Melbourne, a city of stately trees—silver-green eucalyptus, willows, casuarinas. It is more Victorian than Sydney, though, and less colorful even when, as now, decked for Christmas.

To Sherbrook Forest, hoping to see a lyrebird—without success, but we do hear a tinkly bell-bird. Smells of gum-leaf and moss. A grove of charred trunks, and a forest of ferns like an illustration from Humboldt. Each tree is an individual, V. says, but the deeper we wander among the tall eucalyptus the more we feel the absence of individuality and the loneliness of Australia, the silence of the wilderness measured by the cry of a bird.

TAHITI

November 29. Melbourne to Tahiti. Noumea, three hours from Sydney. A white bracelet of coral, an emerald lagoon, hills striped like tigers, a runway scratched in the livid earth like a vaccination. Dry heat and sun sap. And dusky faces, giggling boys to whom I say *"Bonjour"*—this causes sustained hilarity; black-skinned Dominicans in white skirts, rope belts, fedoras; French marines with red pompon berets; *"flics"* in khaki and kepis; women with slit Chinese skirts and faces like statues at Angkor.

Nandi. Rice terraces and watery valleys. A native in a white apron charges through the plane gaily spraying DDT in our faces. The terminal is air-conditioned even on the half-open outside ramps, and its numerous showers are equipped with electric dryers. The sponge-haired Fijians in white skirts serrated at the hem like saws, are gentle and well mannered. We buy batik from them, and sit at tables strewn with purple hibiscus, sipping pineapple juice. I.S. thinks Rousseau was right, if by natural people he could have meant the Sulus.

November 29 (*sic*: we have crossed the International Date Line). 2 AM. Tahiti. The tarmac is lighted by naked flame torches in iron sconces. We turn at the end of the narrow crushed-coral dike, our wings wobbling like the balancing bar of a man on a tightrope. Reception by Tahitian belles in blue sarongs. Suffocating redolence of gardenia leis. An elderly

United States tourist to one of the *taïtiennes*: "Say, young woman, what's that flower in your hair?" "Tahiti flower." "Oh, I see."

The Hotel Tahiti, a cluster of thatched bamboo cottages on the lagoon edge. Inside, a perpetual light wind, like the sound of rain. Other, less romantic, noises: the "chirp, chirp" of lizards and the scuttle of small, unidentified (rodent?) feet.

A rooster debate at 4 AM. Unable to sleep, I go for a walk in the soft silver morning, watching the spray of waves on the outer coral crown. Across the open sea is cloud-crested Moorea, newborn and lovely in the now amethyst dawn.

To the girl who brings breakfast I say *"Maruru"* ("Thank you," my entire vocabulary) and then show that the washbasin faucets produce no water, but only a kind of orange pekoe tea, leaves and all. She giggles and explains in verbless but gesture-full *tutoyer* French that this is because of the rains. She looks around the room and asks if I am alone, and when I admit that this, regrettably, is the case, she disappears for a moment and returns with six other giggling girls who employ the pretext of examining the faucets, but show that the *de facto* object of curiosity is me. They wear flower-patterned gingham sarongs and gardenias over their left ears. All have long hair, braided or loose, and all are barefoot. Gauguin was a good observer of *taïtienne* toes, of the large flat feet, the thick calves, the shapes of heads and of eyes, but the admixture of Chinese has made these girls much more beautiful than any *jeune fille* in Gauguin.

Papeete. A cozy harbor full of yachts, ketches, small steamers. Wooden French colonial buildings with colonnades and open balconies peeling white paint. Chinese shops, with girls leaning over sewing machines and advertisements in ideograms. Bicycles and motor scooters driven by women in sarongs trailing long hair. Buses with benches along the sides and open at the rear, to admit large domestic animals. French officials and French priests on the sidewalks mixed with Polynesians of a thousand complexions. We swim at Fautaua (pronounce five syllables), a cove of sable sand.

Night. The hotel terrace. Orange flares of fishing canoes far
at sea. I sit with two hostesses, one a pure Tahitian, she says,
the other a quarter-cast, both pretty, and we communicate
in barroom French—the girls' English is limited to the names
of the less complicated drinks. At midnight some American
businessmen arrive—neither of my companions has the vaguest
idea where America is, or Europe—and try to dance the twist.
They wear flower-patterned shirts and gardenia crowns, awry
like Bacchus' girdle of grapes and from the same cause. In a
few minutes the superannuated American adolescents have
paired off with the mature child *taïtiennes*. The whole island
is a ready and willing vulva.

November 30. At 3 AM, a marital squabble in the other half of
my hut—the dividing wall is a thin, resonant tympanum. The
husband: "So you think I married you for your money?" (Next
morning we see that that, indeed, must have been the case,
but what can have been her reason?) Switching on the bed
light, I am aware of a hairy object on the floor by my slippers,
and reaching for my spectacles I see that it is a spider the size
of my hand. (Do I actually scream?—I wonder, later, but no, a
totally paralyzed person could not do even that.) Then the
monster flies under the bed on which I huddle, shivering. Suddenly I remember the bug bomb in the bathroom and overcome my fear long enough to jump from the bed to fetch it—
the jump causing infinite confusion amongst the cockroaches
and lizards night-basking there. I spray the area under the bed,
half-asphyxiating myself, until the spider climbs from behind
it to my night table, where I blow the poison at it like an open
fire hydrant. Retreating groggily to the wall, it dodges me there
like a PT boat in an aerial raid, but finally falls to the floor,
where it lands on its back with a terrible thud. The legs twitch
horribly for a moment, then draw in as, tremblingly, I crush
down (cowardly and cruelly, no doubt) with the spray can.
(In the morning the hotel maids laugh at my pallor as they
sweep out the corpse and its crab-size legs. The spiders are
harmless, they say, but "beware of the centipedes." I resolve,

starting tonight, to spray every surface of the cottage before going to bed, and to sleep sitting up, with my bathrobe over my head and all lights on.)

To the Chilean Consul's at Punavia in the district of Faaa (pronounced in three stutters, like a bleating lamb; the Tahitian alphabet has but thirteen letters), the best beach on the island. The women of Punavia are sitting on the steps of their Napier huts and combing their long hair. A sign near the little church of St. Étienne says that "Paul Gauguin lived here 1896–1901." The Consul, a white-haired hidalgo with gentle brown eyes, fondles the hackles of a parrot and tells us how he loves Tahiti. He is sloppily dressed and unshaven, and embarrassed thereof, but he is lonely, too, and happy to talk to us. His *"vahine"* ("wife"; I.S. thinks the word must be a corruption of "vagina") is a teen-age girl with long braids, long fingers, long, animal laugh. The Consulate is cluttered with idols from Easter Island, and the yard with chickens, pigs, mynah birds, monkeys, cats. We swim in the warm lagoon as far out as the coral reef opposite Moorea.

V., at dinner, talks about the first Christmas she remembers. "I received a newborn black lamb with a blue bow, and ever since then lambs and Christmas trees remind me of each other." I.S. says he cannot remember his first Christmas, but he does remember a reminder of it: "I was a baby sitting naked on the sands of a Baltic beach—how agreeable to feel the hot sand on one's bare behind. My mother gave me a bottle, which I filled with sand and emptied, and refilled and emptied again and again. A pine twig fell beside me and I grasped it and tried to push it into the bottle, but without success. I started to study the twig and I thought how like our Christmas tree it was." I.S. also says that he remembers, as a small child, a schoolmate pointing out a cat to him and saying that the cat was skillful in catching fish. "The word skill impressed me, and I have paid attention to it ever since."

December 1. Tahiti is tandem-shaped. We spend the day touring the larger of the two "wheels." Bald white coconuts lying

on the ground look like skulls. The husks have been gathered
into pyres, and the trees themselves have shiny metal armbands, shields against rats. Other island flora: acacias, with
flamboyant pink flowers; breadfruit trees; mango trees with
purple fruit; yellow hibiscus; red ginger bushes; wurra lilies;
elephants' ears; kapok trees (for pillow stuffing); pandanus
plants with aerial roots and leaves joined like spiders' legs
(which shows what is still on my mind); vines of fragrant va-
nilla beans; chestnut trees: the hard straight chestnut wood is
used for making pirogues.

Every few kilometers is a church, usually Catholic, but oc-
casionally Protestant, Mormon, or Seventh-Day Adventist; the
Catholic churches look as though borrowed *in situ* from French
villages. Another architectural incongruity is the tomb of King
Pomare V. Its red-capped dome looks exactly like a bottle of
Benedictine, intentionally it is said, to memorialize the mon-
arch's favorite fluid and cause of his demise. The only other
buildings of any interest are a modern lazaret—the lepers
sit or stroll on a wide, roofless porch—and the ruins of the
Polynesian temple of Arahurahu, where smiling, toothy, preg-
nant-baby idols stand in a rectangle of volcanic cobblestones
on a hillside facing the sea.

Georges Clouzot, with whom we spend the evening, is fox-
eyed and hirsute. He talks about other film directors, actresses
(Monroe and Bardot), musicians (Xenakis, with whom he is
working), and painters, and says that he believes that Nicolas
de Staël killed himself "because he failed to find the rules and
limits of his art." Driving back to Papeete in his jeep, and in
strong, straight-down rain, we see people without coats or umbrellas slowly walking along in the dark, and one old man is
playing a wet guitar.

MEXICO

December 17. Mexico. Christmas evergreens and neon procla-
mations of "*Feliz Navidad*." The trees in the Alameda are a
sugarplum dream of gold, sapphire, and ruby light, but the
wonder-of-wonders is an electric bird-of-paradise that changes

colors and tail positions three times a minute. The streets around the Alameda are full of hurdy-gurdies and pyramids of balloons, and behind it, somewhere in the outskirts, are ferris wheels of exploding fireworks. "Mexican people have much *revolución, señor*, but they very happy people. You see what I mean?" This is from Vicente, himself very happy to see us again. We drive by a cinema with a waiting line five blocks long. "The people stand many hours, *señor*. Mexicans have much time, *señor*."

December 18. Today is the end of the two-week celebrations of the miraculous appearances at Guadalupe, and all day long columns of pilgrims parade to the shrine from starting places miles away in the center of the city. Each of these processions is led by a band of cornets, violins, and guitars—and sometimes cymbals and tubas—playing gay tunes. Behind the musicians are banners with the Virgin image, carried by boys in black suits, and behind them are the marchers, braided Indian women with babies on their backs and gladioli in their hands.

We stand for a moment at the entrance to the Cathedral, next to a kneeling girl in a white Communion dress which she holds up from the floor as if she means to curtsy; next to a poor Indian family, their lips moving in prayer; next to a ragged Indian boy aged six or seven whose feet are calloused and caked with dirt, and who is clutching a green plastic whistle as though it were his only possession. A busload of United States tourists empties into the Cathedral, where by the side of the dark-skinned Mexicans they look as pale as pernicious anemia. "Hold on to your wallets, everybody," their guide says, as they walk by the ragged boy with the whistle. They seem hardly to breathe for fear of the germs and the superstition.

A glass coffin in one of the chapels contains a brown-frocked saint with skin the color of Parian. The body has been piled with coins and paper money, and the surrounding walls are pinned with letters, photographs, wax flowers, babies' shoes. I.S.

buys candles to place on the altar table, though those already there are melting each other and wilting like cane handles. The Indians kneel after planting their candles and pray with their heads to the floor like Muslims.

December 19. The church of Santiago, on ruined revetments of Tenochtitlán, is white inside with black spandrels now looped and twined with ropes of evergreen. Near the door is a striking statue of the captive Christ in a pure white robe with a golden hem, and to the left of the altar an embalmed saint looking like a lump of marzipan.

To the Plaza de Garibaldi to hear the *mariachis*, Vicente helping to corral the band from nearby bars. They wear black velvet jackets and wide-brimmed sombreros tilted forward. (I.S.: "The Mexicans are the only men who know how to wear hats. Even Carlos Chávez's derby is just right.") Their instruments are a clarinet, a cornet, and several sizes of guitar, from the tiny *vihuela* to the big bass. The bass guitarist is also the vocal soloist; his mouth is full of gold. The program, three pieces of music for ten pesos, is the *"Corrida de Pancho Villa,"* the *"Corrida de Emiliano Zapata,"* and *"Guadalajara."* While we listen, a one-legged beggar polishes the car.

The pink palace of Porfirio Díaz is not far from the ramshackle house where Zapata lived in 1914—Vicente: "Zapata no fancy man, *señor*. You see what I mean?"—and both edifices are near the Zócalo. "Seventy Aztec temples stood here, *señor*. I never know how they move so many stones, but I think they must have very strong religion."

December 21. To Toluca, on a steep route with *"curva peligrosa"* warnings most of the way. The slopes are thickly pine-wooded as they were when Mme. Calderón de la Barca made the trip, though they were hiding places for bandits then. The Nevado de Toluca has a brow of black clouds.

The Plaza is a park of ahuehuete trees. Vicente's explanation of this name claims that the Spaniards were unable to pronounce *"ahua"*—which means, of course, that the Mexicans couldn't pronounce "*agua*"; we "see what *he* means" when he points to a group of new buildings and says that they are part of a "housing pro*y*ect." The sidewalks around the Plaza are spread with ceramics, blankets, baskets, Christmas *juguetes* (toys).

Many of the Indian women in Toluca market are barefoot and purple with cold, and the older they are, the more they seem to carry; one poor crone is bent double with a bale of moss that would balk a mule. They sell *churros* (chocolate cake coiled like a rope), hot pigs' knuckles, plucked Christmas turkeys, piles of dried *frijoles*, purple peppers, *pescado frito*. The richer female peddlers wear bright blue wool stockings, matching blue ponchos, straw hats, ladder-like racks strapped to their backs. The men wear cheverel leggings and carry nothing, but they knit as they walk.

According to Vicente, Toluca is still Aztec, and the mountain people still believe in Tlaloc, Huitzilopochtli, Quetzalcóatl. He says the Spaniards called it the *ciudad de los tigres* because the Indian braves wore the heads and skins of wildcats. Toluca, which reminds us of the Andes, is a cold, harsh, indelible place with an uninterrupted ancient life.

On the return ride, Vicente discourses on bullfighting. "The bull he no cry, *señor*, because he is real man. And the bull he is only one in *corrida* who doesn't want fight, *señor*. The crowd want fight and the *matador*. Then why all the people cry so loud when the *matador* is caught, *señor*, but they no cry when bull caught?"

1962

UNITED STATES

January 16. Washington, D.C. Visit from St.-John Perse. He says that his Nobel speech provoked young Swedish physicists to ask if he thought a scientific explanation could be found for the *germination poétique.* "They said they were tired of hearing about the opium of the irrational. I told them to substitute 'experimental' for 'opium'—the experimental irrational—and said that poetry can only begin there, which is to say in the inconsequence of the absurd. The application, in the logic of the word, can be scientized, of course, though I have not tried to do it myself, or anything more than develop my intellectual *maîtrise."* Talking about *"le hazard,"* Perse recalls a conversation with Einstein, who said that "God does not throw dice" and that the idea of a chance universe made him dizzy. I.S. says he simply does not understand chance in art. "One has a nose. The nose scents and it chooses. The artist is like a pig snouting truffles."

Perse criticizes the "canalization into logic," of all philosophy, by English and American "university philosophers," and he defends Heidegger's theory of the beginnings of poetry with quotes from him on Hölderlin and Trakl. I.S. contends that the university today "is really only a department store, because art itself is no longer allowed to be the teacher, and the emphasis is removed to 'the teacher as artist' of 'the art of teaching.'"

Perse's most loving and eloquent words are reserved for Joseph Conrad, "the most perfect aristocrat and the truest friend I have ever known—Claudel and Valéry were close intellectual friends, of course, but hardly more than that." (He declares himself in complete agreement with I.S.'s remarks on Valéry in our book. And he tells a charming story about Valéry. He saw Valéry sitting on a street bench one night head in hands and the picture of despair. After questioning, Valéry finally explained that: "My wife is going to have a baby and that means I shall need money, which means that I shall have to write again, which means the Academy.") "Conrad would never judge a friend morally or intellectually. Friendship was sacred for him. He did *not* love the sea, of course—he lived forty-two miles inland, you know—but man-against-the-sea, and boats, and he never understood me when I talked about the sea itself. (I think he must have disliked my poems, though the only literature that I am certain he positively hated was Dostoievsky.) Conrad once told me about a dinner he had had somewhere in the country with Shaw, Wells, Bennett. When these *savants cyniques* of the literary industry talked about writing as 'action,' poor Conrad, horrified, left the table pretending he had to catch an earlier train. He told me later, in *épouvantable* French, except for one English word I will never forget: 'Writing, for me, is an act of faith. They all made me feel so *dowdy.*'"

Talking about his recent travels in Patagonia and Tierra del Fuego, Perse sounds like a page from *Amers*: "The wind, the ocean, the cold, and the sky and earth empty of the detritus of man." He says that for him, "*La poésie est une façon de vivre, mais je n'ai pas une carrière littéraire et je déteste même à parler de la littérature*. The rationalists invented 'literature' and killed poetry—almost."

Perse says that in 1935 he was sent as a special envoy of the French government to the Kremlin, where "Litvinov translated for me, but adjusted everything I said. Each evening the dinner table was heaped as though for an orgy, and, in fact, a real orgy of toasts did take place, a glass of vodka for each of the commissars present, and a final one for Comrade Stalin. I didn't drink, or, rather, I managed to switch carafes and substitute water, and I noticed that though Stalin appeared to, it did not effect him. I assumed he must have received water too, and I was sure of it when I saw that he ate only goat cheese and fruit. When the commissars eventually discovered me as I poured my vodka into a water glass, and asked me why, I replied that like Comrade Stalin I did not drink. This met with an explosion of silence; apparently Stalin's water-drinking was an open secret. Stalin regarded me severely for a moment, then started to laugh. I had a better opinion of him after that, as I know he did of me. The next day, in the Kremlin museum, I was followed by police. Later I asked Stalin why, and he said: 'I only wanted to know what interested you most.'" Perse cannot hide the fact that he considers the pendulum of Stalin's reputation to have swung a little too far the other way. "He was a man of extraordinary good sense, and I refuse to believe the stories about him as a table-tapping mystic. He was also not vain, and he was never an actor."

Perse recalls that he first began to know I.S. well in 1921, when they were together at the Bassianos' in Versailles and I.S. was preparing the three piano excerpts from *Petroushka*. He says that at the premiere of *Le Sacre* he saw men swinging their canes at each other, and opening and shutting umbrellas. "I was with Debussy before and after that performance, and I remember how excited he was by the music at first and then how he changed when he understood that with it you had taken the attention of the new generation away from him. He felt abandoned, and he began to criticize it."

Perse also remembers I.S. in Boston in 1939, "registering in a very proper hotel and asking the clerk in slow, loud, and abominable English, 'May . . . I . . . bring . . . with . . . me . . . a . . . female . . . companion?' Some adoring old-maid disciples of yours overheard and were stupefied with embarrassment."

In profile Perse resembles E. M. Forster, but full face he suggests a neat and terribly sane Poe. Broad-shouldered, ramrod, and dapper—in a striped suit, vest, bow tie—he is a head taller than I.S., and the heads of the two, side by side, are absurdly disproportionate. I.S., later: "He has one of those brows, dear to phrenologists, that contribute to the inferiority feelings of low-lobed simian types like myself. Don't you think Marino Marini saw me as, simply, *apteros anthropos?*"

I.S. asks Perse's advice about what to say when he receives the Secretary of State's medal this afternoon. "I want to be *méchant*. I do not want to be decorated, like a general." Perse, the professional diplomat: "But courtesy is the nastiest thing of all."

January 18. Dinner at the White House. A presidential limousine calls for us at eight o'clock, and our arrival is timed through the driver's two-way radio. Light snow on the White House lawn. The trees, covered with ice, look like chandeliers. At the door a battery of television floodlights and cameramen like a football team ready to tackle. The President and Mrs. Kennedy step outside to welcome the I.S.'s. Both are taller than we expect, and she is more slender and he more Palm Beach-color. He greets us in a public-speech voice, and she in a dulcet, Marilyn Monroe pant. Photographers push, shout, roll on the ground, like a scene in *La Dolce Vita.* The Kennedys then accompany us through the foyer to an elevator, and from there to an upstairs reception room. Conversation, en route, is about the State Department's medal and the coming performances of *Oedipus Rex.*

Presentation of guests: Leonard Bernstein ("*Cher maître,*" plus a French embrace); Nicolas Nabokov ("*Kak ya rad,*" and a Russian hug); Goddard Lieberson; Max Freedman; Marshall Field; Arthur Schlesinger; Pierre Salinger; the wives of these people; Lee Radziwill; Helen Chavchavadze. The women sit on sofas by the fireplace and the men stand in a circle around the President. Large cocktails too rapidly drained, and caviar. Makeshift and self-conscious conversation with furtive faces of old friends who are betraying insecurity, I think, by coming to talk to me. Unable not to look two steps away to the young

President of the United States. Even less able not to look at
"Jackie." Her light gray eyes—not dark brown as photographed
—are prettier in person, and the thin, haggard look female
America imitates is imaginary. Afterward I remember nothing about the room, but on the corridor wall facing the door
is the portrait of an Indian of the Western Plains, the sight of
which gives me a sudden patriotic shiver.

To the State Dining Room, V. with the President on the
staircase and I.S. with "Jackie" in the elevator. (I accompany
N.N., who is now relaxed and therefore droll and unprintable
about the portraits of Taft and Harding on the walls.) Ushers
help us to our places, the President in the center and V. on
his right; "Jackie" opposite, with I.S. on her right. (I am buffer
between Mr. Salinger and Mrs. Schlesinger, and I talk books
with the latter, which is a relief, as I am politically up-to-date
only on the Australian election.) Near the end of the meal
(*sole mousse, gigot, brie, strawberry soufflé*), on the third
round of champagne, the President toasts I.S. All stand except
"Jackie," who at two shaky moments in her spouse's speech
allows twinges of anxiety to show in her pretty eyes. "We have
been honored to have had two great artists"—I am wonder-
ing if I.S. realizes that Casals is meant by the other—"here
with us in the last months. As a student in Paris, my wife wrote
an essay on Baudelaire, Oscar Wilde, and Diaghilev." (I.S.
later: "I was afraid he was about to say his wife had made a
study of homosexuality.") "I understand that you, Mr. Stravinsky, were a friend of Diaghilev. And I was told that rocks
and tomatoes were thrown at you in your youth." The President's speech is based on V.'s briefing during dinner, and the
story of the *Sacre* premiere amazed him and even made him
laugh aloud. Rocks and tomatoes, I explain later—I.S. has understood the phrase literally—is an American interpretation;
they are thrown at baseball umpires. But the speech is short
and—because an American President is honoring a great *creative* artist, and that is so absolutely unheard of in American
history—it is moving. As I.S. thanks him, the anxiety passes
from "Jackie's" eyes to V.'s.

While we gather at one end of the table, the women retire
to the Red Room. I.S. tries to follow V.—he is so terribly de-
pendent upon the rapidly translated hints with which she puts
him on the right track for what he fails to hear—but N.N.
gently leads him back and seats him on the President's right.
Cognac and cigars appear, and an intrusion of boyish phrases,
including an Anglo-Saxon tetragram in the President's talk,
demonstrating manifest masculinity. The President: "How do
you feel now, Mr. Stravinsky?" I.S.: "Quite drunk, thank you,
Mr. President." Marshall Field asks I.S. a question about
Prokofiev and the USSR, but I.S. does not understand. Leonard Bernstein tactfully tries to cover this by describing the reception of I.S.'s music in Russia. "I saw tears in people's eyes
and not only for the *Sacre* but for the Piano Concerto, which
is, after all, an astringent piece." (I.S., later, is skeptical about
the shedding of much lachrymal liquid over the Piano Concerto.) Duty done, the conversation turns to politics. The
President shows skill as a debater, and ability to bring an argument to a head. And he drops evidence of reading, for example by calling an article on the Berlin crisis in *Encounter*
"playing to the gallery." He is a close listener whose regard
never wanders from another speaker, though this attention is
also defensive, for he must know that every eye in the room
is trained on him. He is open with his ideas, and he seems to
say exactly what he thinks. "We are essentially a conservative
country. The liberal element is and always has been a small
minority, and by liberal I mean open to new ideas." The discussion turns to the syndicated columnists, and the President's
opinions about them are voiced in fair, unguarded, and un-
minced terms. He even talks about Cuba without apologetics.

The Kennedys accompany us to the door and wait with us
fifteen minutes until a White House car appears. They are
warm, gracious, and totally disarming.

I.S., in the car: "Nice kids."

A scrimmage of news-hens in the hotel lobby. Upstairs, I.S.
to V.: "*Le Président me rappel un jeune homme de football
qui ne peut pas jouer à cause de son mauvais dos.*" But V.,

not listening, is only immensely relieved that I.S. did not try to engage the President in a *tête-à-tête* about having his taxes reduced.

January 19. Lunch at St.-John Perse's with Auden, who is wearing not merely dark, but black, glasses that make him look like a blind beggar. The poets sit side by side, but as neither wants to speak the other's language, Auden comes through on my side during most of the meal. At the beginning, Auden to Perse: "By the way, what is the French for *Hühneraugen?*" As Auden's last poem begins with this word (corns), we wonder if the question is really concerned with French translation or whether Auden wishes to discuss his podiatric problems. V. advises him to try space shoes, in any case. The footwear he has on looks as though it had been lent to him by one of Brueghel's peasants.

Auden is in an aphorism/epigram phase, and he instructs us about the difference in typical a) . . . b) . . . form. "An aphorism must apply to everyone, past and present, but an epigram need apply only to particular cases and to one person. Thus, Wilde on fox hunting, 'The pursuit of the uneatable by the unspeakable' is an epigram because only certain people at a certain time would understand, whereas his 'A cynic is a person who knows the price of everything and the value of nothing' is universally comprehensible and therefore an aphorism." French examples are cited first, probably in deference to Perse, but he assures us flatly that the Marquis of Halifax's are better than La Rochefoucauld's, and that Flaubert is only "a provincial manufacturer" of them. Auden's favorite among the French is Proust's "In matters of love it is easier to overcome a deep feeling than to renounce a habit." He asks I.S. for Russian aphorisms, and is told to look in Turgenev and Herzen. Auden: "I got rather frightened of the Russians after the first sentence of *Anna Karenina* which, obviously, should be the other way around. Now, if you are going to do aphorisms surely the first thing is to get them right." He quotes a string of examples from Karl Kraus whom he calls "one of the great people of the century." (Auden, who should soon be at the crest of his Teutonic period, quotes his cablegram to Graves for the inaugural lecture at Oxford last fall, and, naturally, it is in German.) I tell Auden the only Kraus I know, which is how, in 1919, Kraus proposed to change the national anthem from "God Save the King" to "Thank God for Saving Us from the King," but as this contributes nothing to the quotient of aphorisms, Auden only frowns.

Opera talk. Auden: *"Die Frau ohne Schatten* is Hofmannsthal's best, but the ending is pure M-G-M." Then, perhaps to nettle Perse, who could hardly care less: "None of the classical French tragedies can be made into libretti." And, "Karajan has an unusual devotion to darkness. I saw his *Ring* the other day; or, rather, I didn't see it, as it all took place in a blackout, as though we were an audience of owls, and Brünnhilde singing about *'Die Sonne'* the whole time. And not much of the *Ring*, at that, as the stagehands struck after *Die Walküre*."

I.S. talking about *The Flood* says he is puzzled about how to visualize the Devil. "I thought at first that we could photograph a mobile red spot." And, for the flood itself, "I do not want movement back and forth, or waves, or anything large and tumultuous. I have an idea for a single piece of wood bobbing and turning this way and that and always in the same place. Incidentally, I was impressed, not long ago, by an underwater film of the Red Sea. The fish came right up to the bathyscaphe. They were exceedingly confident monsters."

Auden says that a certain book is "the best queer novel this year," and its author is "as ambidextrous as a polyp. He uses his wife more as a shield than as a resource." Apropos of something or other in this conversation, Perse remarks that *"La justice est une invention Suisse."* Auden doesn't hear this, but he jolts to attention when we laugh, afraid that he may have missed a new aphorism (or was it an epigram?). He leaves saying he is on his way to hear a Mass for the Africans. "Heaven knows they need it, poor things. The world has had enough of Uncle Tshombe's Cabin."

FRANCE

May 15. Paris. Isaiah Berlin to discuss "Abraham and Isaac" with I.S. He has a habit of concluding his sentences with an upset belied by the string of preceding adjectives. Thus, X. is "intelligent, charming, capable, and a complete crook." Isaiah claims that his favorite piece of English music is "*On Hearing the First Cuckold of Spring*," and, talking about the group of American composers—Piston, Schuman, Barber, etc.—he says that their pieces are "like *New Yorker* short stories: you don't actually have to read them." He describes a meeting with a Neapolitan impresario to parley a proposed visit to Israel by the San Carlo Opera. "The Israelis wanted to omit the 'San' and have the company appear as the 'Carlo Opera,' to which the Neapolitan replied 'and I suppose you want us to play *La clemenza di Tito*?'" Isaiah says that he was strolling with Auden one afternoon when they were startled by a thunderclap, at which Auden remarked, "Oh dear, the headmaster must be angry."

May 16. Samuel Beckett for lunch. A tall, thin man with the manners and modesty of an oblate. A wrinkled and aggrieved face, a furrowed forehead, long fingers, much silver to be mined in the teeth. Startling blue deep-set eyes which, together with the way his hair stands up, suggest a bluejay, except that he is so shy, gentle, and softspoken—in a light, musical voice. He has motored in from his country house in what he calls his "sardine can." From his description, we are surprised not to find the tires wrapped in rags. He talks about W. B. Yeats, whom he met in Dublin for the first time in 1934. "W.B. never gave the impression that he had any sense of humor, but that was far from the case." But he says he knew Jack Yeats better than W.B. "The father always considered Jack the more gifted son. I don't agree, do you?" V. tells him that in her opinion "critics should be ignored." Beckett: "Yes, but some of them live such a long time." Beckett considers the possibility of notating the tempo of performance in a play, and of timing the pauses in a work like *Godot*. I.S. likes the idea of such controls, of course, but Beckett thinks circumstances are too different. Beckett's best remark is: "The OAS is beginning to sound like Péguy."

An exhibition at the Grand Palais, Ancient Art of the Tchad. Figurines of cows, porcupines, hippos, crocodiles. Many cow masks, and bolas with stone weights shaped like hand grenades. Labrets made of shell and bone are among the commonest artifacts, and the statuettes of dancers and other sanctuary idols from the necropolis of Butte de Medigué all have distended lips.

AFRICA

May 17. Brazzaville. 6 AM. A salmon sky streaked with violet and mother-of-pearl. Plumes of mist above the swirling river. We tilt to the runway over tin roofs surrounded by green the color of frozen peas. Sodden heat even at this hour, and our glasses smear with moisture, but I.S.'s reluctance to step aground pretends to another cause—in fact, a presentiment that "the natives may be anthropophagous."

The restaurant walls groan with the heads of big game. Breakfast—inedible to me because of the smell of palm oil—is served by French-speaking natives in billowing black knickerbockers, like the women's trousers in a Turkish harem. Some of the Congolese selling souvenirs at the entrances to the airfield have almost no clothes, some are in European dress, some are wrapped in blankets, some wear skullcaps and ankle-length robes with blue or green stripes. Most are surprisingly short in stature.

Léopoldville, from the air, is a mixture of thatched huts and Le Corbusier, and the whole Congo basin is covered with a film of blue smoke. We cross the Zambesi, a loop of bronze foil, not far east of Victoria Falls. Thereafter, the red Rhodesian deserts are marked only by jebels—monument-like formations of black boulders—a few lonely trees, and a dirt track on which a car raises a dust cloud a mile high. In Salisbury terminal, the waiters wear stovepipe tarbooshes, long white robes, shoulder-to-waist sword sashes, cummerbunds. I.S. thinks they look like colonels of Toussaint l'Ouverture.

Near Johannesburg the now khaki-colored desert is broken by tracts of erosion-control trees, and the sky is full of slowly dissipating funnels of smoke. The slag heaps of the gold mines, gray, white, yellow mounds, are like giant cake molds or Chichén Itzás.

May 19. Johannesburg is a bilingual city, like Brussels or Montreal. And a new city. I.S.: "How depressing to discover that I am older than it is by a decade." And predominantly "white." Room service in the hotel, as well as higher types of domestic service, is by East Indians, whereas lift boys, porters, and menial workers generally, are Bantus. V. asks our "white" Afrikaans chauffeur if the churches are segregated, and his "Yes" sounds as though the fact should make everybody happy, but he does not know what to make of her "And is heaven segregated too?" The Bantu live in special districts, as do—and apart from them—the "coloreds"—Muslims, half-castes, or anyone neither "white"—Chinese and Japanese are legally "white"—nor Bantu. But the character of the city derives from the customs and occupations of the Bantu; or the attraction, anyway, as one watches them pulling rickshas, carrying head bundles (the women), simply squatting on the curb, or huddling by gutter fires late at night—nights are cool in this altitude.

Johannesburg is a refugee city, too, and all European and many other countries are represented in the orchestra. A cellist, Budapest-born, tells us he was a prisoner of the Japanese in Indonesia, and that he came to South Africa after the war "because of its opportunities." A Yugoslav woman describes how she and her mother and daughter abandoned their automobile on a highway near the border and fled through the woods to Austrian asylum. A young violinist from Amsterdam says that she survived the German occupation there by living like Anne Frank. Our Italian headwaiter tells us that he was interned in Ethiopia; he speaks Gheez. The husband of our elderly German room maid was an archaeologist in Tanganyika until the war, when the British removed them to a camp in Rhodesia, where the husband died. South Africa welcomes these people because they are "white," and as they forget, and want to forget, few of them recognize or protest here the very evils they have suffered from, abroad.

The orchestra and chorus are "white." This leads I.S. to ask whether both ensembles might be improved if the personnel were not restricted to the ruling minority group. "For example," he tells an Afrikaans musician, "can't you imagine that in this vast country some 'non-white' might eventually learn to play the bass drum better than the 'white' now in charge of that instrument in the orchestra? Or, if that seems improbable, you will certainly agree that many 'non-whites' must be blessed with voices that could improve or at least swell the chorus." But the musician replies that the "non-whites" have their own chorus and it is much better than the "white" one. I.S. answers this lamely—it is a segregationalist argument of another kind—by saying that he should have the "non-white" chorus in that case, as his goal is to perform the music in the best possible way. But "best possible" means "regardless of color" and is not a logical argument to the Afrikaans, for whom no parity exists between logic and racialism.

The Dutch-descended Afrikaans "whites" are courteous and hospitable in the way imputed to "Southern gentlemen" in the United States. They anticipate criticism of apartheid, of course, and conversation is always straying guiltily toward it. Their argument is that they have developed the country and achieved the highest living standards, for all the people, in Africa, and they are now being asked to grant a vote that would reduce themselves to a powerless minority and force them to abandon all they have labored so hard to build. They claim to be as much the victims of the colonialist inheritance as the "non-whites," though world publicity has never dared to state that side of the case, and they contend that the "non-white" population is incomparably better off now than a decade ago—which must be true, materially, however incomplete the argument. The "non-whites" do not want integration, they say, less convincingly, and apartheid is a "tradition" as old as European South Africa—in fact, the basis of the culture. We are also told that the "non-whites" are not ready for equality, though no one ever says whose fault it is that after all this time that should be the case. These are familiar arguments in the southern United States, of course, and for this reason American criticism is regarded as hypocritical: "In the United States, integration exists only on statute books. From the White House down, American Negroes are a servant class and a zoned people." To this I can only reply that we are at least trying. And, well, a faint cheer for those statute books.

May 20. Drive to the Western Areas Gold Mine to see tribal dances, passing Diepkloof (of *Cry, the Beloved Country*) on the way, and Carletonville, a mining city of fifty thousand inhabitants that was an empty plateau a few years ago. The road follows the great "reef of auriferous conglomerates," and the country is humped and pyramided all the way by gray, beige, white, and—because of the cyanide used in placer processing —green-blue slag heaps. It is also marked by power stations and hoist towers, corset-shaped cones from which shafts are sunk to below sea level, or a depth of 6000 or 7000 feet.

Bantu loll on the roadside selling watermelons and oranges, prop themselves against trees, amble along the highway two or three together and often accompanied by a musician who encourages them to shuffling dance movements. We stop by one of these groups to look at the instrument, a kind of two-string tabor with a flattened petrol can as a sounding box and a piece of railing as a backboard. The men shade their heads with color-striped parasols, but women's heads are protected only by heavy bundles. We reduce our speed near the mines, a precaution for newly arrived tribesmen who are said to be so unaccustomed to automobiles they may actually run out in front of them like headlight-blinded animals.

The dances are held in the compound of "Blyvooruitzicht" (Bly-*voraussicht*, of Happy Prospects), which sounds like an Orwell-inspired name, as the workers must live like paid prisoners; that is what they look like, in any case, holding out their mess tins to receive a dollop of gruel. The miners work a term of six months, then return, highly prosperous it is said, to their villages. They are tribesmen from the Rhodesias, Mozambique, and Bechuanaland, as well as from the Union and the Swaziland and Basutoland protectorates. The dance arena is bounded by a circular grandstand now filled, principally, with Basutos and "blanket people"—men in blue-violet karosses and tightly wrapped pink or khaki blankets. The Basutos are distinguished by straw hats with pagoda-like knobs on top, and some of them wear European trousers, artfully patched—not necessarily because worn or frayed, but because the owner likes the pattern. Ears, ankles, and upper arms are usually adorned with metal rings, but never two people in the same way. Indeed, no crowd of this size in Europe or America manifests so much individuality, and the dancers' costumes, improvised from contents of dustbins, display far more wit than the *créations* of our most expensive couturiers. The participation of the audience is also non-conformist. The man in front of me sways to the sound of his own Jew's-harp without a regard for the performance. Others laugh or heckle, but never in the mass, and spectators come and go in a steady stream. From time to time the wind raises scarves of dust and sickish, ammoniac smells of perspiration.

Each dance circles the arena, and at about the halfway point the next team, already noisily revving up outside, like the next bronco in a rodeo, starts to agitate for its turn. And each begins in the same way, with a rally of singing and hand-clapping. When these preliminaries become too protracted, and they always do, the leader hectors the company with a whistle. The leader is assisted by uniformed policemen, who cannot resist dancing along and otherwise getting into the act themselves, to the considerable delight of the audience. The music is not intended as a concert for the grandstand, but is directed exclusively to the dancers, and the guitars and concertinas are inaudible to us, though not the clapping and stomping, which precipitates a dust storm, or the Swazi drumming, which inspires feats of rolling, leaping, kicking, high-jumping. The instruments, like the dancers' costumes, have been put together from crude and improbable materials. The subtlest music comes from an orchestra of reed flutes in which each player contributes a single note, like carillons or Webern. And the loudest is a charivari of jingles, rattles, and bells attached to automobile inner tubes wrapped around the dancers' legs. This is to accompany a Xosa ritual in which the dancers shimmy, shiver, squat, crouch, and fling their arms up like the praying mantis. One solo performer wears a miner's aluminum helmet, a dozen neckties strung from his belt, and a flossy mophead tied to each knee. The entire garb of another, a would-be comedian, is a grass skirt and a large comb stuck like a cockade in his stubble hair, but the catcalls he receives drown the laughter. The audience is much more amused by the antics of a great muscular creature in a green beret and a woman's fur boa.

The last dance, by the Machupi tribe from the Limpopo River, is the most spectacular, and so is the dress: white skirts and ankle feathers; purple, blue, black, and green tail feathers; deerskin headgear and shield-covers. The dancers fling their hatchets to the ground at the climax of this very dangerous-looking ballet, and in spite of assurances from the manager of the mine that "it is not a war dance," the gesture can only have intended the extinction of the receiving party. This time the musicians, who wear winglike ostrich feathers, are separated from the dancers, one supposes for safety's sake. They play ratchets and a battery of marimbas made of scrap-metal slats placed on a trestle of empty barrels. The melody is repeated over and over, in *crescendo*, and simultaneously in several ranges, the larger barrels in augmentation with the smaller ones.

It stops after a tremendous gust of sound, as though truncated by an invisible force, and the dancers plunge their hatchets into the earth in blood-freezing silence, hurling their shields to the ground afterward and savagely somersaulting over them.

May 22. Johannesburg. Letter from a woman in Durban who knew I.S. in the Hôtel des Crêtes, Clarens, in 1913, but wants to be sure he is "the same Russian composer who used to pound the piano there all day long."

May 26. The Ndebeli (Mapok) kraal. An olive and yellow landscape stretching to a pink horizon. Near the kraal gate is a monument to the pioneers who "broke the Zulu nation." It reminds us of similar piles of stone in the American west commemorating victories over the Indians. Inside the kraal grounds, the Bantu men we see raise their hats and wave their knobbed clubs in greeting. They are accompanied by dogs and by long-tailed Persian sheep. The land is desiccated and the kraal streams are all dry. They have names like "Sand River" or, more hopefully, "Fountain" this or "Fountain" that.

The kraal huts stand behind a long white wall on which are painted gay purple, green, and orange windows, shutters, doors, diamonds and squares, of which no line is exactly straight, and of which the symmetry is quite drunk. A broad trough cuppers the wall below these brilliant designs. It is used as a sun deck by the Ndebeli women, who sit there in their heavy raiment like queens in their courts. The Ndebelis are an Amazonian society, and the power of continuing the culture is believed to reside exclusively with the female. Wives are purchased with Biblical numbers of cattle and their husbands are sunk in mortgages and denied use of the product until it is paid for in full.

After marriage, the female remains in command—though that, after all, is not so unusual—and she may determine such questions as whether her spouse shall share the hut or sleep outside. The women are shackled in piles of brass bracelets, however, the weight of which should be leash enough to keep them from straying very far. They also wear tubes of woven grass encased in beads around their necks, and these, too, are welded on, and permanent. And they wear colored blankets and beaded aprons; even the baby of the sex has a beaded G-string. The male children, by contrast, are naked except for flies, to which nobody pays any heed. (Their mothers whisk them away from their infant sisters. Incidentally, one wonders about the universality of the Oedipus complex after a visit to Amazonia.) The unmarried adolescent girls are naked from their aprons up, proving that from a mammary point of view the human female is in decline, in an exact sense, from about the age of thirteen. Not so their meridional proportions. The millet staple is swilled in such bulk that the stomachs of the adult women are grotesquely distended. The coiffure of the Ndebeli belles consists of four small hedge tufts, like phylacteries, on a skull otherwise smoothly mown and glistening with pomatum of lamb fat.

The interiors of the huts are painted in the same style as the wall. We buy admittance with gifts of snuff to giggling female elders, and with purchases of beaded figurines. The whole kraal is busily beading to fill a Christmas order from Macy's.

May 27. A concert for the Bantu people of Springs, a mining city surrounded by yellow slag piles. The houses of the Bantu are generally tin-roofed shanties, but new communities are also pointed out to us, with regret that the people are "not yet ready to live in such [palatial] dwellings"—the old argument around any housing development in a United States slum. At sunset, thousands of women appear, balancing tins of water on their heads.

The audience enjoys, above all, the demonstrations of instruments preceding the actual concert, especially the percussion, the trombone when it "slides" and the tuba when it imitates gastroenteritis. At the conclusion of the program, the audience sings a dolorous Methodist piece, as if on purpose to remind us of the cultural confusion brought by colonialism. But why should a people with its own rich and varied music greet us with a dismal captors' hymn? (The city Bantu despise their own "Kaffir culture," or so the Afrikaans people say.) But the reasons for the concert are disingenuous, and the effects of it are disturbing. Wasn't the concert primarily for ourselves, a demonstration to make us see that the Bantu really are savages, benighted blacks not yet ready for European culture? And isn't it just possible that the Bantu might resent the concert for the very reason that it has been uniquely for them, in their own compound, a white orchestra and a black audience? Bantu means men, incidentally, and Muntu, man. How were the poor creatures to know when they formed the words that other Bantu existed in the world and that they were "white"?

Night drive to Pretoria. Veldt fires on the north side of the road, a prehistoric tableau.

May 28. Pretoria. The plaza. President Kruger in bronze, glowering on a pedestal. Pillared porches and Dutch-colonial gingerbread. Our hotel, the Union, is Victorian in physique, style of service, cuisine—copious breakfasts and teas. The Bantu room waiter has heard that I am an American, and he is surprised to find that we speak the same language. I set out to explain why quite a few Americans speak English. Then, "Do you know the American Negro orchestra conductor Dean Dixon?" I say I do, and I laud Dixon, adding that I enjoyed playing under him in my student days in New York, but not admitting that Dixon was unable to find a post in the United States. At the end of the conversation he says, "Thank you, massa," which depresses me for the rest of the day.

At night, in the street, we listen to a quartet of Bantu minstrels playing guitars and *flutes à bec.*

May 29. The road to Kruger Park. Bantu boys carrying cala-
bashes and bags of oranges on their heads. Metal-collared
Bantu women carrying baskets and rolled-up sleeping mats on
their heads. Bantu men comfortably asleep on two-wheeled
bullock carts. All Bantu heads are covered and all "white"
men are bareheaded. The Bantu women are as melonous and
protuberant as fertility idols.

Witbank. A coal-and-carbide city, the beginning of the car-
boniferous beds of the eastern Transvaal. The beginning of
Swazi country, too, and of domed Zulu-style huts. Tall native women stand erect and motionless on the roadside, selling
watermelons. Behind them are fields of sunflowers—the seed
oil is a major export—gerberas, yellow wattles, arums, and
aloes.

Belfast, the highest point of the upper veldt. Bird-rimmed
salt lakes. And scrubby black-stemmed proteas, milk-white
eucalyptus, blue gum trees. The anthills, heretofore small
mump-like papilli, are eight or nine feet tall. Machadadorp is
warmer—a city of willows and lime-colored mimosas—and the
tropical climate, in which the natives carry umbrellas and live
in straw and grass tukals, begins soon after. We stop at a pic-
nic site in which garbage disposal is left to scavenger baboons.

We enter the Park by the Numbi gate. A dusty, tortuous,
narrow road, with immediate signs of spoor—tracks and ordure,
munched and trampled bushes. Weird shapes of trees, especially the flat-crowned thorn tree with the wizened trunk, the
wild fig, the ebonies, baobabs, cassias with pendant pods,
white bougainvillaeas, flame of Africa, red-flowered Kaffir
plum trees with hanging finch nests, tall fever trees—so-called
because they are the complexion of a man with yellow fever.
The dry season has begun, and except for riverbanks the Park
is brown. The anthills are parched and porous, too, like stucco
towers by Gaudí.

Suddenly we see a waterbuck in a glade about twenty feet
from the road: violently twitching ears, black horns, a white
circle like a brand on the rump. He watches us over his

shoulder, poised to run, but does not move until we do. We should expect to find two cows, V. says, but the ladies do not appear, and we drive on. This confrontation turns the Park into a spell, and we go forward with clenched nerves.

An impala herd. Brown backs beautifully sheened, beige stomachs, black grill-striped behinds, pinched tails, dainty white feet, black ankles like Russian ladies' fur-lined boots. The antlered leader, in the center of the pack, wiggles his ears and grunts a warning that frightens a young doe and causes it to leap like Pavlova. They travel in safari, like a cavalcade of camels, but group when they graze.

A duiker appears next, picking its way like a hen in a head-first pecking movement. And then a family of koodoo. The koodoo young do not interrupt their feeding on our account, but the mandarin-bearded buck lifts his streamlined horns and watches us distrustfully. Koodoo have large ears, white lip-stick, white forelegs tufted at the knees like the Greek evzone uniform, lightly striped coats, long black flyswatter tails, and white tickbirds riding perkily on their backs.

At Pretorius Kop, the first entrepôt, a pair of West African rhinoceros await release in the Park. They doze under phency-clidine tranquilizers like wet dynamite. At Skurukwan, armed rangers accompany us to the Hippo Pool; a man was killed here by a lion only a year ago, and it is the only place in the Park where visitors are permitted to leave their cars. The hippos are submerged on a shoal near the other shore, but the surface of the river bristles with conning-tower nostrils and eyes. One great otiose brute raises his keel, yawning—a vast, obscene red maw—and snorting—a truck stripping gears—and the whole herd surfaces after him, an ear-cracking detonation. They blow, bellow, gargle, and spout, like any gang of beach bullies. Suddenly a hippo slips out of the foliage on the mud-bank near us, where it has been bolting branches and fouling the river. A young one is sheltering between its rear legs, how-ever, and this sight makes me regret my unkind epithets above.

Back on the road, we see purple-gray wildebeeste, timorous creatures with black eyes or mascara; and a circle of baboons sitting in the road like stumps. The baboons leap to our hood, fenders, and rear window, which makes I.S. feel as though he were "an important politician in a parade." I fetch a candy in the map compartment and pass it through a slit of window. The receiving baboon is in front of the window in an instant, pointing to the map compartment and demanding more. I.S.: "In another year they'll be saying, 'Go home, Yank.'"

It is now animal rush-hour by the river. A sable antelope crosses the road running with end-to-end, rocking-horse action; and a bushbuck lamb, and a steenbok fawn, and a warthog which, seeing us, charges into the woods with his tail up like a flag; and a hyena with a sloped back, like a gargoyle. For the last mile, elephant devastations, droppings and broken branches, have been more and more in evidence, but they do not prepare us for the sight of a huge bull elephant bursting into the road twenty feet ahead. Taller than the woods, and larger than we remember the proboscideans in circuses or zoos, he thrashes about as though greatly agitated, and his ears flap like sails. We fear that a herd may be following him or, if he is a rogue elephant, that he may attack if he feels trapped. Neither contingency develops, however, as he suddenly turns and re-enters the woods, but we hesitate before passing his point of exit. An elephant in the wild is an awesome thing.

Skukuza Kamp, the largest in the Park, billets five hundred people in rondavels, and almost as many more in tented bivouac areas. But the Skukuza dining room décor—animal trophies, witch doctors' mantic objects, Zulu shields and assegais —offers no respite from the Park, and neither does tonight's outdoor film on *African Arachnids*. On our way to bed, a ranger's flashlight discovers hyenas and baboons on our side of the low wire fence beyond the rondavels. They have come to burgle citrus fruit and leather shoes, the ranger says, and they are adept at opening doors of huts and automobiles. Several times during the night, a lion roars only a few feet away.

May 30. 5:30 AM, by the Sabie River, in alleged elephant and lion country, after a breakfast of delicious Skukuza *pirochki*;

the sun rises orange, but turns white in seven minutes. A baboon sits at the first fork in the road, like a traffic cop. Then, other baboons appear, scratching themselves, nursing pink offspring, clamoring for tourists' handouts. The ranger last night implied that this defection from the forest to the welfare state will disturb the natural system of dependencies, but in the abundance of Kruger Park one supposes that the chain must overlap as well as interlock; the impalas, for example, are so plentiful that a lion only has to reach out as they go by, like grabbing a sandwich in a cafeteria.

Suddenly we see two great glistening black elephants nonchalantly consuming a tree a few feet away. They show no concern for us whatever, and they continue to crunch their morning lumber like any American at his crackle-and-pop breakfast food. As we drive away, a monkey jumps from a tree, grasps our radio aerial, and rides along on the fender like a straphanger in a subway. His face is black, his body gray-white, his testicles billiard-chalk blue. His tail, in contrast to the baboon's, which loops cheekily upward like a girl's ponytail, drops down straightaway.

Eight lions block the road ahead, the elders prowling leisurely in our direction, the young ones playfully pummeling each other. They must already have had their *petit déjeuner*, as an antelope has crossed the road only a hundred yards back —one wonders whether the antelope knew that the lions are replete or whether he was simply on the wrong side of the wind? The lions disregard us and give no ground to the car, as if, like Berkeleians, they could deny its existence by refusing to look. The mother pads by my window and only a foot from it, the glare from her cold, yellow eyes crossing my heartbeat like a shadow of ice. We think the lion intends to use the car to cover its scent, but it soon lopes into a thicket, where it yawns as harmlessly as an actor in a summer theater during intermission of a play about Androcles. The young gambol into the bush too, and in a moment they have melted into the landscape. Who would now suspect this patch of undergrowth to be part lion, and who, seeing what we have seen, would trust the appearance of the jungle?

Birds. Glossy starlings; blue-casqued guinea fowl; yellow, waddling hornbills; purple-crested lories; violet troupands. A black bird with a prima donna breast, long flappy wings, and a tail like a ray fish—indeed, of such length that it seems able only to float from tree to tree, like a glider. Red-beaked honey birds and black butcher birds, the latter skillful bird-callers who impale the victims of their dissembling on thorns. A single bird in a tree perches on the topmost limb, usually, like a hat-pin, or on the tip of the farthest extended side limb. Vultures appropriately prefer dead or totally bare trees. A black whirl-pool of vultures is always somewhere in the sky. They go round and round like fathers in a maternity hospital.

Near Lower Sabie, the road opens along an expanse of river and we see a crocodile basking on the far bank. Its jaws are half open—a most depraved grin. A second crocodile climbs to a rock, midstream, and a kingfisher loops over it like a stunt flyer, alights on its dripping back, stands there vainly preening.

The roadside is dense with impala. Now, in the early morning cold, their coats are a frizzy, gooseflesh fur. We come upon two impala rams fighting in a widely scattered circle of ewes. They charge each other like jousting knights, and the ferocity and the noise of their combat destroy forever the sentimental Disney image of the doe in a dingle.

Only a mile from Lower Sabie we discover a leopard, couchant in a copse a few yards from the roadside. It sniffs the air and twitches its whiskers like any house cat, and it is incomparably more feline than the lioness. Birds scream when it begins to walk—a movement of such litheness that the lion is a hobbler in comparison. And, walking, it displays the sleek white throat, the lustrous rosetted back, and the slowly sloping tail with the upsweep at the end—compared to which the lion's is a mere knout. It wants to cross the road to the riverside, apparently, but can find no egress in the rapidly lengthening barricade of tourists' automobiles.

We return to Skukuza on the northern river road, a good one, by repute, on which to encounter zebra and giraffe. And giraffe we soon see, pruning treetops. They are a pure fantasy animal; a unicorn would be less surprising. A little later we discover several of them at the riverbank. They have white earflaps and horns like Michelangelo's *Moses*, and they cross necks like French generals embracing. They are obliged to spread and sprawl in order to reach the water, a posture of such clumsiness that one marvels at the survival of the freak at all. Another, hitherto unnoticed, giraffe is peering at us over the top of a tree, on the other side of the road, like a gardener over a hedge. It ambles away in a long side-to-side movement like roller-skating, the hind leg of each side touching the ground first and then the longer front leg.

Zebras are less trusting. We come upon twenty or thirty of them nervously prancing in a field—I.S.: "Like the exercise yard at San Quentin"—and though they are a considerable distance from us, the mares carefully shield the foals. Every surface is striped, from dewlap to fetlock, whorled nose to Cathedral-of-Siena legs. Koodoo graze nearby, to pool their more powerful auditory radar with the zebra's more acute olfactory sense, an *entente cordiale*, which I.S. says is "an example of what Peer Gynt meant by 'nature is witty.'"

Campfire at Skukuza, with the chief game warden. Polenta and sosatie—haslets, spitted like shashlik. The warden says he is able to keep a close count of elephants in the Park, and a reasonable estimate of the lion population, but all other censuses are unknown, and especially the impala, which must fluctuate radically at lion lunchtime. The warden says that he once saw a crocodile catch an impala at the riverbank. "The croc does not eat the meat fresh, of course, but stores it under a rock until it gets high." He also tells us of the discovery of a cannibals' ossuary in the Limpopo mountain region of the Park. And he reveals fascinating information about such creatures as the edible lizard (the dthub), the fennec, the rhim, the lemur, and the nearly extinct oryx, now being brought to breed in Africa from Arabia. But his most appealing story describes how a baboon in a tree suddenly saw a lion directly below, and fainted. We feel more sympathetic to baboons after hearing that.

May 31. The sunrise, from a lavender sky, matches every shade on the color chart from blood red to white, and turns the river mist into a cataract of gold dust.

Three lions in the road, a "triangle" evidently, with *monsieur* trying to growl away *le gigolo*. A crapulous trio, too, judging by the vultures overhead. Farther on, two more lions, young ones with incipient manes, bound across the road.

A driver coming from the opposite direction tells us that a large herd of elephants can be seen on the far bank of the Sabie around the next bend, but they are almost entirely hidden by reeds and palms, and are visible only through binoculars. Information about animals seen is shared in this manner throughout the Park—"Beyond the bridge about thirty yards to the left we saw an ostrich . . ." and without it we would have missed a great deal.

The road between Mbyamite and the southern gate is the wildest and loneliest of all, and the animals seem doubly alert, perhaps because of the tall, lion-concealing grass. Two saddle-backed jackals, silver chines and red-clay-colored bellies, run zigzag from us, like professional fugitives. The country is weirder and more savage at each turn, and the anthills suggest to I.S., "the chimneys of the subterranean survivors of the next war, or of H. G. Wells's Morlocks."

As we leave the Park, I.S.: "Animals do not have to *do*, they just *are*"—which sounds like the "A nose is" philosophy.

May 31. To Capetown. The pilot, for our benefit, circles Table Mountain, The Twelve Apostles, and the Bay Area, which lights up as we land. A Riviera climate, palms and umbrella pines. White houses with black shutters and brick houses with iron balconies and tin roofs. English rugby fields. Dutch flower stalls. In the marketplace, two-wheeled Bantu handcarts. Political resistance slogans—Freedom's Going—Remember Sharpe-

VILLE—STOP THE VOERSTER NAZI BILL—are as common as roadside advertisements in the United States. We stay in the
Mount Nelson Hotel. It is as lively as a sanatorium.

June 1. Drive to Groot Constantia, the estate of an early Governor whose vineyards established the first wine industry. The
manor house, a white building with looped, Dutch-style gable
ends, is a museum of colonial furniture: teakwood bidets,
stinkwood tub seats, armchairs with fan-shaped splats and
cabriole legs, Delft celadon and other wine vessels, and books
—a volume of voyages dated Venice 1520 and opened to Vasco
da Gama's description of the Cape.

Returning to Capetown, we overtake a column of "non-
white" boys in their early teens. They are, it is later explained
to us, "a kind of Borstal unit for recidivists." Recidivists at fourteen?

Reception in the City Hall, the Mayor with the gold chain
of office around his neck like a *sommelier* in an expensive restaurant. Speeches and *petits-fours*. Someone tells us that the
Mayor is Jewish and that a "Jewish section" exists in Parlia-
ment, as though this were testament of a libertarian government. V. shocks this person by telling him that her own main
interest in South Africa is the crossopterygian—the armored
fish from which the amphibian emerged, twice captured in
South African waters.

At dinner we try more ordinary fish: hake, kinglip, snook,
steambras.

June 3. Drive to Muizenberg, False Bay, Kalk Bay, Chapman's
Peak Drive. Marshes, yellow heath flowers, blue hydrangeas,
pink watsonia, sand dunes—which from the airplane, at night,
we mistook for snow. Below Chapman's Peak, a fog rolls in on
the surface of the sea, like a tidal wave.

June 5. Kimberley. Strip farming, scrub desert, ponds shaped
like boomerangs, gray slag heaps, burning sun. I.S.: "The Kimberley motto 'Largest man-made hole in the world' sounds so
indecent."

ITALY

June 11. Rome. Reminders of Africa. The elephant with the obelisk by the Chiesa di Minerva (is this Milton's "elephants endorsed with towers"?); and, in the Campo dei Fiori, Giordano Bruno's statue, on the site of his burning, has been whitewashed with the protestation: LUMUMBA ASSASSINATO.

We call on Giacomo Manzù, in his Latino Malabranca studio, to see his "Doors of Death" for St. Peter's. Manzù's nose is notched, his forehead is furrowed, and his hair appears to have been transplanted from the crown to the back of the head and neck, where it curls between shirt and ears in classical *maestro* style. His eyes study I.S.'s head professionally throughout the visit.

The studio is built against an ancient alcove of Roman bricks the height of the eight-meter bronze doors, a full-scale skeleton of which stands in front of it with a Death on the Cross blocked out in gold paper on the upper right panel. The new concrete side walls are covered with tapestries, and the only other furnishings are easels and cavalettes with clay casts of sculptured reliefs for the doors.

The upper left panel will contain a Death of the Virgin, and two smaller spaces, below the Virgin and Christ, are to be filled with *natures mortes*. Next below that will be the deaths of Abel, Moses, saints Joseph and Gregory the Great; and, underneath in panels of the same size, deaths by earth, air (in space), water, and violence (war). Manzù says he has an idea to represent violence by the hanging of a partisan, with his mother at his side. These eight central panels are to be executed in low relief, and the *natures mortes*—and six squares at the bottom with animals symbolizing death—in full relief. The animals are a porcupine, a serpent, a tortoise turned on its back, an owl, a crow, and a *guira*. When I confess that I don't know this word, Manzù quickly draws a squirrel.

The only panel completed in bronze is the Death of Gregory. Manzù and a helper carry it outside into the light. An Angel of Death, helmet visor thrust back, points from the sky to the slumped but still-mitered head of the enthroned

Gregory. The long papal cope flows from behind the head to below the body, which it dwarfs, and the line of this robe is the fixing feature of the composition. Rubbing the patina for the true tincture of the bronze, Manzù tells us that he prefers to work directly in bronze in spite of the risk, because only then does he feel the form is completely his. He claims to make but few sketches and few cloth and paper maquettes, whereas he may try as many as ten castings; he shows us a laundry list of trial moldings for the animals of death, and seven or eight scratches follow the name of each animal. He also professes never to make more than a single copy—"Two is already mass production"—and he tells us that he refused the Vatican's request to depict the Resurrection, because "Resurrections are baroque—too baroque for me, in any case—and their drama is diluted. Death is purely dramatic."

The only other opus in the studio is the head of a cabaret girl, a striptease *artiste* with an unforgettable twist of *je m'en fiche*-ism on her lips.

Manzù takes us later to another studio, this one in an industrial outskirt. High walls and hounds guard a yard full of sculpture and a three-room atelier that, because of busts and figures wrapped in canvas hoods, looks like a morgue. The shelves are piled with unfinished figurines, gesso puddings, and a whole hardware store of hammers, hatchets, chisels, picks, pestles, spatulas, saws, drills. A plaster bust of Kokoschka lies in a corner, and the terra-cotta head of a boxer. In the center of the room, two naked ballerinas in bronze stand tautly on their slippered toes tying ribbons in their hair. As we admire them, Manzù pats their behinds—with pride and a little concupiscence.

Manzù's still lifes, chairs with compositions of vegetables and fruits on their seats, are so real that we want to touch them and do, a cold and macabre sensation. But these technical exercises, as Manzù calls them—and he shrugs a bit showing them—bother us in the same way as the sculpture in the Campo Santo at Genoa. Because a *nature morte* in three dimensions and actual proportions is as morbid as Madame Tussaud's? Because a real chair in bronze seems a waste of that substance as well as of sculptural energy?

Manzù: "Unlike the poet and the painter, when they complete their work, I, when I finish mine, must still endure the suspense of the *fusione*." Commenting on this, I.S. quotes Strindberg, to the effect that "the art of the future will, like nature, leave a lot more to chance."

Manzù wants to do I.S.'s head, though he says he cannot just begin to sculpt, but has to study photographs, think for a long time, and "be inspired." I.S.: "For me the necessary angel will appear only when I am already working, but the lady sometimes takes a lot of nudging before her wings begin to flap."

June 14. Piero's *Misericordia* polyptych is now in the Istituto Restauro, accompanied by technically interesting photographs of each stage of its cleaning. In the center panel the Queen of Heaven spreads Her cape above an apse of kneeling worshipers. The cape is an oil emulsion and Her other garments are pure tempera, which may indicate different periods of painting. One of the kneeling figures wears a black hood, as members of Tuscan Misericordia societies still do, and the man on his left, the most arresting face in the group, is, by tradition, a portrait of the artist. The agony of the Sebastian in the left panel, which is more Masaccio than Piero, is not that of the usual disappointed lover, but of a peasant, dumb and brutalized. The marginal surfaces of the wood beneath the area of the paintings are still daubed with Piero's trial color mixes.

Also in the Istituto is an icon from Santa Maria in Trastevere, a *toile* already restored—placed on cedar boards—a millennium ago; the discovery of this early effort at preservation has excited the workmen, who think that it may be one of the oldest icons in existence. The face is in the Fayum tradition, but the picture is full of movement. The Madonna dandles the Infant as though giving Him a first walking lesson, and the pedestal for Her left foot is, or seems to be—this part of the picture gapes with lacunae—the prostrate person of a Pope.

But the most affecting of the to-be-restored treasures is a chipped and candle-blackened *Ecce Homo* signed *"Antonellus Messinius pixit,"* in a painted banner on the frame. The eyes of the young red-haired model are bloodshot, as though with conjunctivitis, and a shadowed rope hangs around his neck. The flesh is flecked with tears of blood and transparent perspiration. The painter must have prided himself on this pearly perspiration.

SOVIET UNION

September 21. Paris–Moscow, in a Soviet TU-104. Vodka and *zakousky*—spratts, herring, caviar—served by hostesses who have not been to charm school and have no camera smiles. Nearing Moscow, we fly low over forests turning yellow, meadows still green, lakes, boat-busy rivers and canals: an unexpectedly rich and tidy landscape to one who has imagined something muddy and sprawling—the Russia I.S. characterizes as a combination of *"caviare et merde."* I.S., straining to see, is excited and open-mouthed, and V. is choked with emotion; fifteen months of uncertainty have come to an end. Aground, we taxi past airplanes from Poland, Bulgaria, and China, unseen in our world. A reception committee pushes to the door, and I.S. emerges, bowing deeply—a gesture out of another era, as his dark glasses are glaringly symbolic of another kind of life (Hollywood, I regret to say). We move toward television lights blinded, like moths.

Familiar faces among those helping us to a waiting room: Tikhon Khrennikov and Kara Karayev. And familiar-by-resemblance: a woman with the slant eyes Picasso saw in I.S., singing to me in a high voice, *"Je suis la nièce de Monsieur Stravinsky."* A short, stout woman whom I mistake for Jacob Epstein, says *"Ich bin Yudina,"* and plants a wet kiss. Someone else hands me a birchbark basket containing moss, a twig, a blade of wheat, an acorn, a leaf, telling me, in English, she is the daughter of the poet Konstantin Balmont; I thank her, though I am not particularly needing any of the contents. Inside the terminal we shake scores of hands and hear "*Dobro pozhalovat*," over and over, from large, round, smiling faces. Most of those present have waited a seesawing year for this moment, and some have hoped or feared a far longer time still; to Yudina, for example, it must fulfill a lifelong dream. That is why the atmosphere is like a child's birthday party, why everyone, and not least the I.S.'s, is bursting with relief. A neat, bright-eyed young woman introduces herself as my interpreter, Alexandra Alexandrovna, and we pack into a limousine.

A divided turnpike, through birch and pine woods. A cold pink sunset with an Edvard Munch feeling. Less than United States, but more than anticipated, traffic—a statement that suddenly makes me aware of my cold-war "conditioning." Moscow lights up as we enter, and V. vainly studies the miles of new apartment buildings on Leningrad Prospekt for landmarks. At the National Hotel, the airport committee, only slightly diminished, awaits us again, but this time their welcoming is sealed in vodka and sweet champagne. The event of Russian musical history, some say, and others tell me privately that they are still rubbing their eyes, never having believed that it would happen. When I.S. reads a telegram from Shostakovitch, national sentiment flows with the national champagne and gets even thicker.

We escape to the restaurant with Xenia Yurievna, the newfound niece. Thirty thousand people have queued for I.S.'s Leningrad concerts, she tells me, and so earnestly that I fear she may have arrived at this tally by her own footwork. Perhaps the restaurant has ambitions as a nightclub—moldy jazz-type noises are coming from a far corner—and that might explain why single men are relegated to a smaller, adjoining room. The waitresses are blond, uncorseted, and unhurrying, and the customers—Indians in saris among them, a party of Italians very happy to find *espresso* on the menu, and Chinese who are the "best dressed" people in the room—seem to have all the time in the world. But except for the portrait of Lenin on the wall and the absence of neckties, the restaurant is not unlike many in non-midtown Manhattan. The Chinese are "conditioned," too, as much as we are, V. says, a conclusion she reaches after watching them cut their food into tiny pieces.

The hotel lobby is the place of embarkation for a pair of dilapidated elevators and a staircase whose caryatids appear to be holding up the second floor. (Nothing appears to be holding the drapery over the caryatids' private parts, however, and for this reason they look as though about to drop the second floor.) At the front desk we receive folders of the "Lenin-Stalin Mausoleum" on which an unsuccessful attempt has been made to cancel the name of Stalin (it is still distinctly legible). At the second-floor desk we receive our room keys from a governess in a white *kokoshnik*, like the nurses in *Petroushka*. Cuspidors are found in the corridors at convenient distances, and tonight, because of the strong smell of fish glue, they could conceivably be required for serious service. The I.S.'s suite, which the Prime Minister of Singapore has vacated minutes before, could be called the Napoleon Room. The ceiling fresco is a "Lancret" (peacock and naked *femme fatale*), the draperies are Empire-style crushed velvet, the furniture includes chairs with fasces-shaped armrests, and the "Sèvres," on a pedestal in the corner, is adorned with imperial gold eagles and a likeness of the Corsican himself. Incongruously non-imperial are the modern five-pronged lamps and the portrait of a heroic dog. From tomorrow, our meals will be served in this medium-sized ballroom, Alexandra says, and waiters and maids come to take dispositions for breakfast (caviar and coffee). These people are as curious to be talking to the I.S.'s —returning "White Russian" celebrities must be rare—as the I.S.'s are to them. We learn that they work and rest in twenty-four-hour shifts, which is probably not ideal for efficiency, but which they claim to prefer. One girl says she is to leave for her vacation in a few days, and she begs V. for a bit of rouge. I walk, before bed, in Red Square. A few trucks, a few pedestrians. The red stars on the Kremlin towers burn like beacons in the crystal night.

September 22. Rehearse the Moscow National Orchestra in glossy Tchaikovsky Hall, a warmly resonant room that is also a portrait gallery of composers. The conductor Ivanov—yellow hair and the face of a good woodsman in a Russian fairy tale —introduces I.S. to the orchestra. They receive him with applause and bow-tapping, but the greeting seems to me a little quiet and cool. I confide this impression to Alexandra, whose answer is that "artists are not glamorized here as they are in America where, for example, Ulanova's *claques* embarrass the Bolshoi Ballet. We have no personality cult here." Not since Stalin, anyway, one wants to say, and to protest that I.S. and Ulanova are not analogous cases. But, in fact, I like this refreshing democratism, and the absence of that detestable protocol, "Sehr geehrter Herr Professor Doktor," and I like seeing my name on the *affiches*, when I recognize it, in the same type as everyone else's, instead of in the usual pica otherwise reserved for piano-tuners.

A good ensemble, quick to adopt our alien demands of phrasing and articulation, and harder-working than European orchestras generally. And *Le Sacre*, played with an emotion I can describe only as un-Teutonic, is a different piece. The sound does not glitter as it does with an American orchestra, and it is less loud, though still deafening in this small and live room. The musicians prefer the lyric dances to the rhythmic ones, I think, but even in the broadest *cantabile* they do not chew into the visceral fat. This is very agreeable to I.S., and so is the general sobriety; the violinists do not weave with passion as Russian violinists are wont to do abroad. In fact, our only significant criticisms are that no one is attentive to tuning— I think they consider our concern with it exaggerated—and that the harp is thick, honeyed, and weak in volume: two players share the part in *Orpheus*, but it is less penetrating than ever before. The bass drum is another, but satisfying, oddity. It is open on one side—sawed in two, in fact. The *secco* articulation from the single head makes the beginning of the *Danse de la terre* sound like a stampede. I.S. thinks the bassoon timbre different, too. "The *fagotti* at the end of the

Evocation des Ancêtres sound, for the first time, like the *cinq vieillards* I had imagined." But the music is in every respect radically unlike that of the familiar fuse-blowing piece of orchestral exhibitionism.

A reception at the Composers' Union, with Khrennikov, Shaporin, Dankovitch, Kabalevsky. Then a tour, beginning with turbaned St. Basil's and the Kremlin. Alexandra and Karen Khatchaturian, our escort from the Composers' Union, use pre-1917 names that the I.S.'s are likely to recognize, and we go about being told, anachronistically, that the green building on the left is "the Hall of the Nobles," and the rose-colored building on the right "the English Club, which you know from *War and Peace*." The common colors of the old city are pastels of peach and pink, contrasted with strong blues, ochers, and greens. These are the colors of the low, flat nineteenth-century houses with double-windows and circular archways which are found helter-skelter by mammoth gray apartment and office buildings. At Sparrow Hills, on the south bank of the Moscow River, the site of Napoleon's first view of the city, we leave the car for a walk. A russet-and-gold afternoon, with a gauze of blue smoke over the city. The I.S.'s are silent and, I think, more moved than I have ever seen them.

And they are even more so back across the river at the Novodevichy Monastery (which means "New Maidens," and which seems a redundant title unless the place was intended for repentant fallen women, "new maidens in heart"). This excursion, at V.'s insistence, is, I think, against the wishes, unexpressed, of Alexandra and Karen. The Novodevichy, decaying behind ancient walls, is an island of the old Russia. Crosses, graves, and statues of angels are in the gardens, and old women in black kerchiefs, tattered coats and shoes, are everywhere kneeling and praying before them. We enter a church in which a priest in a white cassock is officiating before an elderly congregation. A few of the more fervent lie kowtow in the prostrate crossficall position I.S. sometimes used to assume at his own devotions in the little Russian Church in Hollywood.

This unexpected look behind the door has driven a wedge, however slight and transparent, between the I.S.'s and their escorts, though the visit was in no outward sense opposed by them, and perhaps we are mistaken even in having felt their silent resistance. (In any case, I have felt it more than the I.S.'s, but then, twenty-four hours in the Soviet Union have helped me to realize that my, and my generation's, disease of self-consciousness is infinitely further advanced than theirs.) Inside the church, nevertheless, we are all three aware of a discomfort to them that is due not, I think, to the numbers of people there, but to the too obvious fact of their poverty. And the conversation in the car, later, is inhibited. Karen talks about "the New Soviet Life," the free education, the free medical care and free medicine, the free utilities, the nine-rubles-a-month rent, the wonders of the Metro, and of the street automats where a kopeck in a slot may procure everything from a sandwich to a spray of perfume. Alexandra, taking another tack, uses the Novodevichy as an example of religious toleration. She talks about religion as the relic of an older generation —"Why, even my own mother knows a priest"—that will die a natural death soon and is therefore of no consequence. But the I.S.'s are disturbed not for any religious or political reason, but simply because the Novodevichy is the Russia they knew and the Russia that is a part of them.

Tonight, exchanging impressions with the I.S.'s—this is the first time we have been alone long enough to do so—I am conscious of a desire to push into black or white, no matter the cost in exaggeration. And I am aware of a need, for the first time in fifteen years with the I.S.'s, to feel some co-ordination between my impressions and theirs, or confirmation that our experience has been in some measure the same. The I.S.'s complain that the foreign picture of the Soviet Union is absurdly misleading, even concerning such uncomplicated questions as the condition of consumer goods; V. has come with trinkets, rather as Peter Stuyvesant came to the Indians, except that she is now ashamed to give, and is even embarrassed to dispose of them. And the I.S.'s are indignant at having suffered so many months of anxiety, and they are ashamed, I think, of their suspicions, as recently as yesterday, about being "taken in by flowers and flattery." And Moscow is not "grim," and the people do not appear more "oppressed," or indeed, "happier" or "unhappier," than they do elsewhere. And though, admittedly, "unhappiness" and pride go well together, pride here is of an altogether different order. The I.S.'s profess themselves astounded by "the absence of *nichivo*-ism and of servility," and V. has come back from the post office saying that "servility has been replaced by civility." The man who drives our limousine is not a "chauffeur," the girl who cleans the room is not a "maid," the woman who checks our coats is not an "attendant," the boy who operates the elevator is not the "lift boy." (What they *are* I do not know, but "Tovarishch" is still the most common greeting.) All of this is only an indication of the overwhelming "pro" judgment of all three of us at the end of one day. But do the I.S.'s share my feeling that in spite of all the similarities slightly transposed (and of the knowledge that Paris is only a long lunchtime away), and in spite of admirations and sympathies aroused by everything we see, the sensation remains that intellectually speaking we are on a different (not a better or worse) planet? The answer is "no." They are at home. The schizophrenic US/USSR situation does not bother them at all, and forty-eight years abroad have not brainwashed them in the least. Their abiding emotion is an intense pride of everything Russian. (How wise of immigration departments, though unjust, to put the question of birthplace first and citizenship second.) Forty-eight hours ago, in Paris, I would have denied with full conviction, that I.S., and to a slightly lesser extent V., could ever be at home here again, not in the political Soviet Union, of course (though that could be arranged), but in "Russia." Yet, even a half century of expatriation can be forgotten in a night.

September 23. Passersby in front of the Conservatory at 9 AM: women in boots and kerchiefs, men in leather jackets, some with berets and some with Lenin beards (nobody looks like Marx or Castro).

Solid improvements in the orchestra this morning, especially toward rhythmic steadiness in the strings. Further transformations in I.S., too. V., at breakfast, claims, as part of the reason, that without money and taxes as possible subjects of conversation, sixty percent of his talk is freed for other topics. But another reason is that I.S. has always been a different person speaking his own language, and now, exchanging talk with the musicians, he is more buoyant than I ever have seen him. This, too, is the first time in his life that he has worked with a Russian-speaking orchestra. (The fact that no one speaks a word of any language but Russian makes us feel the decades of isolation more strongly than anything else, orchestras being so polyglot usually.) The musicians call him Igor Fedorovich, and the family feeling common to any group of Russians soon is established. To the eye, I.S. remains outside the family only by virtue of his elegant manners—that courtly bow from the door of the airplane.

Returning to the hotel, we find V. tearful. Her cousin Valodya has come with a packet of family photographs, and an account of her mother's death during the war, which is the first news of any kind concerning her mother in thirty years. This is the moment V. has dreaded ever since the trip became a possibility, though she has sought it, too. Earlier in the morning she has searched for the residence of her first marriage, and though the street was found with no building destroyed or changed, she has failed to recognize the house. This has been almost as disturbing.

Boris at the Bolshoi. *Ancien régime* plush and gilt, and a glittering chandelier. We sit in the first box over the orchestra pit, half shrouded by red canopy. The conductor receives only the faintest greeting on his entrance. This, Alexandra explains, is because "he hasn't done anything yet," though even when he has, and the other performers too, the audience reaction seems to us remarkably restrained. But the visual attributes are consistently superior to the musical. The sets could be *tableaux vivants* in the Kremlin Museum, and actors more richly robed would be difficult to imagine. I.S., who has not heard the music in thirty years, is both moved and—by Rimsky-Korsakov—annoyed. "Mussorgsky accompanied Pimen, as he wrote, by a single bassoon, but Rimsky, to make certain everyone saw the point added other instruments, with the result that an original idea is reduced to a commonplace. Still, I object less to the fact that Rimsky deformed Mussorgsky than to the fact that he tried to export him." I.S. thinks that "the music of the Coronation Scene must have inspired the Emperor's death march in *The Nightingale*," that "Mussorgsky's Fool supplied Berg with a model for the same role in *Wozzeck*," and that the Tsarina's unaccompanied song at the beginning of Act II was almost literally copied by Debussy in Mélisande's "*mes longues cheveux.*'" But I.S. likes the Polish scene above all, "the revelry which, alas, musically speaking, turns to marmalade at the end." During the intermission following this scene, I.S. is feeling extraordinarily compassionate about the Poles: "What a history! But, of course, if you pitch your tent in the middle of Fifth Avenue, it is quite likely you will be run over by a bus."

Another late-night séance, the I.S's again complaining of the misinformation of other visitors, and conveniently forgetting that nobody else has enjoyed a red (no pun) carpet tour like theirs. But by now I.S.'s *volte face* has reached the point at which he is currently appearing in the role of defender of the faith (Lenin's). His "defense of Russia," too, is virtually complete. "What a beautiful factory. *Chudno* apartment house." Heads roll when dinner in Hollywood is five minutes late, but a two-hour delay here is commended as "very good service"; which, indeed, it is, compared with some of the even longer waits. (But perhaps this change is due also to the resumption of that Russian time-scale according to which visitors arrive for tea and talk until midnight.) And when the dinner finally does appear, he will make statements like "What marvelous salt!" and not mention that the *pièce de résistance* would ef-

fectively resist an electric saw—and not want me to mention
it either. In fact, if tonight's meal had been served to him in
France, de Gaulle himself would have received a telegram
about the decline of civilization, but here it was "*vkussno*"
("very tasty")—a judgment not based on an attempt to eat it,
I should add.

Ralph Parker, Hurok's representative, to whom I confide
some of this transformation, asks me whether I am now seeing
"the true" I.S. Well, all I.S.'s are "true" enough, but the picture
of him *has* been given background, and the background does
wash out a great deal of what, heretofore, I had supposed to be
"traits of character" or personal idiosyncracy. And perhaps
I can now see the Soviet point of view of I.S.'s expatriate years
as a pillar-to-post course from circus ballet to Hebrew canticle
to—and indifferently—Roman Catholic Mass, a point of view
blind to the value question of how perfectly fluted I.S.'s pillars
are, and with what exquisite capitals he has adorned the posts.
But, for a time, anyway, I will try to listen to his music from
their perspective, and *sub specie patris*.[2]

V. says that I.S. is slipping into diminutives—a thing he
affects to scorn in other Russians abroad—and she adds that
diminutive forms are not more endemic than they were fifty
years ago, contrary to foreign information. Tonight, for example, he has asked the waiter for a spoon-*chik*, which V. considers a "*petit-bourgeois* solecism of a very revealing kind," even
though she has always held that I.S. is a pure hundred-percent
Russian whose "international sophistication was invented by
and is an imitation of Diaghilev." I.S. has begun to call his
niece Xenia, "Xeniochka," and this seems remarkably inappo-
site. Though Xenia is a good-hearted and courageous woman,
she often appears to regard her uncle as something a new
Soviet invention has retrieved from the moon.

[2] I have, and have discovered Russianisms even in *Pulcinella*; the D-minor
tenor aria, for example, which is a Russian dance, and the horn countermelody
at No. 65 in the soprano aria, which is closer to Tchaikovsky than to Pergolesi.
The Symphony in C seems to me now as nostalgically "Russian" in its way
as *Les Noces,* and Russia haunts Stravinsky's masterpiece *Oedipus Rex.*

September 24. An interview with I.S. in this morning's *Pravda* concludes with what he says is a spurious (but what sounds to me like a true) quotation: "I salute the noble Soviet Union." Ralph Parker telephones advising us to ignore it. A stock phrase, he says, that is tacked on to every interview. But the difficulty in I.S.'s case is that he has annoyed the Western press by receiving *Pravda* and refusing them. When they call, asking for his denial of the statement, they are well aware that he cannot give it without insulting his Russian hosts. Parker succeeds in pacifying the principal reporters, after a time, with the argument that I.S. is not a United States cultural exchange artist, but a guest of the Soviet Government. (The "U.S.A." appears only after my name on the programs and placards, but *could* it have been put after I.S.'s name?) I.S.'s confidence is a little undermined by this, as he calls it, breach of faith, and though he does not mention the matter to Alexandra and Karen, when they appear, everyone behaves sheepishly.

Several surprise visitors at the rehearsal today, such as our friend Carlos Prieto from Mexico, and Lily Brik, Mayakovsky's *amour,* whom V. saw last in Petrograd just before the Revolution. And Lina Prokofiev, not encountered since 1938, in Paris; the I.S.'s are startled to see her, in fact, because Parisian Russians have advised them that even to inquire about her could do her harm: in Stalin's time she was sent to Siberia for eight years, supposedly for consorting too much with British and Americans in the Embassies (she speaks perfect English). She is accompanied by her son Sviatoslav, a gangling, slightly grosser image of the composer. At this rehearsal, the conductor Rozhdestvensky gives I.S. a cover of the second volume of Debussy's *Préludes* on which, after the printed words *"pour piano,"* Debussy has written, *"et pour amuser mon ami Igor Stravinsky, juin 1913."* Rozhdestvensky says he bought the page for a few kopecks in a Moscow bookstall. It leads me to make inquiries concerning I.S.'s house in Ustilug, whence it must have come, but no one has heard of Ustilug, and all Xenia Yurievna knows is that in 1941 I.S.'s Beliankin cousins moved his possessions from Ustilug to a warehouse in

Poltava. Xenia does have a photograph of the Ustilug house with her, though, and of the *shtetl*, the Jewish village, but as I.S. feels more strongly about this happy home than about his largely unhappy childhood one in St. Petersburg, he does not want to look at it, and Ustilug is a subject he will not discuss. The Debussy autograph probably indicates that his possessions there, manuscripts, paintings, books, were sold or distributed after the Revolution.

In the Kremlin Armory Museum (Oruzheinaya Palata) this afternoon, we find ourselves looking less intently at the exhibits than at the other visitors: Tartars, Mongolians, Chinese, Red Army soldiers, kerchiefed Russian women, Uzbeks in black-and-white hexagonal caps. In felt overshoes and in tow of female lecturers, they glide clumsily over the polished wood floors, like tyros on a skating rink. A museum of the church, first of all, it is rich in crosses, Bibles, and clerical garments, all lustrously jeweled: a surplice brocaded with 150,000 pearls; a Bible encrusted with a tutti-frutti of rubies, diamonds, emeralds; another Bible set with tear-shaped amethysts. The Imperial jewels—in orb and scepter, in throne seats, in baldrics, in fur-trimmed crowns and ermine-lined robes—are not less rich, of course, and the Tsars' horse equipages (saddles, bridles, stirrups, whip handles, harnesses, pommels, cantles) are the most extravagantly jeweled objects of all: for example, a horse's bit with a topaz stud the size of a bird's egg. One of the horse blankets, the gift of a shah, is made of the feathers of five hundred yellow parrots. But it is also a museum of fabrics and needlework, of winding-sheets and palls in gold and silver thread, of silks and satins, taffetas and velvets, of sleigh rugs with cloisonné spangles; and it is a museum of Imperial utensils, of silver plate with niello tracery or appliqué gold.

Lermontov's *Masquerade* at the Maly Theater is well acted and so lavishly decorated that the stage picture could be a collective dream-wish of upper-class elegance. (Incidentally, the I.S.'s have been told abroad of a shortage of convincing "aristocratic" accents and "refined" intonation, but they find no evidence of that lack tonight.) The production seems to follow the old Meyerhold staging, and its fast pace depends upon ingenious uses of the revolving stage. The long evening is cleverly relieved, if not shortened, by incidental dancing to a well-chosen potpourri of Prokofiev. But what a curious play! The first two acts are hardly less powerful, in some ways, than the *Othello* to which the plot contains a not overstrained parallel, but the third act falls into bathos. Instead of a dramatic solution, the author pops an "evil genius" out of the bag, and the "tragedy" is laid to a forgotten vengeance-seeker of long ago.

Line for line, for four-and-a-half hours, resourceful translation of this difficult verse play has been piped into my ear by Alexandra, and hers is the most amazing performance of the evening. (She apologizes to our neighbors in advance, but no one gives us even a glance of annoyance.) During intermissions we drink tea with the scene painter and stage director—and talk theater with Alexandra. It is her passion, and play translations are her largest source of income. She asks me for new American plays to translate, but the prescription is that they should be "something like Wesker."

September 25. An official call on Ekaterina Furtseva, the Minister of Culture, an attractive blonde—gossip calls her Catherine the Third—with abundant *charme slav.* She talks to us about the future, giving poetical recitations of production statistics, and descriptions of new orchestras, new ballets, new schools in Tashkent or Siberia, which she graciously invites us to visit.

The policeman at the Lenin Mausoleum allows us to jump the queue, a caterpillar of booted and bundled, capped and kerchiefed people winding around the north corner of the Kremlin. (Some feelings of guilt about doing so, but we couldn't have waited six hours, and those who have waited seem so long-suffering.) We descend a staircase in double file, and in silence. In front of us are turbaned heads from the southeast, fur-covered heads from the far north, red faces, dark faces, yellow faces, square faces, slant-eyed faces. Soldiers keep the traffic moving in the marble corridors, and a soldier faces the glass catafalque from each end, standing, themselves, at near *rigor mortis*. The hair and brows of the small recumbent figure in the black suit are red and not black as in photographs, but surely the figure is a wax doll and no embalmed body. And, as surely, it makes no difference. Seeing is believing, and Mohammed's toenail, the splinter of the True Cross, the "real" remains of Lenin, are all to the same purpose. I.S., later: "The religion of Lenin is the opiate of the masses."

Orpheus, Petroushka, and the *Firebird* performed by the Leningrad Ballet in the Kremlin Theater, a new auditorium with escalators, lounges, bars to accommodate six thousand, and with devices for radioed translations by every seat. We sit with pretty Natasha Khrennikov, and the English-speaking composer Kabalevsky who, though reputedly an oppositionist to I.S.'s visit, weeps at the end of the *Firebird*—though that, come to think of it, is not incompatible with anti-Stravinskyism. At times, both the music and the staging are hardly recognizable, especially in *Petroushka*, which is much less "Russian" to us than Fokine-Benois. The *Firebird* is the best-performed and best-received but, then, it is the prototype of the Soviet ballet in many respects including length, sentimentality, and, I regret to say, musical quality. Shortly before the lights are lowered for it, a part of the audience discovers and applauds I.S. A moment later, Khrushchev, accompanied by several members of his cabinet, enters the loge directly across the hall from ours, and the whole audience stands and applauds. When the *Firebird* begins—or seems to: the *tempo* is strange and the sound unbalanced—a shout of "*Viva* Khrushchev" comes from somewhere below. The cry is taken up by other voices, and an attempt is made to turn it into a rhythmic chant, but shushing noises are heard, too, and they soon have the majority. The demonstration is quelled only when the lights are turned up. "Cubans," says Alexandra, without much sympathy. "It happens all the time." At the end of the *Firebird*, Khrushchev stands to applaud, but he has vanished before the first curtain call.

September 26. Kolya K. is a poet (self-declared) aged twenty-six who has haunted the hotel lobby for three days in hopes of interviewing I.S. He is offended when V. refers to his hero Evtushenko as "a tribune who might have been a poet in another time and place," but V. says the same of Mayakovsky and that is an even less popular verdict. Brecht is another Kolya idol, but Rilke is unknown to him even by name, and Edna St. Vincent Millay is his favorite contemporary English-language poet. The pantheon of painters is even more curious in that it contains no Renaissance masters at all, but only such "moderns" as Cézanne and Renoir, whom he feels obliged to defend as *avant-garde* causes. Confessing his inability to appreciate more recent art, he tells us about "a clump of barbed wire at an exhibition in Paris, that was called 'Dream.' Now what has barbed wire to do with dreaming?" Talking about the arts during Stalinism, he says that the dictator is supposed to have commented on a book of poems by Simenov to his mistress to the effect that "there should be just two copies printed, one for him and one for her." On the new climate of "liberalism for the arts," Kolya's opinion is that "the only serious enemy is the foreign press. Many government officials want to support the so-called rebel poets, musicians, and painters, but as soon as they are published, performed, or shown, the foreign press pretends that they are defying the regime, which, for example, Evtushenko most patently is not." Kolya's political argument, paraphrased, is: "The Russian people have risen from a terrible history to the highest place. They have never known what you call prosperity, but they will know that now, too, and as, inevitably, they go ahead, the United States will become more and more bitter. We do not want war, if only—to obviate other arguments—for the reason that we have so much to develop here. We believe that as long as Khrushchev is in control, war is not a probability, and we think the Americans should realize that, too, and help him against the militarists and the Stalinists. But is it really true that the Americans have bomb shelters? Surely they can't be *that* silly?" This is the first time international politics and the "war scare" have been mentioned. I.S. on Stalin: "He attempted to and, I am afraid, did prove that people do not matter."

Tonight's concert in Tchaikovsky Hall is the most moving in my life, and I think it is for I.S. too, though so far as I can tell the applause is more for the returning Russian prodigal than for the music. *Orpheus*, in any case, is attended with much reading of program notes and other signs of restlessness and boredom, and this is the same in every section of an audience that is at least as stratified as ours, with, as everywhere in the world, eager youth in the balcony and apathetic age *parterre*. As an encore, I.S. conducts his wind-band arrangement of the Volga Boat Song, but it diminishes the ovation somewhat and dampens the mood, partly because the audience has waited in vain for the strings to play on the second time around, but also, I think, because it is a reference to the wrong Russia and the wrong past. The applause continues in rhythmic unison, however, until I.S. appears in his overcoat and tells the audience, "You see a very happy man." In the dressing room, we receive gifts from the orchestra—for me a lacquered box with a "Firebird" on the cover.

September 27. The former Yusupov estate at Archangelskoye, one of the great suburban villas (*podmoskovnaya*) is a showcase of nineteenth-century country life. Geese are on the lawns, and horsecarts are on the rural roads—the dray horses with large surcingles and large horseshoe-shaped shaft-bows (*doogah*) as in nineteenth-century illustrations. The villa is a heavy, ocher building topped by a tall, untapered dome, like the smokestack on an ocean liner. The center room is an oval crown, eight Corinthian columns supporting the white cornice. The side rooms are picture galleries, but the furniture—Karelian birch chairs and cabinets, rugs woven in the Yusupov mills at Poltava—is more attractive than the paintings. In the actual living rooms the ceilings are low, to concentrate the warmth.

A party of Cameroons is touring the grounds with a girl lecturer—in Arabic. One of them recognizes I.S. from a photograph in *Pravda*, and one and all gather around for autographs. This seems to annoy the deserted lecturer, who is obliged to stand dumbly by while the I.S.'s talk to them in French and English, and to each other in Russian. Would the Cameroons believe that V. knew the man whose home this was? In any case, they seem to be regarding their visit as a lesson in medieval history. V., in the car, later: "Yusupov was such a perfect gentleman! When he came to call on us in the Crimea during the Revolution—we lived in a single room without any furniture—he did not look about for a chair, but sat on the floor without hesitation, as though that was the most natural thing in the world for him to do."

Returning to Moscow, we pass *izbas*—log cabins—with fancy wooden lace window frames. Every habitation, to the tiniest *izbushka*, has at least one television pole. And we pass the enshrined hut, scene of Kutuzov's council before Moscow. Kutuzov is no longer merely the hero of strategic retreats, but a newly rehabilitated symbol of aggression, according to Ralph Parker, who says that even the grounds of Borodino have been adjusted to this interpretation.

Prokofiev's *War and Peace* helps establish the interpretation too, for though Napoleon appears as a kind of Fascist neurotic, Kutuzov, the solitary, is a genius as big as Russia, and rather larger than history. The opera is a chain of historical friezes. Visually rather like a series of old-fashioned historical panoramas, it is pictorially very good to look at, indeed. The book cannot be parceled out, of course, or reduced to operatic mold, and if the composer had limited himself to a single tableau, or two or three, Tolstoy's characters would still be too roomy for Prokofiev even on that scale. Nevertheless, the music, especially in the long first-act cotillion, is more pleasing than I.S. makes out, and the performances, most memorably of a soldier in black boots dancing a mazurka, are excellent. A number of Kazakhis are in the audience: skullcaps, caftans cut like Victorian frock coats, beards like Tintoretto's Nicolas Priuli. We sit in the Royal Loge, or whatever it is now called, and in the intervals meet the cast and feed on *pirochki* and sugary champagne. (Later, I.S., feeling slightly tipsy, complains that the champagne "had the wrong nuance.")

A late-night interview at the Moscow television studios. Answering an inquiry about his next composition, I.S. lays an egg as large as Kastchei's, but not magical. At the words "I am writing a Biblical cantata, in Hebrew, for the Israeli government," faces fall, and the program limps to an end. Ralph Parker tells us afterward that the stony reaction was because Israel is regarded as succursal to the United States, and also because of the Soviet attitude to the Bible, and of the Russian composers' feeling that he should be writing in his own language, or, at least, in a language he knows. A newscast immediately before our appearance shows Khrushchev being cheered along the route of his tour, and the new United States Ambassador, Foy Kohler, being made to look as grim and friendless as Gromyko is in the United States.

September 28. To the Scriabin Museum, in Scriabin's old apartment in the Arbat district. Little can have altered since Scriabin's time, which is to say that Blavatsky is still a presence as well as the *clavier à lumières,* now on exhibit as the number one relic. The caretakers are two old ladies madly in love with "Vanya Cleebourne." They introduce a young "electronic composer" who plays his "tape filter" for a film *Cosmic Space,* the techniques for which are mysteriously purported to have been developed from Scriabin's ideas concerning the *clavier à lumières.* We also hear a recording of Scriabin's "Black Mass" Sonata played by the late white (red?) hope of all the Soviet pianists, Safronitski.

Among sundry other visits, the Kamerny Theater, where V. played in Beaumarchais's *Svadba* early in 1917; this is on the Nikitski Boulevard, the "bark" of the old city, on the analogy that Moscow grew in successive circles like a tree. And the Chekov House, a red brick *fin-de-siècle* eyesore. And the Tolstoy House, which is in a neighborhood of attractive lime-colored buildings with white, arched window frames. A tall dovecote stands at a nearby street corner.

Our second concert, a repeat of the first. At intermission, I.S., pale and perspiring, complains of nausea but refuses to see a doctor. I send Alexandra for one anyway, an elderly woman, as it happens, who tells me that I.S. "was a legend already in my childhood." She finds his pulse weak and refuses to sanction any more conducting, at which I.S., furious, drinks brandy and coffee, stalks on stage, and does rather better than at the first concert. The forty-minute intermission puts the foreign press on the trail, however, and newsmen perch outside our hotel rooms afterward like carrion crows. The Soviet medics are dumbfounded at the extent of I.S.'s private pharmacy, and incredulous at the—true—story that he has swallowed ten drops of an opium paregoric before the concert and washed it down with two tumblers of whisky.

September 29. Most of the day is spent in answering cables about I.S.'s "stroke" and in denying press reports that he had had one. At night we go to the Obratzsov Puppet Theater and see a parody of posh music, that is without a moment of *longueurs.* Child prodigies are mocked by an infant in a perambulator who howls for its bottle and babbles baby talk, but then smashes into the Rachmaninov Second Concerto. The "dark" singing of gypsies is lampooned by a teen-age girl with a bass-baritone bray. United States tap-dancing, Hope-Crosby type comedian singing, and "sexy"—"sex-appeala" the Russians call it—adolescent blues singing are all neatly spoofed, but our main interest in these burlesques is in seeing how United States physical characteristics are typed. The drollest of the American parodies is a takeoff on television commercials, an elaborately developed choral "fugue" about vitamin pills "that keep you alive until you die." These gentle satires are well timed and in good taste. But though they are not, I think, the highlight of the show, they receive the most vigorous applause—from an audience that must be at least half foreign, judging by the switchboard of languages in the lobby. (The performance can be followed without knowledge of Russian, though the spectator must be able at least to recognize it, as in the skit with a French poodle who growls angrily when its mistress bids it *"Bonjour,"* but barks with pleasure when she says *"Zdrastvooite."*) The highlight, for me, is a parody of beatnik poetry-readings. The reader has a huge mouth, terrible grammar, and atrocious manners: before beginning, he rudely clears his throat and expectorates on the floor. After affectedly announcing "The first chapter of my new novel," he utters a few obscure and disconnected words, then says, "I will skip the next sixteen chapters, as they are concerned only with the psychological development of Chapter One." The word "psychology" takes a severe beating, and not only here, as we have discovered in conversations.

September 30. Today, V.'s name-day (St. Vera's), is celebrated by our new non-believing friends with at least as much zeal as the church-going "White Russian" regulars in Hollywood. They bring her broadloom linens, an electric samovar, lacquered trays (the old arts of Palekh and Mstera), wood and terracotta miniature animals, and they bring a new covivialty, too, in which all trace of the official manner of a week ago has disappeared.

October 1. Pravda today has a large photographic spread of hate-ugly faces with captions about "the racial war in Mississippi." And the Russians ask us, with genuine incredulity I think, how such things are possible "in a country as advanced as *Ameriki.*"

Lunch at the United States Embassy with Ambassador Foy Kohler and Krilov of the Soviet Embassy in Washington. The Ambassador begins a speech in Russian, but switches to English midstream, asking an aide to translate the latter part. What he says, in substance, is that I.S., as a Russian American, is a unique link in cultural relations. But the Russians— Krilov, Furtseva, Khrennikov—listen with blank faces, do not reply, and do not applaud. (Their attitude is that I.S., as a guest of the Soviet Union, is not a United States cultural exchange artist.) But I.S.'s position *is* extraordinary, for though he is one

of the few Russian creative artists since the literary giants of
the nineteenth century to have attained a high order of world
prestige, he has been *persona non grata*, until now, only in Russia. After lunch he makes the point, privately, that the big
cultural exports of the United States and the Soviet Union are
the same: pianists, orchestras, ballets—"In other words, not
creative talent, but performing talent—which is fine, of course,
though the prospect of more and more *Wunderkinder* playing
Tchaikovsky concertos is not exactly my idea of a musical
Eden." He also says that whereas in the United States the
artist complains of the government's rejection of responsibility
to help art, in the Soviet Union he might decide that the highest duty of government is to leave it alone.

Reception by Madame the Minister of Culture and the lead-
ing Soviet composers, in a private room at the Metropole.
(The dinner, white veal and Kievski *kotleti*, proves that very
good food exists if ordered by the right person.) This is the
most extraordinary event of the trip, a kind of "Last Supper"
(for non-disciples) during which I.S. reveals his Russian-ness
more completely than at any time in the fifteen years I have
known him. Mme. Furtseva presides at the center of the table,
with I.S. to her right and Shostakovich to her left; seeing the
two St. Petersburg-born composers so close together, one is
struck by the fact that their complexions and sandy hair are
exactly the same. V. sits *vis-à-vis* Furtseva and between
Aram Khatchaturian and Kara Karayev, and I am next to
Karayev and my "earphones," Alexandra, who translates word
for often unbelievable word. Shostakovich's is the most "sensitive" and "intellectual" face we have seen so far in the USSR.
He is thinner, taller, younger—more boyish-looking—than expected, but he is also the shyest and most nervous human being I ever have seen. He chews not merely his nails but his
fingers, twitches his pouty mouth and chin, chain-smokes, wiggles his nose in constant adjustment of his spectacles, looks
querulous one moment and ready to cry the next. His hands
tremble, he stutters, his whole frame wobbles when he shakes
hands—which reminds us of Auden—and his knees knock

when he speaks, at which time the others look anxious for him, as indeed they might. He has a habit of staring, too, then of turning guiltily away when caught, and all evening long he peeks illicitly at I.S. around the rounded corners of Mme. Furtseva. (No betrayal of the thoughts behind those frightened, very intelligent eyes.) His new wife sits beside him. An adoring pupil, perhaps, but by age, looks, and her equally shy, serious, distant manner, a daughter. Then it starts. *Confiteor me*. Each musician proposes a toast that is, in effect, an invitation to return to the fold. And each speaker begins by baring his soul, confessing to some guilt, some shortcoming of his own, some misunderstanding of I.S., some prejudice or lack of sympathy—and it is the nature of these confessions that I find so biologically "Russian" and also so characteristic of I.S.; I mean all those remarks in our books which seem to Anglo-Saxons so lacking in reticence. Oblomov may have disappeared in the Revolution, but Stavrogin is still very much around. Only a little of this is needed to turn the room into a Finnish bath, in the vapors of which, proclaiming and acclaiming each other's Russian-ness, everyone says almost the same thing. I.S.'s human qualities are lauded—they are Russian qualities, after all—and the man . . . well all who have met the man have seen how truly *genuine* he is. No one says a word about the composer, and only Shostakovich toasts future works by him—though, to be fair, none of them has or could have any idea of the stature of the composer, and they certainly do not intend to slight the composer. Again and again they abase themselves before the mystery of their Russian-ness, and so, I realize with a small shock, does I.S. In fact, his replies are soon overtaking the toasts. In a very sober speech—he is less alcoholically elevated than anyone else in the room—we hear that "The smell of the Russian earth is different"—it is—"and such things are impossible to forget"—they are, and so far so good. But he goes on to tell Khatchaturian and Khrennikov of a desire to know more of their music, which is not so good, not only because untrue, but also because they have avoided mention of *his* music. All that Khatchaturian has said was that I.S. had been a "legend" to him all his life, "but now that I have seen the man I am greatly moved by his sincerity" (cheers) —a non sequitur that leaves little doubt about the nature of the "legend." I.S.'s serious confessing gets under way in his reply to Mme. Furtseva who, after a patriotic preamble, advances the somewhat dubious proposition that "all really great men are optimists"—commenting on an "optimistic" remark by I.S. Not "in effect," but in actual quotes, I.S. says: "A man has one birthplace, one fatherland, one country—he *can* have only one country—and the place of his birth is the most important factor in his life. I regret that circumstances separated me from my fatherland, that I did not bring my works to birth there and, above all, that I was not there to help the new Soviet Union create its new music. But I did not leave Russia only by my own will, even though I admit that I disliked much in my Russia and in Russia generally—but the right to criticize Russia is mine, because Russia is mine and because I love it. I do not give any foreigner that right." (Bolshoi applause.) An astonishing speech to at least *this* criticizing foreigner who, accordingly, is beginning to feel more foreign every moment; so astonishing, in fact, that the I.S.'s are slightly embarrassed to have had it overheard, even by me. But it is believable, and so is every word he says tonight except the professed interest in Khrennikov's and Khatchaturian's music. I.S. does regret his uprooting and exile more than anything else in his life, which I say not because of a few emotional speeches, even though they have come from the depths, but because of his change of nature in Russia, and the perspective of it from Russia outside. In Hollywood, for instance, where his domesticity is entirely Russian, where he still slurps his soup, Russian style, from the same spoon with which his *babushka* used to feed him in Russia seventy-five years ago; where, if possible, he will go through the day speaking only his mother tongue. Or in Baden-Baden, five years ago, when he flew into a rage at the news of Sputnik, and forbade us even to mention the achievement. Was the power of this jealous hate (the mother's deprived love) responsible for his acquisition of "western sophistication"; that is, as a weapon to prove his superiority, or that of other cultures, to the Russia that failed to recognize his talent? I offer no answer, but I am certain that to be recognized and acclaimed as a Russian in Russia, and to be performed there, has meant more to him than anything else in the years I have known him. And when Mother Russia restores her love, forty-eight years are forgiven with one suck of the breast —several sucks of vodka, in fact, at this deeply Dostoievskyan dinner.

October 2. Reception at the Canadian Embassy. Stalin came here once, mistook a photograph of King George V for the Tsar, thought he was being insulted, fled. So says the Ambassador, anyway. And he tells the popular story about the child who asks its *babushka* if Lenin was a great man. The *babushka* says yes, of course, and then the child wants to know about Stalin. A very bad man, says the *babushka.* "And, *babushka,* Khrushchev?" "Hush, my child, he is still alive." The Ambassador has a fine collection of abstract paintings by Karitnikov and other artists who are not shown publicly, and he takes us to see the Kostaki collection of icons and paintings by the pre-Revolution *avant-garde:* early Kandinskys—an especially fine one on glass—Gabos, Larionovs. Kostaki's gallery is his three-room flat in a huge apartment house many kilometers from the center of Moscow.

Tonight is our first concert with Kiril Kondrashin's orchestra. The musicians are younger than those of the Moscow State Orchestra, their ensemble is drier and more exact, and the varnish on the sound is less thick. I receive flowers from the *New Statesman* and from my soloist in the *Capriccio,* Tatiana Nicolayevna, who looks and plays as though she could have won several events in the Olympic Games. The orchestra presents me with its recording of Shostakovich's Fourth Symphony inscribed by about fifty of the players.

October 3. A buffet, by Ralph Parker, for I.S. and the performing plutocrats, Rostropovich, Gilels, Kogan, Oistrakh, Bez-
rodny, etc. Parker now functions as liaison man between our
hosts and ourselves, as he is our chief "outside" source of information as well, which is to say that he relays the tenor of
the Soviet reaction. Parker is shy, intellectual, helpful, hungry.
He is passionate about painting, and he has good prose style,
with a delightful sense of humor. Over the years, now twenty-
one in the Soviet Union, he has developed the discretionary
habit of whispering. He will sweep into the room, look as
though ready to shout "Eureka," but then sidle up and softly
buzz something in your ear. I.S. calls him "Signor Sotto Voce."

October 4. Fog obscures even the towers of the Kremlin, but
does not delay our afternoon flight to Leningrad. We eat at the
airport, ordering from a menu in Russian and Chinese. A
smooth flight (one class), during which Alexandra talks to
me about psychoanalysis. "Self-indulgence," she says. "We
should be taught to master ourselves with will power, and to
solve our own problems." I try a utility argument, pointing out
that capitalist psychotherapy with its bourgeois-objectivist
rationalisms has helped many people to lead useful lives,
and I suggest that it will appear in the Soviet Union *pari
passu* with the rise of the culture elite. I even try to compare Freud to Marx, in the sense that the ideas of both
men changed the world—one finds oneself in that sort of argument here simply because of the lack of example; Alexandra is
probably better read in pre-twentieth-century European and
American literature than I am, but she has never heard of a
single one of the books I cite as "Freudian." And "Freud"
leads to "Society," which, she says, is only a question of "what
is good for the people." When I imprudently ask who decides
what that good is, she accuses me of "philosophy, which is
only putting the world in parentheses. The Good is better living
conditions and the freedom to pursue one's inner life." We
also talk about "the parasitism of the bourgeoisie," and whether
or not the United States is "a common denominator society

using 'individualism' as a slogan." But Soviet planes are fast, and no conclusions are reached.

The Leningrad welcoming committee is smaller, older, poorer than the Muscovite. One pale elderly gentleman greets I.S. and starts to weep. It is Vladimir Rimsky-Korsakov, and I.S. has failed to recognize him, apparently because he has a mustache instead of, as when last seen, a beard, but the real reason, I.S. tells me later, was that he said "Igor Fedorovich" instead of Guima. "He always called my brother Guri, and me Guima." Vladimir lives in the same apartment house in which I.S. wrote *The Firebird* (in the English Prospekt). Relatives of I.S.'s friend and co-librettist Stepan Mitussov are present too, and a nephew of Diaghilev, a man with an old-fashioned and most un-proletarian manner who speaks English and French; and a daughter of M. K. Ciurlionis, the Latvian Odilon Redon, and again the daughter of Balmont, with another basket of posies and moss, and a photograph of her father in goatee and shoulder-length hair, like Buffalo Bill. The Leningradski are more European than the Moscovichi; they bow, kiss hands, do not shy from foreign, and especially German, expressions.

After driving an hour through postwar suburbs, I.S. recognizes the old Riding School, and from then on it is home. To right and left, everything is "*chudna*" or "*krassiva*," and he has a story to tell about each building. We pass along the Neva to the green-and-white Winter Palace—rose-and-white when the I.S.'s saw it last—and down Nevsky Prospekt to the Yevropaisky Hotel. V., who stayed here on visits to St. Petersburg in her student years, says that the furnishings—German pianos, Louis Seize clocks, Empire ormolu in beds, desks, chairs—are exactly the same.[3]

In the evening we see Tolstoy's *The Living Dead* at the Alexandrinka which, like all of the old theaters we have seen in the USSR, is spectacularly beautiful. But the title of the play is also a perfect description of the performance, and as

[3] In spite of the reports that the furniture had been used as firewood during the war when the Yevropaisky was a hospital.

our seats, in the first row, tip uncomfortably toward the orchestra pit, and as the gypsies singing in Romany are a Himalayan bore, we depart after the first act.

A late-night floor show in the hotel roof restaurant. A magician is sawing a woman in half on a platform at the end of the room, and a party of Cubans at the center table keeps shouting "VI-VA KHRUSH-CHEV" and applauding in rhythm. Are they vivisectionists?

October 5. After the morning rehearsal we drive to Peterhof, now Petrodvorets, and Oranienbaum, now Lomonosov, the city of I.S.'s birth. On the road out of Leningrad, we pass women shouldering large nets of cabbages which, says Alexandra, they are taking home to salt. Views of the Gulf of Finland, of the derricks of the Kronstadt shipyards, and of war scars: charred buildings and woods half cropped from artillery fire. Petrodvorets itself has been badly shot up, though in spite of that, and of systematic German demolition, admirably restored. A Russian tank has been fixed as a monument at the point of the farthest German advance; unlike Petrodvorets, Oranienbaum was never captured by the Germans.

The principal Petrodvorets palace is said to be Rastrelli's magnum opus (by those in our company), but Nature—romantic rustication as arranged by Rastrelli and others—is at least as great an attraction. We walk in Peter III's Dutch tulip garden (where Lermontov conceived *The White Sail*), in bosquets, and on pollarded poplar avenues; poplar petals have fallen or blown over the fir trees like yellow snow. We walk by fountains, cascades, stairs, statuary—a gold Samson, Russian strength, destroying a Swedish lion—and a pond in which, two centuries before Pavlov, fish came to be fed at the sound of a bell.

The long rows of unpainted wooden *dachkis* in nearby Lomonosov hardly can have changed from the time of I.S.'s birth except for the forest of TV poles, but I.S. has not seen the city since he was a few days old, in any case, and he has no clue as to where he was born. From the group of delectable rococo palaces outside and above the city, the architectural fancier may choose Menshikov's, which is domed the shape of a Grand Duke's crown, or Catherine's pale-rose Chinese palace, or her *"palais des montaignes russes."* The Peter-period palaces are low, long, flat, and colonnaded. With them is an artificial lake on which the Tsar's mock naval battles were fought.

Reception at Monferrand House, now the Leningrad Composers' Union. About thirty of us sit at a "T" table, with I.S. at the intersection, directly under a portrait of Glazunov. From this ironic position issues what must have been the Union's first two-hour monologue on the "twelve-tone system." But it is received by people incomparably better informed than any gathering has been so far, and the young men reveal themselves almost as *frondeurs* in comparison with their Moscow colleagues. The atmosphere is that of a provincial club welcoming a hometown hero, though the evening has none of the stuffiness of an "historical occasion"; the meeting is lively and the hometown boy has never enjoyed himself more. In fact, only Glazunov seems not to be having a good time.

One of the "twelve-tone" apaches is Dmitri Tolstoy, son of the writer, Alexei, a stately and corpulent young man (a pronounced pyknic-cyclothymic type, in fact), who presents I.S. and myself with little piano pieces of that description dedicated to us. After proclaiming himself an admirer of I.S.'s music he makes a ludicrous and heartbreaking request: "Could you please send me a score of *The Firebird,* and anything else you have written."

At midnight, as we return to the hotel, a hundred or so queuers are waiting on the sidewalk by Philharmonic Hall. According to Parker, each of them represents a block of a hundred seats. They will remain there all night, too, though each watch may be broken into several reliefs. Parker says that the queue is a year old, and that each place in it has had to be checked every month and, as the date drew near, every week, and, finally, twice a day (before and after working hours). An eighty-four-year-old cousin of I.S. has told Parker that she received the number 5001 and that therefore she will have to see the concert on television.

October 6. The queue, this morning, stretches around the corner to Mikhailovsky Square.

The "Scythian" gold in the Hermitage basement includes art and artifact from the whole Russian geography, and from history as well as prehistory. Early Sarmatian culture is represented, treasures from the Chaltamlik burial sites, works of Greek-period craftsmanship from Theodosia and the Bosporus, and Peter the Great's Siberian collection. All the gold has this in common: it is light in color and the forms, whether ornaments or utilities, rarely tend to the geometric and abstract. The principal objects are harness buckles, scabbards, goblets (one with a relief showing a tooth extraction, not unlike backwoods dentistry today), laurel leaves—a surprising number of them—carcanets, crowns. A great quantity of bibelots can be seen—tiny gold flowers, acorns, sheaves of wheat (for prehistoric Miss Balmonts), sea urchins, dancing humans, birds in flight; or perhaps these are all totems too, like the bulls, eagles, serpents, and winged humans that the young girl guide reproves me for comparing with angels. (They are a kind of "geniuses," she says.) Tsarist-era gold, in clocks, snuffboxes, toys, has this in common: it is all useless, all too richly jeweled —a gold lion paperweight with diamonds for teeth—and it all looks as though made by Fabergé. The visit to this Scythian Fort Knox involves a mile hike through corridors stuffed with grotesquely large bowls made of purple agate, lapis lazuli, and malachite. The largest, a jasper punch-bowl, would do nicely in Beverly Hills as a swimming pool. What appear to be enormous bathtubs are stored here too, but they prove to be tureens for cooling champagne (jeroboams only, one supposes). We emerge feeling properly lilliputian.

A concert of I.S.'s Septet and Octet and an exhibition of Stravinskyana at the Composers' Union. Five hundred guests gather in the paneled oak library under large likenesses of

Tchaikovsky, Mussorgsky, Glinka, Glazunov, Lenin. The instrumentalists, all students, are excellent, but their *tempi* are erratic and the Octet Finale is played faster than we had ever supposed possible. The music stops, too, exactly where the sides come to an end in somebody's old recording, even though the phrase is in mid-career. For the Septet, Professor Maria Yudina steps to the piano, an instrument she plays with skill and control, though the music, the Gigue anyway, makes little sense here and cannot have pleased the audience, no matter how earnest the applause.

It is Yudina's night of glory. She escorts I.S. through the exhibit, listens to the Octet sitting at his side, receives him "humbly" on stage at the end. Her own stage behavior might have been learned from Klemperer. She will not bow or smile, and our most energetic applause is acknowledged by a trifling nod. She will, reputedly, cross herself before playing, and with passionate ostentation (it it said), and one supposes that Soviet audiences are conspicuously not moved by this. She will read impromptu lectures, too, or poems by Pasternak, and she stopped once in a Prokofiev sonata, saying, "I cannot continue with *this* after Beethoven." Yudina has carried I.S.'s banner in the Soviet Union longer than anyone else, and in recent years, through I.S.'s Paris friend Pierre Suvchinsky, she is in communication with Stockhausen and other composers of that generation. Not unexpectedly, she does not sit smoothly with the powers of the Composers' Union, and when today, at their luncheon party, she pops a book from under the table and attempts to make them listen to her read religious philosophy from it, strong expressions of dislike are exchanged on both sides. Yudina's Stravinskyana fills walls and glass cases in several rooms, and includes photographs of Schoenberg, Berg, and Webern which are probably being seen for the first time in the USSR. After tonight's concert she flies to Moscow to play I.S.'s piano concerto, and then back here for another performance Monday. In profile, playing, she looks something like my idea of Bach without his wig. Full face, in the street, with her cane and handbag—from which she is forever pulling books, jars of honey, sweets, poems by Pasternak—she looks like (and is) a Doctor of Philosophy.

October 7. We listen to tapes of four new Soviet compositions, at the Composers' Union. The first is part of a cantata, a triptych on texts by Essenin, Blok, Mayakovsky. The music, by Sviridov, a pupil of Shostakovich, is steady, solid, unhurried (all euphemisms for "boring," of course, but I *am* at least trying). It does not venture beyond a primitive triadic scheme, and of the one or two pleasing instrumental ideas, the piccolo-contrabassoon octaves were more effective in *Alexander Nevsky.* In the context of the Sviridov, the second piece, a quartet by Salmanov, qualifies as experimental music. The Bartók *pizzicato-glissando* is used, and naïvely repeated, but perhaps the device comes from Gnessin, who was the composer's teacher, and not Bartók. The third piece is a violin-piano sonata by Ustvolskaya, who appears to have been exposed to Bartók too—those so terribly sad falling minor thirds—but who is, in fact, another student of Shostakovich. Our friend Mirzoyan is the author of the final piece, a symphony for strings and timpani that starts with a steppe-like *largo,* goes on to some *Schelomo* (equally profound, I regret to say), and concludes in a fast movement—half rhapsody, half Moscow two-step, and all *kitsch.* (After these samplers, no doubt carefully chosen to please good old radical us, how can I.S. continue to proselytize for a school whose musical logic is at least a light-year away, and whose emotional world is on the other side of the galactic field? But he has had the same reactions, in fact, and he tells me later that "that was the real *fer rideau.*")

In his reminiscences, I.S. has hardly mentioned the green, white, and gold Nikolsky Sobor, which is an architectural marvel even in this city. The omission is surprising because the Nikolsky is so near his home that the belfry, a separate building, can be seen from the street in front of his house; and not to mention that belfry—he never has—is like living a block from, but not mentioning, the Taj Mahal. But all of I.S.'s descrip-

tions of the city in our books are greatly misleading as to scale
and space. The Nikolsky is a double-decker church of which
the upper part is a sun-filled but otherwise empty room, and
the low-arched lower part is a sanctuary for old women. The
lower church is illumined by oil-wick lamps suspended from
the ceiling, and by tallow candles carried by a few votaries.
V. joins a queue to buy a candle, but she is made to pay four
times more than anyone else, which is a social justice, no
doubt (Robin Hood type), but which leaves her with the in-
ference that in the new Russia, experiences of this sort occur
only in churches. I.S.'s niece's husband and son-in-law accompany us, albeit with an air of derring-do. They have lived a
block away most of their lives, and both are architectural en-
gineers, but they have not ventured inside the church before.
They watch I.S. with amazement as he dips his fingers in the
stoup, crosses himself, genuflects. Leaving the Nikolsky, we
pass a synagogue bulb-domed like a church, with a large
gathering of the bearded and black-hatted in the street in front.

The Krukov Canal, in front of I.S.'s old apartment, is about
twenty-five feet wide. The buildings on the other side are all
new, but the iron railings on the canal are the same, he says,
and so is the wooden footbridge at the corner. The street is
still cobblestone, too, and tramcars still skid loudly by on their
rails. A plaque commemorates the residence of the "composer
and conductor" Napravnik in the house next door to the blank
wall commemorating the thirty years' residence there of the
composer of *Le Sacre du printemps*. I.S. says nothing as he
looks at the door I have so often heard him describe—it opens
directly on the street—and he shows no trace of emotion. Contrast this with his reaction, around the corner, to the Conservatory and the Maryinsky Theater. As soon as he recognizes the
former, an involuntary "Glazunov" comes out (after fifty
years!). He then looks the other way, at the green-and-white
Maryinsky, and his whole face ripples with pleasure. Anyone
seeing this could not doubt that he had learned to hate music
at the one place and to love it at the other.

A family dinner at Xenia Yurievna's, number 72 Ulitsa

Glinka. I.S.'s old apartment, next door, at number 66, is identical to this one, Xenia says, and her statement drastically shrinks the scale of I.S.'s published recollections. Xenia's husband fought at Stalingrad, and from there to the end of the war at Magdeburg. She herself was in Leningrad throughout the siege, working in an *opolchenie* and then with a burial battalion: a third of the city's civilian population died from starvation.[4] Xenia's family, children and in-laws all in their twenties, are attractive, shy, cheerful, scientifically-minded, and they all have a smattering of English. Xenia's Stravinskyana contains a large number of ancestral portraits, medallions, and photographs, most remarkably, a daguerreotype of Ignatievich, I.S.'s great-grandfather, a mutton-whiskered old tomcat aged 110. (Ignatievich died aged 111 as a result of a fall suffered while climbing over the fence on his way to a forbidden outing: the doctor had ordered him to stay home, and the family had locked the gate.) The photographs of I.S.'s father include several of him in the costumes of such basso roles as Holofernes and Sparafucile. Of a thousand or so family group photographs, I.S. figures in perhaps a third, and of the third, about a half were posed in Ustilug and Petchisky. In a photograph of I.S. in his room, dated 1899, the walls are as crowded with pictures and mementos as they are now in Hollywood, except that Berlioz and Wagner were prominent among the deities then. But the most striking photograph shows I.S. writing down the music of an itinerant and blind old concertina-player. Xenia also owns a small landscape, in oils, by I.S., dated 1900. And packets of letters from I.S. to her father Yuri; these break off in the 'twenties and, after a decade of silence, conclude with a note from *Editions Russe de Musique* in Paris announcing the deaths of I.S.'s mother, wife, and daughter. And several letters of Rimsky-Korsakov, though whether or not with references to I.S. I have no time to discover. And

---

[4] See Leon Goure, *The Siege of Leningrad*, Stanford University Press, 1962. One hundred thousand people died horribly but quickly in Hiroshima. In Leningrad, a million people died horribly and slowly. Leningrad in the winter of 1941–42 was a Last Judgment in which the people's only testament was their ration cards.

programs and press books concerning every performance of I.S.'s music in Russia both before and after 1917: Petrenko singing the *Pastorale*, Gorodetzsky's *Spring*, and, with Warlich and the Court Orchestra, *Le Faune et la bergère*, January 22 (O.S.), 1908; Ansermet conducting *Mavra* and the Symphonies of Wind Instruments in 1927–28; Klimov conducting *Les Noces* in 1926 and *Oedipus* in 1928; Stiedry conducting the Little Suites and *Le Sacre* in the same years.

An emotionally disturbing occasion for I.S., one would have thought, but I have seen no sign of it. V. says, though, that he reverted to childhood expressions several times during dinner.

In the evening we go to the Maryinsky Theater, to see *it* and not *Lohengrin*, of course, which is in the way. (I.S. had wanted to see *Kitezh*, in fact, but the Composers' Union resisted that idea with mysterious excuses. A susurration from Parker finally explains that the performance is famously bad.) I.S. is again wildly wrong on scale. At seventeen-hundred seats, the Maryinsky—light blue and gold, with a blue ceiling and a chandelier—is less than half the size of his description. I.S. says that portraits of singers, including his father, stretched across the hem of the curtain when he was a child. The Intendant tells us the *Lohengrin* was mounted to honor Ribbentrop's visit in August 1939 and also was scheduled for performance the day of the German invasion. (I am misquoting him, though, for he will not say "German," but only "Fascist.") Tonight's performance is the first since then, he announces proudly, but we would have been happier with the ban. A bust of Lenin now stands in the upstairs foyer where I.S., as a boy, saw Tchaikovsky.

October 8. Following the morning rehearsal, I.S. informally lectures a group of young musicians on "the seriation principle" but some of today's questions are of a different stamp: "Doesn't it constrain inspiration?" "Isn't it a new dogmatism?" I.S.: "Of course it is a dogmatism, but don't dismiss it because of that. So was 'the old system' constricting and dogmatic, to bad composers." Then, turning to Khrennikov, "You, too, Tikhon

Nikolayich, will be trying it soon." Everyone laughs at this and, most magnanimously, Tikhon Nikolayich himself, who recently informed a composers' conference that "the twelve-tone system has no place in Soviet music," and to whom, therefore, the laugh must have had a sharp edge. All the same, I.S.'s colonizing has gone about as far as it can on a verbal level—though he has yet to recommend pieces to perform. My own feeling is that to the custodians of this outward-growing society, Webern's music can only seem like the nervous ticks of a moribund culture. I feel no need for it here, in any case, or correspondence between it and what I have seen of Soviet life, while on the other hand, a Stravinsky-shaped hole did at least exist.

The turquoise palace of Tsarskoe-Seloe, now Pushkin, was savagely gutted by the retreating Germans, but the cupolas now gleam as though newly splashed with gold, and one wing —that containing Cameron's Chinese Room, Peacock Room, Blue Drawing Room (with intarsia woods from Vietnam), and the bedroom and green dining room of Catherine II—is a masterpiece of restoration. The satellite buildings in the surrounding parks are inspired by *dix-huitième* examples—a Trianon, an *orangerie*, a monopteral pavilion—and so, perhaps, are the groves of sycamore and the gardens trimmed and colored like *hors-d'oeuvres*. In the tall, uniquely Russian, birch forests children are making sport of gathering leaves.

Verst stones still measure the royal road from Tsarskoe-Seloe to Leningrad. At Nevsky Prospekt we are held up for what seems likely to be a parade, but turns out to be a ski team on two-wheel roller skates poling along in snow-country costume. "They are practicing for the Olympic Games," Alexandra explains. And no wonder if they win.

Our first concert, at eight. A last-minute request for tickets by teen-age boys from the "Stravinsky Club of Kharkov." I.S. tells the audience that he attended his first concert in this hall, and: "Sixty-nine years ago I sat with my mother in that corner"—he points to it—"at a concert conducted by Napravnik to mourn the death of Tchaikovsky. Now I am conducting in

the same hall. I am very happy." This moving little speech is
even more of a success than the music, which was, as I.S.
quips, "half Tchaikovsky" (*Le Baiser de la fée*) "and half
Rimsky-Korsakov" (the *Fireworks* and the *Firebird*). We have
asked the Composers' Union to invite Nadejda Rimsky-Korsakov, Rimsky's daughter, to the concert—the *Fireworks* was composed to celebrate her marriage—but we learn now (a whisper
from Parker) that the old lady has refused because she had
always known that I.S. was not fond of her husband, the composer Maximilian Steinberg, or, for that matter, herself.

October 9. A wet day, but we walk from the Hermitage Bridge
to the Pushkin Museum. Traffic in the Moyka River: several
punts and a kayak. Dmitri Tolstoy waits for us at the Museum,
looking like my idea of Pierre Bezuhov, except for the too-
luxuriant hair. Pushkin's death mask emphasizes the big brow,
the dilated nostrils, the small mouth. The library is half foreign-language, and the relics include the vest he was wearing
at the duel. From Pushkin we go to V.'s former residence at the
Moyka corner of the Champs de Mars (this was a sand-graded
parade ground when the I.S.'s knew it, but it is now a garden
with a mammoth war memorial); and the Aptekarsky Ostrov,
the island where she was born[5] (but which would have been a
more appropriate birthplace for I.S.: Aptekarsky means apoth-
ecary). On Kammenoi Ostrov we see the tree, now in the
middle of a street, planted by Peter the Great; the Peter and
Paul fortress; a corvette (is this the *Aurora*?), the first to mu-
tiny in 1917, now a naval museum; the house of Kschessinska
with a plaque by the balcony from which Lenin addressed the
crowd.

Fourteen kilometers of the Hermitage this afternoon, or so
says Alexandra. We go through being surprised by the dimensions of familiar pictures—the *Madonna Constabile*, which
can be circumscribed by the hands of a pianist—but nothing
else I can say about the Hermitage will satisfy me.

Leningrad is tall, regular, Western, straight—in comparison

[5] At Pesochnaya Ulitsa, 4.

to circular, haphazard, oriental Moscow. And in Leningrad, the royal city, after Moscow, the proletarian one, the population does look drab, if only because the buildings are so sumptuous. I.S.: "The best thing in Leningrad is St. Petersburg." St. Petersburg is a city of romantic bridges and islands, and small cobblestone streets and byways—not yet macadamized like the large thoroughfares. St. Petersburg must be the only great city in which the ugliest buildings are churches: the Issaksky, which is a heavy, black roost for imperial eagles, and which deserves to be in Berlin; the Kazansky, which imitates St. Peter's and deserves to be in Rome, Georgia; the Spassa Nakrovee on the site of Alexander the II's assassination; and the Gastinny Dvor (the "upside-down trousers," as I.S. calls it). And St. Petersburg is a polychrome city: the ocher Dance Academy (which, incidentally, is the size of an American aircraft factory); the green Gorky theater; the red Anichkov palace; the peach-colored stables by the Champs de Mars; the yellow Yusupov palace (in which Rasputin's murder took place—the first stages of it, anyway). And St. Petersburg is a city of classical angles and perspectives, and of planned space —uniquely, of the semicircular space cut back from the corners of the streets contiguous to the Fantanky River. But St. Petersburg is a lonely, melancholy city at night, like Venice in winter. Even now, in October, it is deserted after six o'clock and very dark—street lamps are far apart. At midnight the fog hangs low over the canals and the city has a ghostly gloom. One imagines the Yusupov palace full of light and gaiety, as it once was, but the beautiful old building is empty, dark, and dead.

Tempting generalizations I will never pronounce in public. Russians are: hospitable; sentimental; optimistic (more so than Americans, at any rate); patient (an amazing capacity to stand on queues, especially in Leningrad); garrulous (I.S. has not stopped talking since he arrived, and heavy artillery wouldn't interrupt most of them, but the voices and the language are less grating than French and German ditto); direct (the compliments, not to say encomia, they tell in their toasts), but not frank (they will hide the reason for something they do not wish to reveal, like dogs burying bones); fundamentally friendly (they are more friendly to us than we are to them, certainly, even though they are the more suspicious of political sentiments); generous ("You like it? Here, take it"—never the spirit of "*Klein aber Mein*"). Russians do not have "good manners" in our sense, but they have a much readier affection. I, at any rate, have never known a more affectionate friendship, in such a short time, than with Karen Khatchaturian, with whom I am able to speak only very haltingly. Russians have no commercial spirit—none of our venal pursuit of money, in any case—and no wasteful competition. American and European composers hate one another, the younger ones especially, and though Russian composers may dislike each other intensely— some of them ought to, for sure—they co-operate and function as a professional unit in a way United States and European composers might envy. "Sophisticated" conversation—which means, I suppose, a wide reference of intellectual bric-a-brac —is in short supply. It is replaced by "enthusiasm."

To the midnight train for Moscow after the concert, carrying bags and bouquets. As we pull out of the station, Diaghilev, Tolstoy, Rimsky-Korsakov, Balmont run alongside for a moment, like another era trying to catch up.

October 10. Sunrise through green forests touched with gold. From Klin to Moscow, we press noses to the corridor windows. Colored barns and *izbas*, people in shawls, caps, and boots on their way to work—a feeling of I.S.'s world in the *Pribaoutki*, and of Kandinsky and Chagall of a half century ago. Back in the National Hotel, I.S. receives a letter and a genealogy from a Polish branch of Stravinskys living in Danzig. At noon, Khrennikov and Khatchaturian arrive laden with farewell gifts of samovars, gold spoons, gold tea-glass holders, inscribed scores.

Farewell banquet at the Metropole, a happy occasion, with no speeches and no formality; in fact, it becomes somewhat too relaxed as bread pellets and then apples are flipped about the room. Wives and husbands sit next to each other at these affairs; the wives we meet are physicians, or chemists, or archaeologists, or, in any case, scientists. Shostakovich, this time at I.S.'s side, looks even more frightened and tortured than at the first conclave, probably because he thinks a speech is expected of him. He converses neutrally at first, then like a bashful schoolboy blurts out that he had been overwhelmed by the Symphony of Psalms when he first heard it and that he had made his own piano score of it which he would like to present to I.S. Seeking to return the compliment, I.S. tells Shostakovich that he shares some of his high regard for Mahler. Poor Shostakovich starts to melt, then quickly freezes again as I.S. rather cruelly continues: "But you should go beyond Mahler. The Viennese troika adored him also, you know, and Schoenberg and Webern conducted his music." Toward the end of the evening, and after drinking several *zubrovkas*, Shostakovich pathetically confesses that he would like to follow I.S.'s example and conduct his own music. "But I don't know how not to be afraid."

I.S., going to bed, says he can already imagine a conversation on the other side:

"The Russians have skyscrapers."
"Yes, but they are built on mud and will soon collapse."
"Well, they do have very good roads."
"Of course, but they are the work of slaves."

October 11. A telephone from the Kremlin at noon fixing an appointment with Khrushchev, who has returned late last night from a twelve-day tour. We enter by the Bashnya Borovitskaya at one-thirty. Khrennikov says, simply, "Nikita Sergeich," and the guard asks no identification. We drive beyond St. Ivan's, gleaming white and gold, to the Council of Ministers building. Suslov waves a greeting from the sidewalk, as we arrive, but he walks by, which surprises Khrennikov, who has expected him at the meeting. A solitary soldier stands at the door, and a civilian secretary, who leads the I.S.'s to a

tiny elevator and who walks the two flights with me. A large
cloakroom, a long corridor, a waiting room like a doctor's office, with a table of foreign-language magazines and a portrait of Marx on the wall, like the doctor's old professor. After
five minutes here, the same secretary ushers us to a long room
with a long conference table covered in green billiard cloth.
Khrushchev, behind a desk at the far end, sees I.S.'s limp and
hurries to approach. I.S., addressing him as "Nikita Sergeich,"
apologizes "for taking time that must be doubly crowded after
your long absence." Khrushchev, hardly taller than I.S., with
brown, swivel eyes—you would not be able to look if they were
larger—gives us short, energetic handshakes with a pudgy,
short-fingered paw. "But I wanted very much to meet you."
We sit at the head of the billiard table, I.S. and V. facing
Khrushchev, myself and Khrennikov next to him. Lenin is
present too, in a photograph on the wall behind Khrushchev's
desk, and in a frame on his blotter next to a file marked
"Tass"; and Marx, beyond racks of pull-out maps, over the
door. Khrushchev rests his rimless spectacles on the green felt,
asserts his elbows there, and begins to talk about his trip. "I
had been promising to visit Turkestan and the Aral Sea region
for a long time, and though I was too busy now, I felt I had to
do it. I was so impressed by what I saw that I came back by
train to have time to think about it." He describes the irrigation of the "Hungry Desert," in which "skeletons of camels
have been found, though no humans have been able to exist
there. We have built a canal thirteen-hundred kilometers long
and redirected the once dried-up Amu-Darya. Rice and cotton
are now growing, and in a few years the whole region will
flourish." Anticipating the future, and not only of these regions, Khrushchev beams with pleasure and becomes even
more excited and energetic. He smiles, then, exposing a gallery
of dental gold, but he does not smile all the time, which is
one's impression of him from newspapers. "The world's largest
and fastest supersonic jets are being built in Tashkent," he
says, smiling at the prospect of the Soviet lead in "inertial nav-
igation." He describes a territory, near Samarkand I think, in

which "the English found gold—mere gold—but where we have discovered fountains of naphtha and inexhaustible deposits of copper. The gold is still mined, but as a quaint sideline industry." He says that the women in these regions "like to display their wealth by wearing heavy red velvet, even in that oppressive heat, but they live in squalid houses which they will not improve because of an old fear of being taxed. When, recently, television sets, refrigerators, and laundry machines came to stores there, everything was sold in an instant and paid for from barrels of money." Talking about the good living conditions on the Soviet side of the border, and the misery on the Indian side, his tone is slightly aggressive and boastful. (I.S., later: "I think he wants India.") I.S. asks him if the people in these regions speak Russian or if he uses a translator. Khrushchev: "All *my* republics speak Russian, and I have never used a translator in our country."

But I.S. translates, for me, this being the only occasion in the tour at which Alexandra has not been present. Conversation studded with statistics and geographical names is easy to follow, however, and, of course, no speaker could be more concrete. Afterward, the I.S.'s remark his "very correct Russian." Khrushchev is acutely sensitive to whatever we say, and even more sensitive, I think, to whatever we might say, and clearly he does not want I.S. to talk about music. (But what are his thoughts about this elderly emissary from the Russian past?) Almost all of the talking comes from Khrushchev, in any case, and because he can hardly contain himself on the subject of his trip, nearly all of the forty minutes are devoted to that. We do exchange observations about Moscow, though, and when the I.S.'s tell him how beautiful they have found the city, Khrushchev says: "Yes, not long ago I drove around really looking at it and I was impressed myself, but for eight hundred years it was a pigsty." As we leave, he repeats Khrennikov's invitation to stay in a *dacha* in the Crimea, carefully including myself. I say *"Bolshoi spassiba,"* and he, graciously, *"Prieyzhiety opiat"* (come back). I.S., in the car: "He is like a composer playing you the composition he is working on, and of which he is very full and very proud."

Sheremetievo airport. Reporters, tape recorders, television cameras. United States reporter to V.: "I understand you had an interview with Khrushchev." V.: "It was a visit, not an interview. *This* is an interview." Reporter: "And did you talk about music and the arts?" V.: "Mr. Khrushchev is not a musician. We did not exchange banalities about 'art,' therefore, but listened to him recount fascinating things about his trip."[6] Reporter to I.S.: "Will you say something about the beauties of Russia?" I.S.: "Beauties are to be loved, not talked about." And, "Mr. Stravinsky, what was your impression of Khrushchev?" I.S.: "I was pretty certain that there are no palace eunuchs running his affairs." A hundred new friends and now familiar faces crowd around stuffing our arms and pockets and hearts with all kinds of presents, and bottles of vodka, tar-like lumps of pressed caviar, photographs, flowers, kisses, embraces, tears.

FRANCE

October 14. Paris. Visit from Jean Genet. A small man—for some reason I had expected a large one. And, in spite of the leather jacket, open shirt, necktie slack like a noose, unexpectedly soft-boiled. His gray-brown eyes are at the same time frightened and as impertinent as a stethoscope. He likes or doesn't like, and he lays it down short and sharp, usually with "*Ça m'emerde,*" or "*Ça m'embête,*" but after a round or two this becomes predictably perverse. When someone mentions Dostoievsky, he says "*Tout ça m'emerde beaucoup,*" and his only reaction to Tolstoy is "*Connais pas.*" He was unable to finish Kafka's *The Trial,* he says, "*parce qu'on a trop parlé de ça.*" He laughs with us from time to time, but soon looks dangerous again and ready to bite. When the punch line of someone else's joke has been delivered he has a prickly way of saying, "*Eh, alors?*" V. describes an actor as handsome, and Genet

[6] Next day in the Western press: "As Khrushchev is ignorant of music, he talked banalities about his trip."

contradicts: "*Même à dix-sept ans il était très moche,*" and when she speaks well of a film, Genet finds it "*Abominable.*" He flatters I.S., though, or attempts to, telling him that his voice is like "the sound of the instruments in *Histoire du soldat,*" but when I.S. asks him, innocently, "Do you like to read at night?" he appears to think deeply for about thirty seconds before coming back, wickedly, with "*Oui, peut-être.*"

VENEZUELA

October 28–November 3. Caracas. The principal hotel having been bombed by saboteurs, we stay in the Circo Militar, an officers' club—in fact, a private village—"built in the great days of the dictatorship." The marble bars, ballrooms, restaurants are empty except for us—in spite of which every table is fully set at every meal—but the gates are watched by guards with submachine guns. The Circo is a perfect example of the corruption of the "in" party. The officers' entertainments include a cinema, a stadium, swimming pools, and a perpetual concert piped into every room and hall and even into outdoor space.

Caracas resembles Los Angeles in the thermometer-like glass elevators on the outsides of buildings, and in the freeways on which traffic regulates itself entirely by threat, but it is covered with a more outspoken political *graffiti:* "*Vivan los guerrillas,*" "*Muera Fidel,*" "*Romulistos asasinos,*" and so on back and forth. Unlike Los Angeles, too, is the mountain wall between the city and the sea, the peaks of which, like elderly courtesans, lift their veils only at night.

A reception on the terrace of the United States Embassy, which looks over the city from a hill. "Like San Francisco without the bay," the Ambassador says, but what with the ring of armed guards it feels more like Alcatraz without San Francisco. A time bomb was exploded in the Embassy laundry chute a few weeks ago, and the Ambassador himself is unable to attend our concert because the police cannot guarantee protection in the University auditorium.

The lisp and elimination of the "S" are more marked here than I have ever heard. Some of the musicians address I.S. as

"*Maetro Travithky.*" And when I start to rehearse Debussy's *Gigues*, it is re-pronounced "*Heeg.*" At the rehearsals, incidentally, I.S. tells the *Petroushka* pianist to open the lid all the way, to use the left pedal only, to play *forte* and *secco*, and as I have heard these directions a hundred times, I should record them as definitive. He also instructs the strings to play the triplet in the *Cantique* (*Four Etudes*), and the augmentation of it in the first and last measures, with three up-bows on one bow.

Across the highway from the Circo are hills swarming with shacks. Rich people tell us that the indigent peoples who have drifted here consider themselves better off than ever before, no matter what; and the "what" means no plumbing, no water, no latrine but the street, no electricity—except what can be filched from other people's outlets during the night. We have been warned against walking here—the dirt labyrinths are impassable to automobiles—because of the savagery and the stench, but we walk, nevertheless, and find huts made of billboards, with the advertised products—a woman drinking Pepsi-Cola, for example—still showing on the walls. And we see girls of nursery-school age carrying toy submachine guns.

Commenting on the extremes of poverty and wealth, Federico Schlesinger, late of Vienna and now proprietor of a local hotel, tells us that Venezuela "does not spend its money, but throws it away." Federico's own treasure is a tooled morocco guestbook inscribed by every celebrity who has dared to come within the three-mile limit. No doubt irritated by the sight of a fulsome testimonial, Ernest Hemingway has written, I think with malice, "To Federico, may his luck continue."

A visit to the Institute of Scientific Research, several thousand feet above the city, with its director Marcel Roche, and his beautiful wife. Roche describes the work to combat such tropical diseases as the *schizotrypanum cruzi*, which is transmitted by cockroach-type vermin and already has caused cardiac damage to a tenth of the population.

Late-night farewell party in the garden of Ríos Reyna, president of the orchestra; we leave tomorrow for Curaçao. Creole songs sung by girls with tall spun-sugar coiffures. Giant moths alight on the walls, and grasshoppers with chassis the size of large peapods.

UNITED STATES

November 17. New York. Auden for dinner. Loose folds of skin, like an elephant's behind. Trouser cuffs that hang ten inches above flat, platypus-type feet. He says that in the club car on his way to lecture at Yale, two Yale boys sent him a note: "We can't stand it a minute longer; are you Carl Sandburg?" He says he wrote back: "You have spoiled mother's day." After telling the waiter to bring him a "veg" he tells us that "Cardinal Newman could have become a saint, but he thought it too fruity to do a miracle." Recalling his examination for United States citizenship, he says: "It didn't look too good at first because I admitted I was a writer. When I said that, the interviewer told his secretary to put down 'can read.' One question demanded whether I intended to kill the President, and I am quite certain if I had answered 'Yes,' no one would have noticed."

Opera talk, touched off by Auden's discussion of his ideas for a libretto on the *Bacchae*, and including the confession that "the *Elegy* was our version of *Arabella*." According to Auden, "The beginning of *Die Walküre*, Act Two, is a Victorian breakfast scene, Wotan meekly cracking his morning egg behind 'The Times' and Fricka furiously rattling the teacups." Auden on *Pelléas:* "It is an underwater opera. And, nobody can be that refined. The opera succeeds only because it flatters the audience. But imagine devoting an opera to people with a mania for losing things!" And, on a line in *Vanessa:* "Now where do you suppose the author had seen 'weeping deer'?" Defending opera against other types of music, Auden says that people who attend chamber music concerts "are like Englishmen who go to church when abroad."

A steady flow of epigrams and aphorisms, but the references are all German: "Lichtenberg's essay on Hogarth gives a better translation for '*The Rake*' than '*Der Wüstling*,' but I can't remember what it is." He complains that "the Germans tend to regard one of their classic authors as Jesus Kleist," and he suggests that "a whole category of females might best be described as the Rilke-girl-friend type." He manages to get lost returning from "the loo," and this must have given him an unpleasant turn—"*schwarze gedenken*," he would probably prefer to say—for shortly after he announces: "When my time is up I'll want *Siegfried's Funeral Music*, and not a dry eye in the house."

INDEX

COMPOSITIONS BY STRAVINSKY MENTIONED IN THE TEXT